PROFESSIONAL RESPONSIBILITY

James E. Moliterno

Tazewell Taylor Professor of Law
College of William & Mary School of Law

The *CrunchTime* Series

ΛSPEN

PUBLISHERS

1185 Avenue of the Americas, New York, NY 10036
www.aspenpublishers.com

© 2003 Aspen Publishers
A Wolters Kluwer Company
www.aspenpublishers.com

Permissions
Aspen Publishers
1185 Avenue of the Americas
New York, NY 10036

Printed in the United States of America

1 2 3 4 5 6 7 8 9 0

ISBN 0-7355-4474-3

This book is intended as a general review of a legal subject. It is not intended as a source of advice for the solution of legal matters or problems. For advice on legal matters, the reader should consult an attorney.

About Aspen Publishers

Aspen Publishers, headquartered in New York City, is a leading information provider for attorneys, business professionals, and law students. Written by preeminent authorities, our products consist of analytical and practical information covering both U.S. and international topics. We publish in the full range of formats, including updated manuals, books, periodicals, CDs, and online products.

Our proprietary content is complemented by 2,500 legal databases, containing over 11 million documents, available through our Loislaw division. Aspen Publishers also offers a wide range of topical legal and business databases linked to Loislaw's primary material. Our mission is to provide accurate, timely, and authoritative content in easily accessible formats, supported by unmatched customer care.

To order any Aspen Publishers title, go to *www.aspenpublishers.com* or call 1-800-638-8437.

To reinstate your manual update service, call 1-800-638-8437.

For more information on Loislaw products, go to *www.loislaw.com* or call 1-800-364-2512.

For Customer Care issues, e-mail *CustomerCare@aspenpublishers.com*; call 1-800-234-1660; or fax 1-800-901-9075.

Aspen Publishers
A Wolters Kluwer Company

Summary of Contents

Table of Contents

FLOW CHARTS

CAPSULE SUMMARY

EXAM TIPS

Preface

Thank you for buying this book.

The *CrunchTime* Series is intended for people who want Emanuel quality, but don't have the time or money to buy and use the full-length *Emanuel Law Outline* on a subject. We've designed the Series to be used in the last few weeks (or even less) before your final exams.

This book includes the following features, most of which have been extracted from the corresponding *Emanuel Law Outline:*

- *Flow Charts*—We've reduced many of the principles of *Professional Responsibility* to a series of 19 Flow Charts, created especially for this book and never published elsewhere. We think these will be especially useful on open-book exams. A list of all the Flow Charts is printed on p. 1.

- *Capsule Summary*—This is a 50-page summary of the subject. We've carefully crafted it to cover the things you're most likely to be asked on an exam. The Capsule Summary starts on p. 47.

- *Exam Tips*—We've compiled these by reviewing dozens of actual past essay and multiple-choice questions asked in past law school and bar exams, and extracting the issues and "tricks" that surface most often on exams. The Exam Tips start on p. 101.

- *Short-Answer Questions*—These questions are generally in a Yes/No format, with a "mini-essay" explaining each one. The questions start on p. 141.

- *Multiple-Choice Questions*—These are in a Multistate-Bar-Exam style, and are not published elsewhere. The questions start on p. 171.

- *Essay Exam Questions*—These questions are actual ones asked on law school or bar exams. They start on p. 189.

We hope you find this book helpful and instructive.

Good luck.

James E. Moliterno
College of William & Mary School of Law
July 2003

FLOW CHARTS

CONTENTS

FIGURE 1

SUBJECT TO DISCIPLINE*

Discipline may be based on an incredibly wide range of conduct both within and without the lawyer's role. It may be imposed for violations of the ethics code rules, for acts involving moral turpitude, for criminal conduct, for dishonesty, fraud and deceit, and for acts that are prejudicial to the administration of justice. MR 8.4

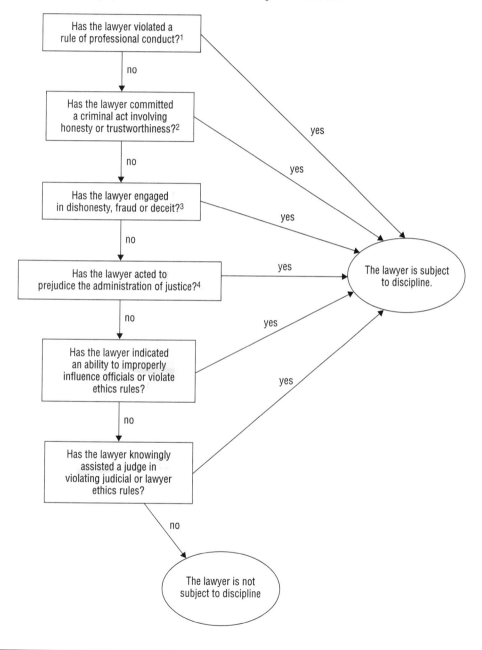

---

*Because of the need for brevity and precision in the flowcharts, language is sometimes drawn directly from the Model Rules without quotation marks. To a great extent, footnote material directs attention to the provisions from which quotes are drawn. Credit for such language is owed the Model Rules and this paragraph is meant to provide a general attribution.

Notes to Figure 1
SUBJECT TO DISCIPLINE

[1] A lawyer is subject to discipline when she violates a mandatory rule of the relevant state's adopted ethics code. All other grounds for discipline are implicitly included in this category, since the adopted ethics code typically includes provisions that in one way or another require a lawyer to refrain from conduct that is criminal, is fraudulent, involves moral turpitude, or prejudices the administration of justice. MR 8.4.

[2] Formerly, the standard for whether an act reflected adversely on a lawyer's fitness (and therefore subjected the lawyer to discipline) was whether the act involved **moral turpitude.** DR 1-102(A)(3). This standard, thought too broad and amorphous, is no longer the explicit standard under the Model Rule. See MR 8.4. Nonetheless, moral turpitude language, particularly in cases of lawyer sexual misconduct, finds its way into the court decisions applying Model Rule 8.4. Now the standard, under MR 8.4, is more functional. The act is disciplinable misconduct if it "reflects adversely on the lawyer's honesty, trustworthiness, or fitness as a lawyer in other respects."

Example: Client retained Lawyer to represent her in divorce and custody proceedings. Because Client was unemployed, she had no money to pay Lawyer's retainer fee, but Lawyer agreed to represent her and began work on her case. Client then offered to engage in sexual intercourse with Lawyer for money. Lawyer told Client that he would give her money as a personal loan if she did not want to have sex, but she advised him that she had no means to pay back the money. Therefore, Client suggested that she would reimburse him with sex. Lawyer gave Client $50 and they had sexual intercourse.

The sexual contact between Lawyer and Client in a professional context constitutes professional impropriety and an act of moral turpitude. It carries a great potential of prejudice both to Client and to her children in the pending court proceedings. Further, Lawyer's conduct reflects negatively on the integrity and honor of the legal profession. Therefore, Lawyer's license was suspended for three months. Committee on Professional Ethics & Conduct of the Iowa State Bar Ass'n v. Hill, 436 N.W.2d 57 (Iowa 1989).

A lawyer is subject to discipline when he engages in criminal conduct that reflects adversely on the lawyer's fitness as a lawyer.

Example: Lawyer was convicted of willfully and knowingly attempting to evade income taxes. In addition to the criminal liability, Lawyer was subject to discipline. In re Colin, 442 N.Y.S.2d 66 (N.Y. App. Div. 1981).

Minor criminal conduct, such as small-amount possession of controlled substances or criminal trespass during a civil rights demonstration, that says little about the lawyer's honesty, trustworthiness or fitness as a lawyer in other respects, will not subject the lawyer to discipline. Under the Model Code rubric, such conduct amounts to a criminal act not involving moral turpitude.

[3] Acts, whether in or out of the lawyer's role, that involve dishonesty, fraud and deceit, even if not rising to the level of criminal conduct, subject the lawyer to discipline. MR 8.4(c). This rule overlaps coverage with a variety of other ethics code rules that prohibit deceitful conduct of one kind or another. See, e.g., MR 3.3, 3.4, and 4.1.

Example: Lawyer represented Client, who was converting several buildings into condominiums. Prospective Purchasers agreed to close immediately on several units on the condition that Client deposit $10,000 in an escrow account to cover the costs of completing necessary work on the units in case Client failed to perform. If Client satisfactorily performed the work, the money would be released back to him. Lawyer agreed to act as an escrow agent even after learning that Client's check for the account was worthless. Purchasers relied on the availability of the escrow funds and paid a non-refundable deposit.

While a client is entitled to representation for any objective within the bounds permitted by law, he is not entitled to affirmative assistance by his attorney with conduct that the lawyer knows is illegal or fraudulent. When an attorney confronts a situation in which the client's wishes call for illegal or fraudulent conduct, the attorney is under an affirmative duty to withdraw from the representation. Lawyer is subject to discipline. In re Austern, 524 A.2d 680 (D.C. 1987).

[4] This prohibition is a broad, catch-all category including various forms of misconduct, much of which is also prohibited by more specific rules. MR 8.4(d).

FIGURE 2

TORT LIABILITY FOR MALPRACTICE

Malpractice is a civil claim for relief intended to remedy a wrong done by a professional (in this case a lawyer) to an individual client or group of clients.

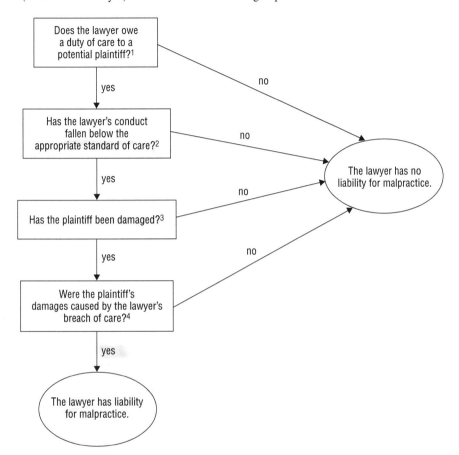

TORT LIABILITY FOR MALPRACTICE

[1] The lawyer's duty to the client is measured by the skill and knowledge of ordinary lawyers in the community.

A lawyer owes this duty to a client irrespective of whether any fee is being paid for the lawyer's service. Thus, appointed counsel and pro bono counsel, for example, owe the same duty as a lawyer who is charging a fee for service.

The duty begins when a client begins to talk with a lawyer as a lawyer. Any reasonable expectation of service that is created by the lawyer at that time creates a duty of care. The duty does not wait for a formal retainer, nor for payment of a fee. It begins when the client reasonably expects that the lawyer has undertaken to provide legal service.

Example: Lawyer is attending a PTA potluck dinner. Acquaintance asks Lawyer a question about a neighbor of Acquaintance who had some years ago built a fence that encroached onto Acquaintance's property. Lawyer, irritated at being asked a legal question at a social function, says, "I'll ask my partner about that." The evening goes on, and Lawyer forgets about Acquaintance's question. Lawyer owes Acquaintance a duty of care. Eight months later, after the statute of limitations has run on her possible claim, Acquaintance calls Lawyer to ask what his partner thought about her fence problem. Lawyer has breached a duty to Acquaintance. See, e.g., Togstad v. Vesely, Otto, Miller & Keefe, 291 N.W.2d 686 (Minn. 1980).

[2] Breach of the duty owed is a required element of a malpractice action. Actions by a lawyer that are below the applicable standard of care breach the duty to the client. Failures to do legal or factual research, failure to correctly analyze straightforward legal principles, losing critical evidence, and allowing statutes of limitations to expire are examples of actions that fall below the general standard of care.

Lawyers are not guarantors of particular results. Often, a variety of reasonable strategies will be available from which to choose. When a lawyer chooses a reasonable course of action, and that course later produces bad results, the lawyer has not breached the duty of care owed to the client.

Example: Lawyer represents Client at trial. Witness testifies against Client, but Opposing Lawyer forgets to draw a particularly damaging fact from Witness during direct examination. Lawyer has available impeachment material that would all cast Witness's credibility in doubt. But engaging in cross-examination risks drawing out the particularly damaging fact that has not yet been admitted in evidence. Lawyer's choice between the two reasonable alternatives of engaging or not engaging in cross-examination of Witness will not breach Lawyer's duty of care to Client.

Watch for questions that say that the lawyer acted "reasonably" or "with due care." Such language means by definition that the lawyer has not breached the tort duty and is therefore not liable for malpractice.

[3] As with any tort action, the wrong is insufficient to create a claim for relief in the absence of damages. Often the value of a lawyer malpractice claim's damages will be determined by the value of the client's claim that has been lost or diminished because of the lawyer's acts.

[4] For a malpractice claim to exist, the lawyer's breach of duty must **cause** the client's damages. Often, this means that the client will have to prove that she would have prevailed in the original matter had the lawyer not breached the duty of care. This requirement is called the **"case within a case."** The malpractice plaintiff must prove the value of the underlying case in order to prevail in the malpractice case.

Example: Lawyer undertook to investigate a possible litigation matter brought to her by Client. Lawyer procrastinated and the statute of limitations for filing the action expired. Lawyer owed Client a duty and Lawyer has breached the duty. Upon examination, however, the matter originally brought by Client to Lawyer has no merit. In other words, even if Lawyer had timely investigated and filed the action, Client could not have recovered damages in that matter. Client cannot prove the case within a case, and therefore Lawyer's acts were not the cause of any injury to Client. Lawyer has no liability for malpractice to Client.

FIGURE 3

REPORTING MISCONDUCT

Among the chief features of the legal profession's claim to be **self-governing** is the requirement to report a fellow lawyer's or a judge's serious misconduct to the appropriate professional authority. MR 8.3.

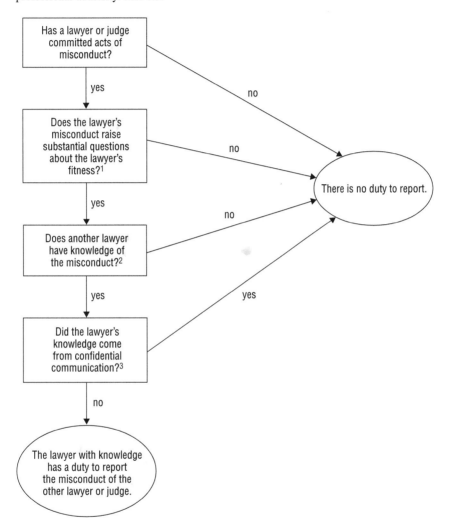

NOTES TO FIGURE 3

REPORTING MISCONDUCT

[1] The rule does not require a lawyer to report all misconduct of which the lawyer has knowledge. It requires a lawyer to report misconduct "that raises a substantial question as to that lawyer's honesty, trustworthiness or fitness as a lawyer in other respects. . . ." MR 8.3(a). "Substantial" means a "material matter of clear and weighty importance." Model Rules, Terminology 1.0(l).
Example: Lawyer 1 and Lawyer 2 practice law in State A. State A has a rule prohibiting financial assistance to clients from lawyers when litigation is pending or contemplated. Lawyer 1 represents Client in a litigation matter. Client is indigent. Lawyer 1 gives Client $50 to help Client make an overdue rent payment, allowing Client and his family to remain in their apartment rather than be evicted. Over a casual lunch in which Lawyer 1 and Lawyer 2 were relating as friends rather than as lawyer and client, Lawyer 1 tells Lawyer 2 that he made the $50 gift without realizing that it violated the ethics rules in State A. The rule does not require intent and Lawyer 1's conduct has violated the rule. Lawyer 2 need not report Lawyer 1's misconduct. The misconduct does not raise a "substantial question as to [Lawyer 1's] honesty, trustworthiness or fitness as a lawyer in other respects. . . ."

[2] Before a duty to report misconduct can arise, the lawyer must "know that another lawyer has committed" the **misconduct.** MR 8.3(a). Personal knowledge of the misconduct obviously satisfies the "knowledge" requirement. While it would be counterproductive to require a lawyer to report every courthouse rumor about another lawyer's misconduct (i.e., the lawyer in such an instance does not "know" of the misconduct), the knowledge requirement is satisfied when a lawyer has been informed of the misconduct from a credible person and there is some independent corroboration. Weber v. Cueto, 568 N.E.2d 513 (Ill. App. Ct. 1991). Put another way, "knowledge" as used in this rule means actual knowledge, but actual knowledge may be inferred from the circumstances. Model Rules, Terminology 1.0(f).

[3] The rule does not require a report of misconduct when the lawyer has learned of the misconduct through confidential communications that would be protected by the ethical duty of confidentiality under Model Rule 1.6. MR 8.3(c).

Clearly, this provision eliminates the reporting requirement when a lawyer is consulted as a lawyer by the lawyer who has engaged in the misconduct. But it must also be remembered that the exceptions to the duty of confidentiality (such as, e.g., the future harm exception) continue to apply with equal force in this setting as in any other.
Example: Lawyer 1 has misappropriated funds belonging to a client. Lawyer 1 consults with Lawyer 2 regarding Lawyer 1's potential liability. Lawyer 2 now knows that Lawyer 1 has committed misconduct of a substantial nature, but Lawyer 2's duty of confidentiality relieves her of the duty to report (or viewed alternatively, prohibits her from reporting) Lawyer 1's misconduct to the bar disciplinary authorities. A benefit of this rule is the creation of an opportunity that might not otherwise exist for Lawyer 2 to counsel Lawyer 1 to rectify the misconduct.

Less clear is whether the confidentiality aspect of Model Rule 8.3 eliminates the reporting requirement when a lawyer learns of another lawyer's misconduct from a client who is not a lawyer. The following example, drawn from the *Himmel* case, is based on the view that the reporting requirement trumps a client's desire that the misconduct of the client's former lawyer not be reported. This view is not unanimously held; authority from other states have opined the contrary. See, e.g., Md. Ethics Op. 89-46 (1989).
Example: Client hired Lawyer to recover settlement proceeds from Client's former attorney. Lawyer discovered that Client's former attorney had misappropriated the funds. The former attorney agreed to return the money to Client if Client and Lawyer would agree not to initiate any criminal, civil, or attorney disciplinary actions against him.

Any contact between Client and disciplinary authorities regarding former attorney's actions did not satisfy Lawyer's duty to notify the authorities of the former attorney's misconduct. Client's request that Lawyer not report the former attorney's misconduct did not relieve Lawyer of his professional duty to do so. In re Himmel, 533 N.E.2d 790 (Ill. 1988).

Figure 4

FEES

Although the regulation of lawyer's fees is relatively light and rarely enforced, it does exist. MR 1.5. Fees are regulated for their amount and their nature.

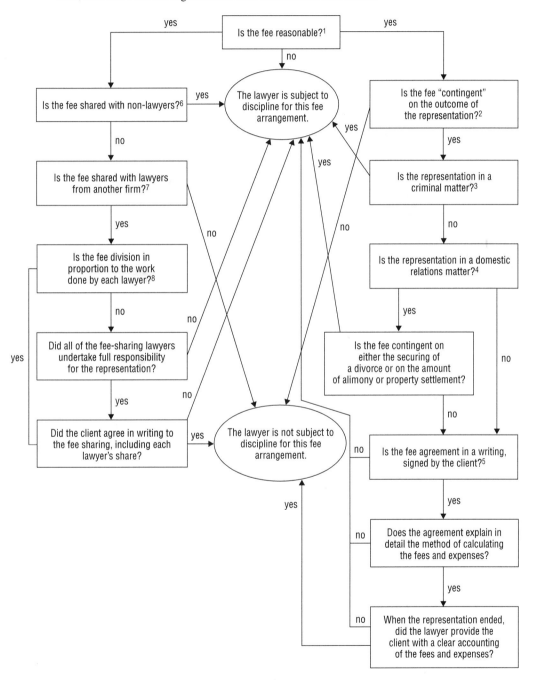

NOTES TO FIGURE 4

FEES

[1] A lawyer's fee must be reasonable. MR 1.5. Under the Model Code, the fee regulation required that a lawyer's fee not be "clearly excessive." DR 2-106(A). Under the 1908 ABA Canons, which preceded the Model Code, a fee was only subject to discipline if it was "so exorbitant and wholly disproportionate to the services performed as to shock the conscience of those to whose attention it was called." Goldstone v. State Bar, 6 P.2d 513, 516 (Cal. 1931).

Example: Client retained Lawyer to represent him against a battery charge. Lawyer demanded a $5,000 fee, and Client paid him. Lawyer sent another attorney to appear at Client's court date. At that time, the complainant dropped all charges, but Lawyer refused to refund any part of his fee. Lawyer charged a clearly excessive fee in violation of DR 2-106. In re Kutner, 399 N.E.2d 963 (Ill. 1979).

A range of factors may be considered in setting a reasonable fee. MR 1.5(a).

—The time and labor involved in the representation may be considered. MR 1.5(a)(1).
—The commonness or by contrast the novelty of the legal work involved in the representation may be considered. MR 1.5(a)(1).
—The amount of skill required of the lawyer to perform the representation successfully may be considered. MR 1.5(a)(1).
—Some representation may preclude other employment for the lawyer, either because of the time and energy needed to represent the client or because of conflicts that will arise that will prevent the lawyer from engaging in representation of other clients. If the client is aware of these limitations, then they may be considered. MR 1.5(a)(2).
—The fee charged by other lawyers in the community for similar services may be considered. MR 1.5(a)(3). Note, however, that this factor is not an authorization to follow what amounts to an informal minimum fee schedule.
—The magnitude of the client's economic or other interests that are involved in the representation and the results obtained by the lawyer may be considered. MR 1.5(a)(4). These factors are chief in what is called "value billing." In value billing, the fee is a function of the value that the lawyer's services have brought the client.
—Time restrictions that either the client or the circumstances impose on the lawyer may be considered. MR 1.5(a)(5).
—The way in which the particular lawyer-client relationship has developed may be considered. MR 1.5(a)(6).
—Lawyer quality: The experience, ability, and reputation of the particular lawyer may be considered. MR 1.5(a)(7). The rule permits a seasoned, well-known lawyer to charge more for the same service than a lawyer fresh out of law school charges.
—Whether the fee is fixed, hourly, contingent, prepaid with a retainer, etc., may be considered in determining whether the amount of a particular fee is reasonable. MR 1.5(a)(8).

[2] With a few exceptions and restrictions, a lawyer is permitted to charge a fee that is contingent on the outcome of the matter. For example, a lawyer may charge a fee that is equal to 40 percent of the recovery on the client's claim that results from a trial verdict. The fee is contingent on the amount of the recovery. **Contingent fee** arrangements have traditionally been thought of as a way for a client with a meritorious claim but little money with which to pay an hourly or up-front fee to get the claim handled by a lawyer.

Generally, cases that produce a **res,** a pool of recovery money from which the contingent fee may be paid, are appropriate for contingent fees.

[3] A lawyer is prohibited from charging a contingent fee to a defendant in a criminal matter in part because no res is produced from which the fee may come and in part because of the special public interest involved in criminal matters. MR 1.5(d)(2).

[4] A lawyer is prohibited from charging a contingent fee in a domestic relations case when the fee is to be contingent on obtaining a divorce or on the amount of property, child support, or alimony recovered. MR 1.5(d)(1). The intrusion of a lawyer whose fee depends on such matters into sensitive domestic relations matters is thought to be too risky to the sensitive and important relationships between spouses and between parent and child.

[5] Because of the heightened dangers of client misunderstanding and of lawyer overreaching, additional restrictions apply to contingent fee arrangements. MR 1.5(c).

Although ordinarily a fee agreement need not be in writing, a contingent fee agreement must be in writing. The written agreement must explain the way in which the fee will be calculated and, in particular, the way in which deductions for expenses will be calculated. MR 1.5(c).

The lawyer must provide an ending statement in writing to the client explaining the outcome of the matter and providing the calculation of the fee and expenses. MR 1.5(c).

[6] Fees may not be shared with non-lawyers except under quite limited circumstances. Fee sharing with non-lawyers is thought to compromise the lawyer's independence and to inject into the lawyer-client relationship the interests of someone who is not bound by the ethics code.

[7] Lawyers in the same firm routinely share fees with one another. That process is a central part of what it means to be a partner in a firm. However, when lawyers who are not members of a firm share fees, or when lawyers seek to share fees with non-lawyers, special problems arise.

[8] The fee-splitting lawyers must share the fee either in proportion to the services rendered by each lawyer or in some other proportion if the lawyers agree with the client in writing that the lawyers shall have joint responsibility for the representation. MR 1.5(e)(1).

FIGURE 5

WITHDRAWAL

Under some circumstances, lawyers are required to withdraw from representation, thereby terminating the lawyer-client relationship. Failure to withdraw under these circumstances subjects the lawyer to discipline. MR 1.16(a). In some instances lawyers are permitted but not required to withdraw. The practical effect of this rule is to allow lawyers to withdraw from representation in the enumerated circumstances without breaching a duty of continued representation to the client. MR 1.16(b).

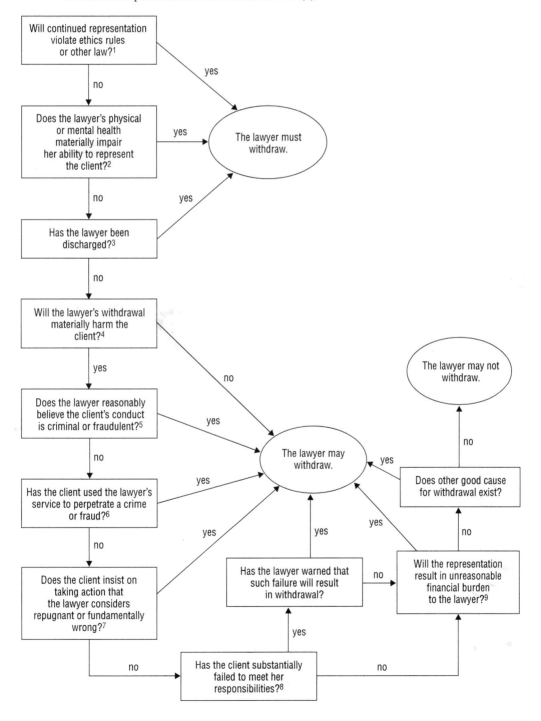

Notes to Figure 5

WITHDRAWAL

[1] When continuing the representation will violate an ethics rule, the lawyer has a duty to withdraw. MR 1.16(a)(1). *Example:* Lawyer agrees to represent Driver and Passenger as co-plaintiffs in a personal injury action. As the representation proceeds, Lawyer realizes that Passenger has a good claim against Driver and that Passenger would be ill served by forgoing this claim. Lawyer's continued representation of either Driver or Passenger would violate conflict-of-interest and confidentiality rules. Providing full representation for Passenger would compromise Driver; using confidences of Passenger or Driver in the continued representation of either Passenger or Driver against the other would violate confidentiality rules. Lawyer must withdraw from representation of both Passenger and Driver.

When continuing representation will violate law other than an ethics rule, the lawyer has a duty to withdraw. MR 1.16(a)(1). *Example:* Client approaches Lawyer to request that Lawyer represent Client in a real estate transfer. Lawyer agrees. Lawyer comes to realize during the representation that the Client is using Lawyer's services to further Client's illegal gambling operation. Because Lawyer's continued representation of Client would violate the criminal aiding and abetting statute, Lawyer has a duty to withdraw from representing Client.

[2] When a lawyer's health will prevent the lawyer from delivering competent service to the client, the lawyer has a duty to decline the representation. MR 1.16(a)(2). *Example:* Client requests that Lawyer represent him in an auto accident matter. The statute of limitations expires on Client's claim in four weeks. Lawyer has scheduled herself to enter an alcohol rehabilitation program for the next four weeks. Lawyer has a duty to decline to represent Client.

[3] A client has an absolute right to discharge a lawyer. When the client discharges a lawyer, the lawyer must withdraw from the representation. MR 1.16(a)(3). *Example:* Lawyer represents Plaintiff-Client in a personal injury matter. Without cause, Client discharges Lawyer. Believing that she is acting in Client's best interests and wanting to prove her value to Client, Lawyer engages in settlement negotiations with Defendant's Lawyer purporting to act on Client's behalf. Lawyer is subject to discipline for failing to promptly withdraw upon discharge by Client.

[4] Without regard to any cause for withdrawal, a lawyer may withdraw if it can be done without material adverse effect to the client. MR 1.16(b)(1). *Example:* Client retains Lawyer to pursue a personal injury action. The statute of limitations does not expire on Client's claim for another three years. After agreeing to represent Client, Lawyer decides to turn his practice away from personal injury representation and toward criminal practice. Lawyer's withdrawal will have no material adverse effect on Client: Client has sufficient time to retain new counsel and pursue his claim. Lawyer may withdraw.

[5] A lawyer is **required** to withdraw when the lawyer **knows** that the client is using the lawyer's services to perpetrate crimes or frauds. MR 1.16(a)(1). When there is somewhat less certainty that the lawyer's services will result in crimes or frauds, but the lawyer nonetheless **reasonably** believes that the client is engaging in conduct that is criminal or fraudulent, the lawyer **may** withdraw. MR 1.16(b)(2).

[6] When the lawyer learns that past services of the lawyer have been used by the client to perpetrate a crime or fraud, the lawyer may withdraw even if it does not appear that the lawyer's current services for the client are being so used. MR 1.16(b)(3). This rule permits a lawyer to withdraw from a client's representation and distance herself from the client's crimes or frauds at the earliest possible opportunity to do so. *Example:* Lawyer first represented Client in Client's efforts to obtain loans from Bank and now represents Client in Client's efforts to merge her corporation with another. Lawyer learns that in the loan representation, Client used Lawyer's services to perpetrate frauds on Bank. Lawyer has no particular indication that Client is currently using Lawyer's services to perpetrate frauds. Lawyer may withdraw from the current representation.

[7] When, after the lawyer has advised to the contrary, a client intends to continue with a course of conduct that the lawyer finds morally repugnant or imprudent, even though lawful, the lawyer may withdraw. MR 1.16(b)(4). *Example:* Lawyer represents Insurance Company. Impecunious Plaintiff has filed a claim for benefits that is meritorious except for the fact that it was filed one day beyond the required filing period. Lawyer advises Insurance Company to pay the claim despite its lawful authority to refuse to do so. Despite Lawyer's advice, Insurance Company determines to deny the claim. If Lawyer finds Insurance Company's action to be morally repugnant, Lawyer may withdraw.

[8] When a client has failed to meet the client's obligations, most often to pay the lawyer's reasonable fee, the lawyer must first warn the client that the lawyer intends to withdraw if the client does not meet his obligations. If the client persists in failing to meet obligations after the warning, the lawyer may withdraw. MR 1.16(b)(5).

[9] If the representation will result in unreasonable financial burden to the lawyer, the lawyer may withdraw. This financial burden is not a mere loss, but is on the same order as the sort of financial burden that would permit a lawyer to decline a court appointment. MR 1.16(b)(6). *Example:* Client retained Firm to represent her in a divorce action against Husband. Client paid a retainer fee and a nominal amount for initial costs and acknowledged her responsibility for future fees and expenses. Firm then worked extensively on client's complicated case, making court appearances on her behalf and logging more than 110 hours in office time. Client then lost her job, began receiving welfare payments, and had insufficient funds with which to pay Firm. Firm moved to withdraw from further representation of Client.

When Firm accepted Client's retainer it impliedly agreed to prosecute her case to a conclusion. Firm did not have cause to abandon that agreement. Its duty to Client did not evaporate because the agreement was not as profitable as first imagined. Firm's motion to withdraw was denied. Kriegsman v. Kriegsman, 375 A.2d 1253 (N.J. Sup. Ct. App. Div. 1977).

FIGURE 6

CONFIDENTIALITY

The duty of confidentiality is the most visible, oft-discussed component of the lawyer's duties to a client. There is a close relationship between the evidentiary privilege (see chart 7) and the ethical duty of confidentiality.

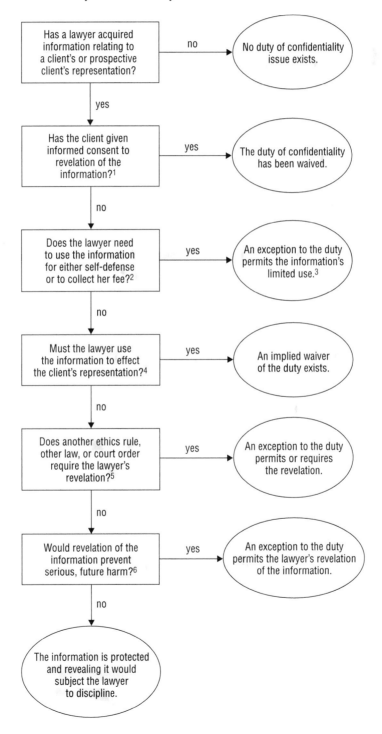

Notes to Figure 6
CONFIDENTIALITY

[1] The client is the holder of the evidentiary privilege and controller of the duty of confidentiality, the party whose communication is being protected. A client may give informed consent to disclosure of information that would otherwise be protected by the duty of confidentiality. MR 1.6(a).

[2] A lawyer is permitted to reveal (and use for her own benefit) information that would be protected by the duty of confidentiality in three self-defense type situations. The three self-defense type situations are "to establish a claim or defense on behalf of the lawyer in a controversy between the lawyer and the client, to establish a defense to a criminal charge or a civil claim against the lawyer based upon conduct in which the client was involved, or to respond to allegations in any proceeding concerning the lawyer's representation of the client." MR 1.6(b)(2).

Example: After sustaining substantial losses on stock purchased in an initial public offering, Plaintiffs brought an action against Corporation, Firm, and certain Firm Partners for willful violations of securities law. Plaintiffs claimed that Corporation's Securities and Exchange Commission registration statement and prospectus had provided materially false and misleading information. They alleged that the defendants did not disclose payments due to and a compensation arrangement made with Firm in connection with the offering. Asserting that Corporation and Firm had concealed the fee arrangement from him, one Partner met with Lawyers representing Plaintiffs and convinced them to drop the claims against him. The remaining defendants then moved to disqualify Lawyers from further involvement in the litigation, alleging that Partner had revealed confidential information obtained from Corporation while discussing the case with Lawyers. A lawyer may reveal confidences or secrets necessary to defend himself against accusations of wrongful conduct. Partner had the right to make appropriate disclosures with respect to his role in the public offering and the right to support his version of the facts with suitable evidence. Further, Partner's duty of confidentiality applied only to information gained from Corporation, not information regarding events at Firm. Because Partner's conduct did not violate his professional responsibilities, his contacts with Lawyers did not disqualify them from representing Plaintiffs. Meyerhofer v. Empire Fire & Marine Ins. Co., 497 F.2d 1190 (2d Cir.), *cert. denied,* 419 U.S. 998 (1974).

[3] With respect to any of the three categories of permitted disclosure, the lawyer must limit disclosure to those facts necessary to self-defend.

Example: Lawyer was discharged by Client. Client sued Lawyer for malpractice. In his Answer to Client's Complaint, Lawyer included the following allegation: "Client constantly worried about everything, including an affair her husband supposedly had with Client's sister eight years ago." The allegation bore no relationship to the Complaint's allegations. A lawyer may reveal those confidences that are necessary to self-defend, but revelation of confidences beyond those necessary to defend is subject to discipline. Dixon v. State Bar of California, 187 Cal. Rptr. 30 (Cal. 1982).

Lawyers must also limit their self-defense disclosures to those who need to know for the lawyer's self-defense or fee collection purpose.

Example: Lawyer represents Client. Client willfully refuses to pay Lawyer's fee without cause. Lawyer is angry. Lawyer tells Hairstylist that Client has "stiffed me on my last three billings even though she has loads of readily available cash." Lawyer is subject to discipline because Hairstylist does not need to know the confidences of Client for Lawyer to collect his fee.

[4] In order to carry out the purposes of the representation, some information that would be subject to the duty of confidentiality must be disclosed.

Example: Lawyer represents Client, who wants to purchase Art's art collection. Client has told Lawyer various facts about Client's creditworthiness, his cash reserves, his interest in the collection, and so on. Client authorizes Lawyer to approach Art and engage in negotiations for the purchase of the collection. In carrying out Client's instructions, Lawyer may need to reveal some information relating to the representation that would otherwise be protected by the duty of confidentiality.

[5] Lawyers may reveal confidences when required to do so by other law or by order of court. When a court orders a lawyer to speak about matters that will reveal protected client information, usually after an unsuccessful assertion of the attorney-client evidentiary privilege, the lawyer may reveal the information without risking disciplinary liability. MR 1.6, Comment 11.

Despite a presumption against other provisions of law superseding the duty of confidentiality (see MR 1.6, Comment 10), in several circumstances, provisions of law outside the professional responsibility rules require or permit lawyers to disclose information that would otherwise be protected by the duty of confidentiality.

[6] In certain circumstances, lawyers may reveal confidential information to prevent **future crimes** or harms by clients. The circumstances defined by the Model Code and Model Rules are quite different from one another. MR 1.6(b)(1) and DR 4-101(A)(3). The 2002 amendments to the Model Rules have changed the focus of the exception from future crimes of clients to future, preventable harms. These harms may be the result of past client acts.

[7] Even when some others in addition to the lawyer and client know the protected client information, the duty of confidentiality continues to protect the information. If the client has shared the information with even a few others, the evidentiary privilege will be lost, but not the duty of confidentiality. When the information **is generally known,** however, its continued protection by the lawyer will in some cases serve little purpose and most would say that the duty of confidentiality is lost as well. Nonetheless, the lawyer's general duty of loyalty to the client counsels for the lawyer's exercise of discretion; if the client's lawyer speaks about information, even information that is generally known, there may be harm to the client's interests that the lawyer is duty-bound to refrain from causing. A lawyer is specifically permitted to use to the disadvantage of a **former client,** information that is generally known. MR 1.9(c)(1).

Example: Lawyer represents Client who is attempting to purchase a piece of property for development purposes. Newspaper prints a story indicating that Client is about to make this purchase. The confidence is now generally known and the duty of confidentiality may be of diminished importance. Nonetheless, Lawyer should refrain from speaking about Client's plans. Revelations by a client's lawyer will in many instances be more meaningful than revelations of the same facts by newspapers or other sources that have no duty of loyalty to the client.

FIGURE 7

EVIDENTIARY LAWYER-CLIENT PRIVILEGE

The parameters of the evidentiary privilege vary to some extent from jurisdiction to jurisdiction. Evidentiary privilege is a creature of the evidence law rather than professional responsibility law. It is meant to further many of the same interests as the duty of confidentiality. In general, the evidentiary privilege is created when a client or prospective client communicates in confidence to a lawyer or a person the client reasonably believes to be a lawyer who is being consulted as a lawyer.

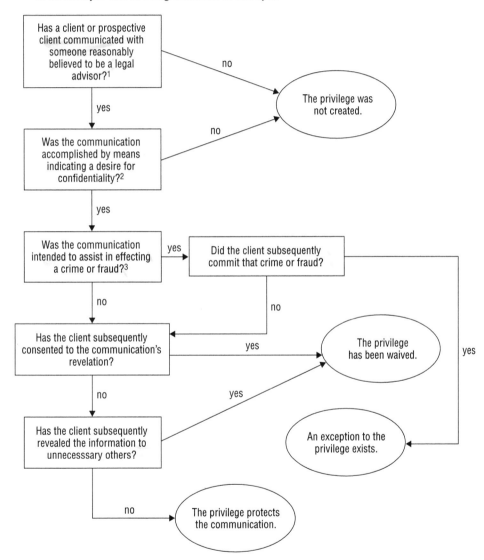

NOTES TO FIGURE 7

EVIDENTIARY LAWYER-CLIENT PRIVILEGE

[1] The privilege applies to communication from a client or a prospective client.

Example: Prospective client walks into Lawyer's office and says, "I did it. I poisoned my boss's decaf cappuccino. Now he's dead. What should I do?" Lawyer responds, "I have no idea. My practice is confined to tax law. But here's the name of a good criminal defense lawyer I know. See her." Client leaves. The attorney-client privilege protects the communication from Client to Lawyer and Lawyer is bound by the duty of confidentiality.

[2] The privilege is not created when the communication is made in circumstances that do not indicate a desire for confidentiality by the client.

Example: Client, accompanied by Acquaintance, consults Lawyer at Lawyer's office regarding a possible action for divorce. Client communicates all the private circumstances of his marital difficulties to Lawyer in the company of Acquaintance. Because Acquaintance was not necessary for Client's communication with Lawyer and because the presence of Acquaintance indicates an absence of a desire for confidentiality on the part of Client, the privilege is not created. Note that the ethical duty of confidentiality attaches nonetheless because the revelation of this information by the attorney would be embarrassing or detrimental to the client, and under the Model Rules language is "information relating to representation of a client. . . ." MR 1.6(a).

The privilege may also protect lawyer observations that result directly from the client's protected communications, as long as the lawyer does nothing to prevent other interested parties from making the same observation.

Example: Criminal Defendant-Client told Lawyer that the murder victim's partially burned wallet could be found in a burn bin behind Client's house. Lawyer went to the house and retrieved the wallet. After examining it in her office, Lawyer turned the wallet over to the Prosecuting Lawyer. The wallet, as physical evidence, is **not** subject to the attorney-client privilege; Client's statements to Lawyer, as communication from client to lawyer, are subject to the attorney-client privilege. The location at which the wallet was found is not subject to the attorney-client privilege because Lawyer, by her conduct of retrieving the wallet, has prevented the government from discovering by independent means the wallet's location. Had Lawyer merely observed the wallet and left it in the burn bin, Lawyer would have had no duty to submit the wallet to the Prosecuting Lawyer and Lawyer could not be required to reveal the wallet's location. People v. Meredith, 631 P.2d 46 (Cal. 1981).

[3] Communications that further future crimes or frauds are excepted from protection by the evidentiary privilege. This is called the **crime-fraud exception.**

The crime-fraud exception to the attorney-client privilege is much broader than the future crime exception to the duty of confidentiality. When a communication is within the crime-fraud exception to the attorney-client privilege, but is not within the future crime exception to the duty of confidentiality, the attorney-client privilege does not protect the communication, but the lawyer continues to have an ethical duty to maintain the confidence. If eventually a court rejects the assertion of the attorney-client privilege and orders the lawyer to testify, the "orders of court" exception to the duty of confidentiality will permit the lawyer to reveal the confidence.

FIGURE 8

CONFLICTS OF INTEREST

(see separate chart for imputed disqualification)

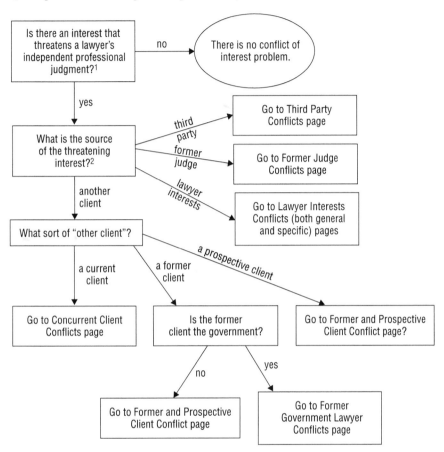

CONFLICTS OF INTEREST

[1] Basic to the lawyer-client relationship is the premise that lawyers owe clients a duty of **loyalty.** Lawyers owe clients a duty of **independent professional judgment.** When the independence is threatened by some interest other than the client's, a conflicts question is present and requires analysis.

Many conflicts questions are primarily about breaches of confidentiality. When a lawyer who is serving multiple clients has confidences of one that would benefit the other, a conflict-of-interest problem exists. Such a lawyer must either breach the confidences of one client or serve the other's interests less well than would be possible through the breach of the first client's confidence. Either choice is a breach of lawyer duty—hence, the conflict-of-interest problem. Relatively easy cases of conflict-of-interest analysis occur when the lawyer attempts to represent directly adverse interests.

The application of many of the conflicts rules is triggered by a determination of whether there "is a significant risk that the representation of a client will be materially limited by the [encroaching interest]." See, e.g., MR 1.7(a)(2). This standard is objective. It requires an examination to determine whether the lawyer's options on behalf of the client will be limited in ways of consequence by interests other than the client's.

[2] There are various sources of encroaching interests that may create conflicts. Primarily, third parties, the lawyer's own interests, and other clients will be the source of the encroaching interest. Former judicial duties may also be a source of conflict. Follow the chart from the encroaching interest to the various other conflicts charts to analyze your particular conflict problem.

FIGURE 9

CONCURRENT CLIENT CONFLICTS

A major source of conflicts is the interaction of **multiple clients** interests. Largely because lawyers owe a duty of confidentiality (and to a limited extent loyalty) to both prospective and former clients, multiple client conflicts can implicate not only concurrent representation of multiple clients but also conflicts between former and current clients, or prospective and current clients, or prospective and former clients.

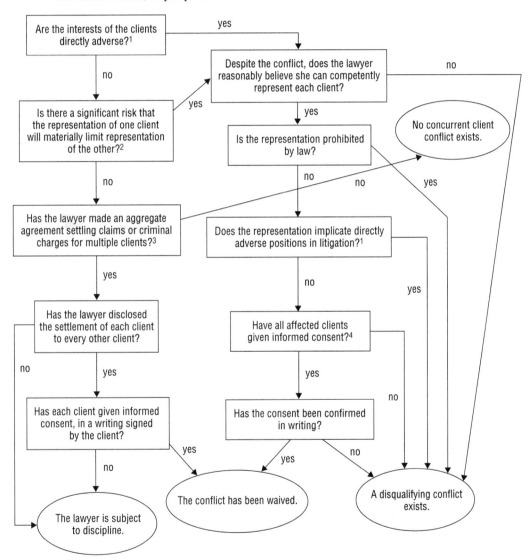

NOTES TO FIGURE 9

CONCURRENT CLIENT CONFLICTS

[1] The easiest cases involve multiple representation of clients whose interests are in direct conflict. Simply put, lawyers may not represent clients on opposite sides of the same matter, especially when litigation is involved. Such a direct conflict cannot be effectively waived by the clients on the theory that it is too gross a conflict. MR 1.7(a)(1).

Example: Firm has offices in City A and City B. Lawyer is a partner in Firm. Firm's City A office represents corporate Defendant in antitrust actions in two markets and sought to represent Defendant against claims of Plaintiff that Defendant had conspired to create a monopoly in a third market. Firm's City B office represented Plaintiff in the "third market" suit. Lawyer owes a duty of undivided loyalty to each of his clients. Because such adverse representation is improper, Firm is disqualified from representing Plaintiff. Cinema 5 Ltd. v. Cinerama, Inc., 528 F.2d 1384 (2d Cir. 1976).

[2] Some examples of such interference follow. A lawyer may find herself representing one client against a second client in a matter unrelated to the representation of the second client. The authority is mixed on whether such a conflict may be waived. It may depend on the context of the lawyer-client relationships involved and on the magnitude of the adversity. Both loyalty interests and the appearance of impropriety are offended by such representation. In general, such a conflict may not be waived, but when the adversity is general, waiver has been permitted.

Example: Lawyer represents Criminal Defendant against burglary charges. Lawyer also represents Grocery Store Owner as a regular matter in filing small claims to collect on bad checks and unpaid credit charges. Grocery Store Owner has such a claim against Criminal Defendant and wants Lawyer to file it. Lawyer should be subject to discipline for engaging in the representation against Criminal Defendant, unless both clients consent after consultation. MR 1.7, Comment.

Example: Lawyer regularly represents Bank 1 and Bank 2 in a variety of matters. Bank 1 and Bank 2 are generally competitors. This generally adverse simultaneous representation should be permitted without the necessity of client waiver. MR 1.7, Comment.

Even multiple representation of clients who are at least initially on the same side of litigation or a transaction implicates conflicts analysis.

Joint representation on civil claims brought simultaneously by multiple clients is permitted if the clients consent after consultation and if both the objective and subjective elements of the waiver test are met. When such representation is permissible, withdrawal from all representation may be the only adequate remedy if non-waivable conflicts later develop. When that is the case, the lawyer may represent none of the multiple clients.

Example: Driver and Passenger approach Lawyer with a potential claim against Careless Driver who went left-of-center and collided with Driver's car. Lawyer interviews both Driver and Passenger and files a Complaint on their behalf against Careless Driver. Later in the litigation, Lawyer learns that Driver had been drinking prior to the collision. Under these circumstances, Passenger has a claim against Driver as well as the claim against Careless Driver. To continue to represent Passenger, Lawyer must advise the filing of a claim against Lawyer's client (or former client) Driver, and would have to use the information Lawyer learned in the representation of Driver, namely Driver's drinking, against Driver. To continue to represent Driver, Lawyer would have to refrain from revealing the confidences of Driver to Passenger. In either instance, Lawyer will have to breach duties to a client. Therefore, Lawyer must withdraw from representing both Driver and Passenger.

[3] In both civil and criminal matters, a lawyer is prohibited from engaging in **aggregate settlements** of multiple clients' claims or charges unless all clients consent after consultation. MR 1.8(g).

Example: Lawyer represents Co-defendant 1 and Co-defendant 2. Prosecutor approaches Lawyer with a plea bargain proposal. Prosecutor proposes that he will dismiss charges against Co-defendant 1 if Co-defendant 2 pleads guilty to a reduced charge. Lawyer may not participate in this aggregate settlement of claims against his two clients.

[4] **Whether a conflict is waivable is often the critical, deciding point. Be careful to distinguish between the conflicts that may be waived and those that cannot. Recognize that even if a conflict exists and is waivable, a lawyer will be subject to discipline if she goes forward with anything less than a client's informed consent. Many questions will have the lawyer giving notice to the client, or merely disclosing the conflict to the client, neither of which satisfy the waiver requirements.**

Because most conflicts put client interests at risk and because client autonomy and decision-making are values worthy of some respect, clients are empowered to **waive** most conflicts of interest. By doing so, a client may then be represented by counsel of the client's choice in spite of the existence of a conflict-of-interest concern. Two important exceptions to this general rationale exist.

After consultation, a client must consent if waiver is to be effective. The client consent must be freely given and not coerced. It may be partial or conditional, consenting to some but not all potential conflicts. See Restatement of the Law Governing Lawyers (Third), sec. 122. The general rationale of honoring client autonomy does not apply when the conflict is sufficiently gross to make any client waiver suspect. Some conflicts rules that allow for client waiver include an element that is independent of the client's preferences, requiring that the lawyer "reasonably believe" that despite the conflict, the lawyer will be able to competently represent the client. MR 1.7(b)(1). This test implicates both objective and subjective standards. The lawyer must in fact believe that the representation will not be adversely affected. In addition, the lawyer's belief must be one that would be shared by a disinterested, reasonable lawyer.

Example: Client is a tenant, renting an apartment at Awful Arms Apartments. Client approaches Lawyer with Client's interest in pursuing a claim against Awful Arms based on breach of the warranty of habitability. Lawyer's spouse is the sole owner of Awful Arms Apartments Inc. In effect, if Lawyer undertook this representation, Lawyer would be filing a claim on Client's behalf against Lawyer's spouse. Even if Client asked that Lawyer engage in the representation despite the conflict, Lawyer cannot "reasonably believe" that despite the conflict, Lawyer will be able to competently represent Client, and must therefore decline to undertake this representation. Some of the conflicts rules that allow waiver require more than consent after consultation. Some require informed consent, e.g., MR 1.8(b), MR 1.8(f); some require informed consent, confirmed in writing, e.g., MR 1.7(b), 1.9, 1.12; some require informed consent in a writing signed by the client, e.g., MR 1.8(a); and some have additional, specific requirements, e.g., MR 1.8(a) and 1.8(h).

FIGURE 10

FORMER AND PROSPECTIVE CLIENT CONFLICTS

(begins with a current client and either a former client of a prospective client for whom representation was not undertaken)

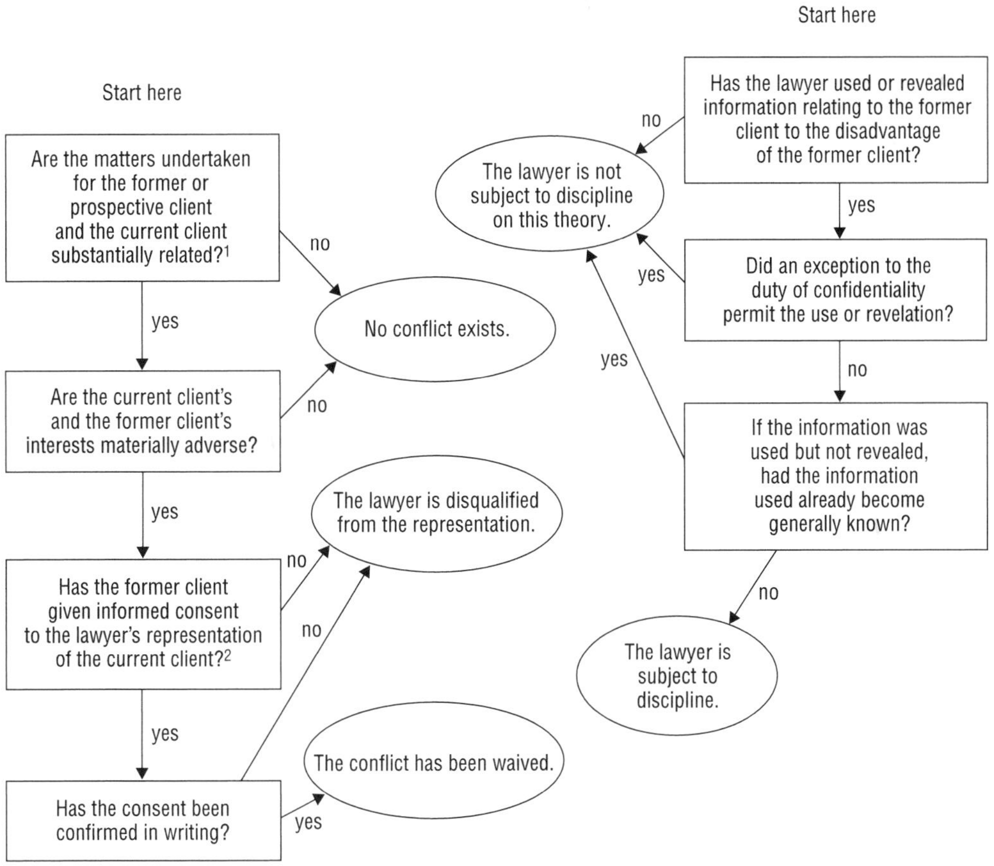

Start here

Are the matters undertaken for the former or prospective client and the current client substantially related?[1]

no → No conflict exists.

yes ↓

Are the current client's and the former client's interests materially adverse?

no → No conflict exists.

yes ↓

Has the former client given informed consent to the lawyer's representation of the current client?[2]

no → The lawyer is disqualified from the representation.

yes ↓

Has the consent been confirmed in writing?

no → The lawyer is disqualified from the representation.

yes → The conflict has been waived.

Start here

Has the lawyer used or revealed information relating to the former client to the disadvantage of the former client?

no → The lawyer is not subject to discipline on this theory.

yes ↓

Did an exception to the duty of confidentiality permit the use or revelation?

yes → The lawyer is not subject to discipline on this theory.

no ↓

If the information was used but not revealed, had the information used already become generally known?

yes → The lawyer is not subject to discipline on this theory.

no → The lawyer is subject to discipline.

NOTES TO FIGURE **10**
FORMER AND PROSPECTIVE CLIENT CONFLICTS

[1] Because lawyers owe clients a continued measure of loyalty after representation ends and because lawyers owe clients a full measure of the duty of confidentiality after representation ends, conflicts between former and current clients arise when their interests are directly adverse or when there is a **substantial relationship** between the two representations. Such a conflict may be waived by both clients by giving informed consent, confirmed in writing. MR 1.9.

Example: Lawyer worked as in-house counsel for Corporation before joining Firm A. After Lawyer joined Firm A, Firm A represented Plaintiff in a suit against Corporation. While employed by Corporation, Lawyer had access to confidential information relating to Corporation's business practices relevant to the litigation between Plaintiff and Corporation. While working for Firm A, Lawyer had personal involvement in the litigation between Plaintiff and Corporation.

Whether or not Lawyer *actually* shared information about Corporation with Firm A, Lawyer is disqualified from the case. Haagen-Dazs Co. v. Perche No! Gelato, Inc., 639 F. Supp. 282 (N.D. Cal. 1986).

[2] **Whether a conflict is waivable is often the critical, deciding point. Be careful to distinguish between the conflicts that may be waived and those that cannot. Recognize that when a conflict exists and is waivable, a lawyer will be subject to discipline if she goes forward with anything less than a client's informed consent. Many questions will have the lawyer giving notice to the client, or merely disclosing the conflict with the client, neither of which satisfy the waiver requirements.**

Because most conflicts put client interests at risk and because client autonomy and decision-making are values worthy of some respect, clients are empowered to **waive** most conflicts of interest. By doing so, a client may then be represented by counsel of the client's choice in spite of the existence of a conflict-of-interest concern. Two important exceptions to this general rationale exist.

After consultation, a client must consent if waiver is to be effective. The client consent must be freely given and not coerced. It may be partial or conditional, consenting to some but not all potential conflicts. See Restatement of the Law Governing Lawyers (Third), sec. 122.

The general rationale of honoring client autonomy does not apply when the conflict is sufficiently gross to make any client waiver suspect. Some conflicts rules that allow for client waiver include an element that is independent of the client's preferences, requiring that the lawyer "reasonably believe" that despite the conflict, the lawyer will be able to competently represent the client. MR 1.7(b)(1). This test implicates both objective and subjective standards. The lawyer must in fact believe that the representation will not be adversely affected. In addition, the lawyer's belief must be one that would be shared by a disinterested, reasonable lawyer.

Example: Client is a tenant, renting an apartment at Awful Arms Apartments. Client approaches Lawyer with Client's interest in pursuing a claim against Awful Arms based on breach of the warranty of habitability. Lawyer's spouse is the sole owner of Awful Arms Apartments Inc. In effect, if Lawyer undertook this representation, Lawyer would be filing a claim on Client's behalf against Lawyer's spouse. Even if Client asked that Lawyer engage in the representation despite the conflict, Lawyer cannot "reasonably believe" that despite the conflict, Lawyer will be able to competently represent Client, and must therefore decline to undertake this representation. Some of the conflicts rules that allow waiver require more than consent after consultation. Some require informed consent, e.g., MR 1.8(b), MR 1.8(f); some require informed consent, confirmed in writing, e.g., MR 1.7(b), 1.9, 1.12; some require informed consent in a writing signed by the client, e.g., MR 1.8(a); and some have additional, specific requirements, e.g., MR 1.8(a) and 1.8(h).

FIGURE 11

FORMER GOVERNMENT LAWYER CONFLICTS[1]

Special conflicts rules apply to lawyers who move from government practice to private practice. MR 1.11. At least two facts distinguish former government lawyers who move into private practice from private practice lawyers who have moved from employment in one law firm to employment in another law firm. First, government lawyers represent the government (or the public, or the particular agency within which they worked). As a result, in later private practice, any representation of private parties against the government might be seen as former client conflicts. Because of the breadth of the potential disqualification from representation, this result must be ameliorated. Second, as a government lawyer, the stakes of the appearance of impropriety are raised. The possibility of abuses of either relationships with former colleagues still in government practice or of confidential government information create greater concern regarding private practice subsequent to government practice. Both of these facts have effects on the formulation of the special conflicts rules that apply to former government lawyers.

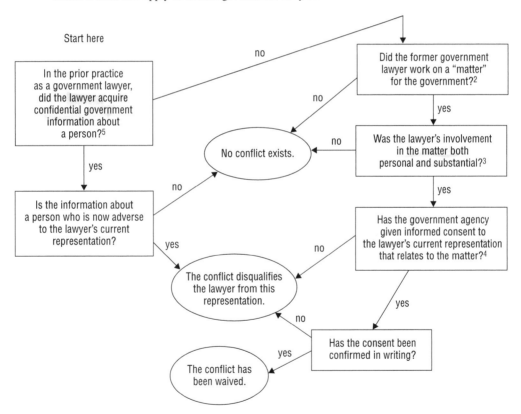

NOTES TO FIGURE 11

FORMER GOVERNMENT LAWYER CONFLICTS

[1] A former government "lawyer shall not represent a private client in connection with a matter in which the lawyer participated personally and substantially" as a government lawyer. MR 1.11. Notice that this conflict rule applies without regard to whether the lawyer has effectively changed sides in the matter.

Example: The SEC investigated and prosecuted Defendants for misappropriating money and property from a group of investment companies. Following a default judgment against Defendants, Judge appointed Receiver to recover the judgment from Defendant. Receiver retained Firm to assist in litigation against Defendants. However, Firm employed Lawyer, a former SEC official who had had supervisory authority over the original prosecution of Defendants. Although Lawyer had not participated on a daily basis, he was generally aware of the facts of the case and the status of the litigation. Lawyer may not participate in the representation of the Receiver absent agency consent. Armstrong v. McAlpin, 625 F.2d 433 (2d Cir. 1980), *vacated on other grounds,* 449 U.S. 1106 (1981).

[2] The rule defines what it means by a "matter." It is only later private representation in connection with a government service "matter" that triggers a conflict-of-interest analysis. A matter includes a wide variety of instances and actions that engage the agency with a particular party or parties. The definition excludes rule drafting and other agency actions that have more general application.

Example: Lawyer worked in the IRS policy office. Lawyer's primary task was to draft a new set of regulations for determining the deductibility of business travel expenses. The regulations Lawyer drafted became law through normal agency procedures. Later, Lawyer leaves the IRS and goes into private practice. Client hires Lawyer to defend an action being brought by the IRS. At issue is the interpretation of the business travel regulation that Lawyer had written. Lawyer may represent Client because the regulation drafting activity is not a "matter." MR 1.11(d).

[3] Similar to the treatment of former judges, the mere fact that a lawyer was employed in a particular agency while that agency was involved in a matter does not disqualify the lawyer under the conflicts rules. Only when the lawyer has participated personally and substantially will the conflicts rule's disqualification threshold issues be satisfied.

[4] The agency may waive the conflict by giving its consent. In the absence of a specific statute that applies to the specific agency to the contrary, an agency may waive all future conflicts for its departing lawyers.

[5] Except when law otherwise expressly permits such representation, a former government lawyer is also prohibited from representing private parties who are adverse to parties about whom the lawyer has confidential information gained in the government practice that could be used against the adverse party. MR 1.11(b).

Example: Lawyer formerly worked for the IRS. In that capacity, Lawyer was privy to confidential information about Taxpayer's finances and assets. In private practice, Client approaches Lawyer requesting representation against Taxpayer in a complex matter that involves the finances and assets of Taxpayer. Lawyer has a conflict of interest and may not represent Client against Taxpayer unless Taxpayer consents.

The private party's interests are the ones at risk in such a case. As such, it is the private party and not the agency that must waive the conflict if the lawyer is to be permitted to proceed. Such a waiver is, of course, highly unlikely in such an instance.

FIGURE 12

FORMER JUDGE CONFLICTS

Former judges' conflicts differ from those of lawyers who move from one practice setting to another, and they require special conflicts rules. MR 1.12.

In their judicial role, judges do not represent parties and thus have little of the loyalty transfer concerns of lawyers representing multiple clients. In addition, judges are not the confidants of clients and thus carry forward into private practice no former client confidences. Nonetheless, the appearance of impropriety considerations are stronger in the case of certain former judge conflicts situations than are the like concerns with lawyers' similar conflicts.

A former judge shall not engage in private representation in a matter in which the judge participated personally and substantially as a judge, unless all parties to the matter consent after consultation. MR 1.12.

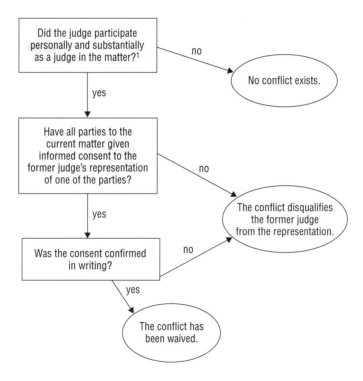

FORMER JUDGE CONFLICTS

[1] Judges in most courts are members of a group of judges who individually hear cases brought before their court. The mere fact that a judge was a member of a group of judges that variously hear cases brought to a particular court does not disqualify the judge from all matters that were in the court while the judge was there. Only when the judge has participated personally and substantially will the conflicts rule apply.

FIGURE 13

THIRD PARTY CONFLICTS

Third party interference conflicts occur when someone who is not a party to the lawyer-client relationship seeks to affect or becomes positioned to affect the independence of the lawyer's judgment on behalf of the client. See MR 1.7(a)(1) for the general rule. Such conflicts may be waived if the client gives informed consent.

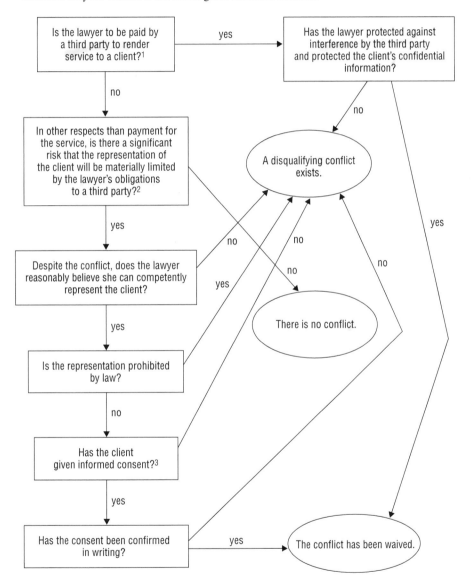

NOTES TO FIGURE 13

THIRD PARTY CONFLICTS

[1] The most common third party interference example occurs when a third party pays the lawyer's fee for the lawyer's representation of a client. MR 1.8(f).

Example: Harry has retained Lawyer to represent him in a divorce proceeding. Lawyer has agreed to represent Harry at a reduced fee. Harry's Mother approaches Lawyer and offers to pay Lawyer's full fee on Harry's behalf. Lawyer may not agree to this proposal unless Harry consents after consultation. Even then, Lawyer must instruct Harry's Mother that Lawyer represents Harry and not Harry's Mother and that Lawyer owes the lawyer's professional duties, including confidentiality, to Harry alone. MR 1.8(f).

[2] Many practice settings place the lawyer in a position of guarding against inappropriate third party influence as a regular, daily part of practice. Some of these involve third parties who pay the lawyer; others are less direct but no less real.

Lawyer for an organization: The lawyer who represents an organization (e.g., a corporation or a labor union) represents the organization, not the individual directors or managers of the organization. MR 1.13. Nonetheless, the organization's lawyer talks and interacts with the directors and managers; indeed, the primary way in which the organization's legal needs and interests can be made known to the lawyer is through the communications of the directors and managers. To the extent that the managers and directors articulate the organization's interests, the lawyer is hearing from her client. But when the directors and managers interpose their personal interests between the lawyer and the organization-client, a third party interference conflict of interest occurs.

Example: Lawyer is in-house counsel to Corporation. CEO confides in Lawyer that CEO has been engaged in an ongoing series of frauds on behalf of Corporation and instructs Lawyer to maintain this as a confidence. CEO has an interest in not being discovered and in continuing the frauds. Corporation has an interest in discontinuing CEO's actions and in distancing itself from the unauthorized and wrongful actions of CEO. CEO is a third party attempting to interfere with Lawyer's lawyer-client relationship with Corporation. Even though CEO ordinarily speaks for Corporation, Lawyer's duty is to Corporation, the entity that is Lawyer's client.

Legal services practice: Lawyers who provide legal services to the poor through an organized legal services or legal aid office represent their clients but are paid to do so by the organization for which they work. The legal aid organization is typically a not-for-profit corporation, with a board of directors, that obtains grants from the government and employs lawyers to represent people who meet low-income and asset eligibility requirements. Two sources of third party interference are present and must be guarded against.

The organization, usually through its board of directors, will typically establish case acceptance priority guidelines that restrict the lawyer's freedom to accept the cases that the lawyer might prefer to accept. Members of the board of directors of a legal services organization are not lawyers for the purpose of the lawyer-client relationship with the organization's clients. MR 6.3. Therefore, board members may represent clients who are adverse to the organization's clients, but may not participate in decisions of the organization that materially affect the interests of the organization's clients when the board member represents a client adverse to the organization's client. MR 6.3.

Government regulations, especially those of the federal Legal Services Corporation, restrict the type of services that may be provided by organizations that receive the applicable category of funding. For example, a Legal Services Corporation grantee legal aid lawyer is prohibited from engaging in legislative lobbying services for clients. These restrictions are interferences by third parties with the lawyer-client relationship.

Insurance defense: In some insurance contexts, a lawyer is hired and paid by an insurance company to represent the insured. When the insurance company is not also a party to the matter, the company is a potential third party interference with the lawyer-client relationship between the lawyer and the insured.

[3] **Whether a conflict is waivable is often the critical, deciding point. Be careful to distinguish between the conflicts that may be waived and those that cannot. Recognize that when a conflict exists and is waivable, a lawyer will be subject to discipline if she goes forward with anything less than a client's informed consent. Many questions will have the lawyer giving notice to the client, or merely disclosing the conflict with the client, neither of which satisfy the waiver requirements.**

Because most conflicts put client interests at risk and because client autonomy and decision-making are values worthy of some respect, clients are empowered to **waive** most conflicts of interest. By doing so, a client may then be represented by counsel of the client's choice in spite of the existence of a conflict-of-interest concern. Two important exceptions to this general rationale exist.

After consultation, a client must consent if waiver is to be effective. The client consent must be freely given and not coerced. It may be partial or conditional, consenting to some but not all potential conflicts. See Restatement of the Law Governing Lawyers (Third), sec. 122.

The general rationale of honoring client autonomy does not apply when the conflict is sufficiently gross to make any client waiver suspect. Some conflicts rules that allow for client waiver include an element that is independent of the client's preferences, requiring that the lawyer "reasonably believe" that despite the conflict, the lawyer will be able to competently represent the client. MR 1.7(b)(1). This test implicates both objective and subjective standards. The lawyer must in fact believe that the representation will not be adversely affected. In addition, the lawyer's belief must be one that would be shared by a disinterested, reasonable lawyer.

Example: Client is a tenant, renting an apartment at Awful Arms Apartments. Client approaches Lawyer with Client's interest in pursuing a claim against Awful Arms based on breach of the warranty of habitability. Lawyer's spouse is the sole owner of Awful Arms Apartments Inc. In effect, if Lawyer undertook this representation, Lawyer would be filing a claim on Client's behalf against Lawyer's spouse. Even if Client asked that Lawyer engage in the representation despite the conflict, Lawyer cannot "reasonably believe" that despite the conflict, Lawyer will be able to competently represent Client, and must therefore decline to undertake this representation. Some of the conflicts rules that allow waiver require more than consent after consultation. Some require informed consent, e.g., MR 1.8(b), MR 1.8(f); some require informed consent, confirmed in writing, e.g., MR 1.7(b), 1.9, 1.12; some require informed consent in a writing signed by the client, e.g., MR 1.8(a); and some have additional, specific requirements, e.g., MR 1.8(a) and 1.8(h).

FIGURE 14

LAWYER INTERESTS CONFLICTS (GENERAL)

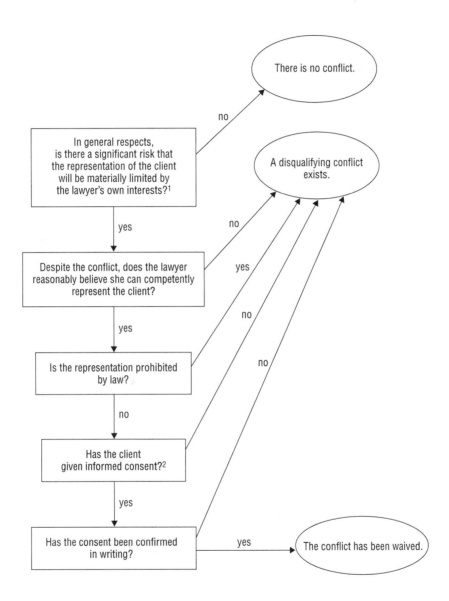

LAWYER INTERESTS CONFLICTS (GENERAL)

[1] As a general matter, a conflict of interest exists when "there is a significant risk that representation of a client will be materially limited by the lawyer's . . . own interests." MR 1.7(a)(2).

[2] **Whether a conflict is waivable is often the critical, deciding point. Be careful to distinguish between the conflicts that may be waived and those that cannot. Recognize that when a conflict exists and is waivable, a lawyer will be subject to discipline if she goes forward with anything less than a client's informed consent. Many questions will have the lawyer giving notice to the client, or merely disclosing the conflict with the client, neither of which satisfy the waiver requirements.**

Because most conflicts put client interests at risk and because client autonomy and decision-making are values worthy of some respect, clients are empowered to **waive** most conflicts of interest. By doing so, a client may then be represented by counsel of the client's choice in spite of the existence of a conflict-of-interest concern. Two important exceptions to this general rationale exist.

After consultation, a client must consent if waiver is to be effective. The client consent must be freely given and not coerced. It may be partial or conditional, consenting to some but not all potential conflicts. See Restatement of the Law Governing Lawyers (Third), sec. 122.

The general rationale of honoring client autonomy does not apply when the conflict is sufficiently gross to make any client waiver suspect. Some conflicts rules that allow for client waiver include an element that is independent of the client's preferences, requiring that the lawyer "reasonably believe" that despite the conflict, the lawyer will be able to competently represent the client. MR 1.7(b)(1). This test implicates both objective and subjective standards. The lawyer must in fact believe that the representation will not be adversely affected. In addition, the lawyer's belief must be one that would be shared by a disinterested, reasonable lawyer.

Example: Client is a tenant, renting an apartment at Awful Arms Apartments. Client approaches Lawyer with Client's interest in pursuing a claim against Awful Arms based on breach of the warranty of habitability. Lawyer's spouse is the sole owner of Awful Arms Apartments Inc. In effect, if Lawyer undertook this representation, Lawyer would be filing a claim on Client's behalf against Lawyer's spouse. Even if Client asked that Lawyer engage in the representation despite the conflict, Lawyer cannot "reasonably believe" that despite the conflict, Lawyer will be able to competently represent Client, and must therefore decline to undertake this representation. Some of the conflicts rules that allow waiver require more than consent after consultation. Some require informed consent, e.g., MR 1.8(b), MR 1.8(f); some require informed consent, confirmed in writing, e.g., MR 1.7(b), 1.9, 1.12; some require informed consent in a writing signed by the client, e.g., MR 1.8(a); and some have additional, specific requirements, e.g., MR 1.8(a) and 1.8(h).

FIGURE 15

LAWYER INTERESTS CONFLICTS (SPECIFIC)

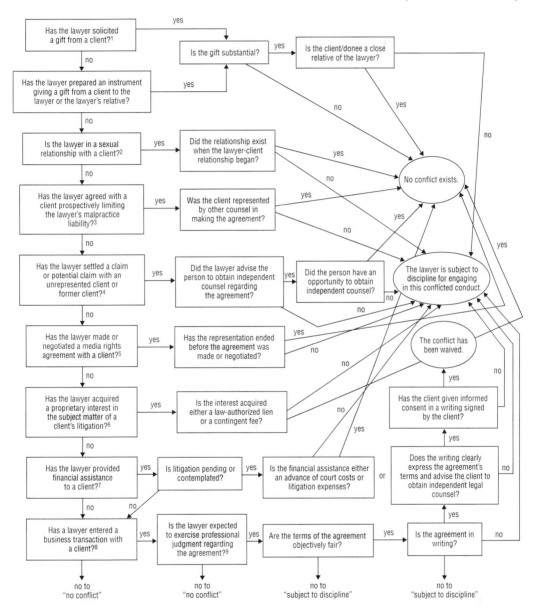

LAWYER INTERESTS CONFLICTS (SPECIFIC)

[1] A lawyer is prohibited from drafting a document that makes a substantial gift to the lawyer or the lawyer's close relatives. This restriction does not apply when the donee is related to the donor. MR 1.8(c).

[2] Because of the complicated mixture of interests that can develop when a professional lawyer-client relationship is mingled with an amorous one, lawyers are well advised to avoid amorous relationships with current clients. Some states have used a conflicts rationale to prohibit such relationships while others have used a moral turpitude rationale. MR 1.8(j).

[3] A lawyer is prohibited from entering into a contract with a client that prospectively limits the lawyer's liability for malpractice unless state law permits and the client is represented by independent counsel with respect to the agreement. MR 1.8(h)(1).

[4] A lawyer is prohibited from settling malpractice claims with unrepresented clients or former clients unless the lawyer first advises the client or former client that independent counsel is advisable. MR 1.8(h)(2).

[5] Lawyers are prohibited from negotiating for literary or media rights based on their clients' stories until the conclusion of representation. A lawyer's judgment may be compromised if the lawyer has an interest in the client's matter being handled in a dramatic fashion. MR 1.8(d). No waiver of this conflict is permitted.

Example: Murder Defendant is the son of a famous movie star. Lawyer agrees to represent Murder Defendant in exchange for Murder Defendant's agreement to cooperate only with Lawyer and with no other writer working on books or movie projects based on his story. Without more, Lawyer is subject to discipline. Government offers Murder Defendant a very favorable plea agreement. Lawyer's interests are furthered by rejection of the plea agreement (who wants to watch a movie-of-the-week with a negotiation session as the climactic scene?). Lawyer's independent judgment on behalf of Murder Defendant has been impaired.

[6] A lawyer is prohibited from acquiring an interest in litigation or its subject matter, whether that interest is consistent or inconsistent with the client's interests. This prohibition is not a restriction on the lawyer's contract with a client for a reasonable contingent fee. Client waiver of a violation of this rule is not permitted. MR 1.8(i).

Example: Client is engaged in a dispute over ownership of 22 acres of prime commercial property. Lawyer agrees to represent Client in this dispute in exchange for a 5 percent interest in the property conveyed to Lawyer from Client. Lawyer's interest is worth nothing unless Client prevails in the dispute. Lawyer is subject to discipline because a lawyer's interest may impair her independent judgment and because a lawyer's purchase of an interest in the subject matter of litigation is thought to violate the champerty policy against stirring up litigation. The same would be true if Lawyer had purchased a 5 percent interest in the property from Client's Opponent, but for different reasons. In this instance, Lawyer's interests would be adverse to Client's interests. By contrast, however, Client could pay Lawyer's fee by conveying a 5 percent interest in some other property of Client's that was not the subject matter of the dispute.

[7] Lawyers are prohibited from advancing financial assistance to clients when there is pending or contemplated litigation, except that the lawyer may advance court costs. Client waiver of this "conflict" is not permitted. MR 1.8(e).

Example: Lawyer advanced money to three clients for purposes other than the cost of litigation (e.g., to help pay the clients' rent or grocery bills). He did not aim to obtain legal business or collect interest but merely to provide charitable and humanitarian assistance to clients in extremely dire financial need.

The rule proscribing Lawyer's conduct makes no exceptions. It is intended to prevent an attorney from procuring an interest in a legal matter but does not require proof of such intent or effect. Lawyer's conduct is subject to discipline. Committee on Professional Ethics & Conduct of the Iowa State Bar Ass'n v. Bitter, 279 N.W. 2d 521 (Iowa 1979).

[8] Model Rule 1.8(a), which addresses business transactions between lawyer and client, requires that the client's consent be in writing, that the client be "given a reasonable opportunity to seek the advice of independent counsel," that the transaction be objectively reasonable, and that the transaction itself be in writing and in terms that can be understood by the client.

Example: For several years, Lawyer advised Client on a number of business and personal matters. Client then decided to replace his small boat with a larger model, paying a deposit and requesting Lawyer to arrange for the financing of a $30,000 balance. Lawyer was unable to obtain sufficient funds for payment of the balance. Insisting that he did not want to lose his deposit, Client agreed to borrow $30,000 from Lawyer, with title to the new boat as security. Further, Client conveyed a parcel of real estate and all of the personal property on it and his small boat to Lawyer. Client also signed an agreement indicating his awareness of the drawbacks of the deal and containing his acknowledgment that Lawyer had advised against the transaction. When Client defaulted on the first payment on the note, Lawyer took possession of the new boat without notice to Client, as permitted by their agreement.

The transaction between Lawyer and Client was fundamentally unfair. At a minimum, Lawyer should not have proceeded with the transaction until Client had an opportunity to receive independent advice on the matter. Lawyer breached his fiduciary duty to Client. Lawyer had to return the fair market value of the assets transferred, plus interest. Goldman v. Kane, 329 N.E.2d 770 (Mass. App. Ct. 1975).

[9] The business transactions restrictions of MR 1.8(a) apply only when the client expects the lawyer to exercise legal judgment regarding the transaction. As such, lawyer and client may enter ordinary business transactions with one another without restriction.

Example: Lawyer and Client live in the same neighborhood. Lawyer attends Client's garage sale and purchases Client's used lawn mower at a very reasonable price. Because Lawyer was not expected to exercise legal judgment regarding the transaction, the business transaction restrictions do not apply.

FIGURE 16

IMUPTED DISQUALIFICATION

If you are beginning this chart, you will have determined that a conflict exists for a lawyer that is either non-waivable or has not been properly waived. As a general rule, when a lawyer has a conflict of interest, that conflict imputes to (transfers to, extends to) all of the lawyers in the law organization (usually a law firm) in which the lawyer works. MR 1.10.

This **imputed disqualification** rule is mainly based on the notion that confidential information possessed by one lawyer is effectively possessed by all lawyers in the same firm. In addition, loyalty and appearance of impropriety concerns arise when one lawyer in a firm engages in representation from which another lawyer in the firm would be disqualified for conflict-of-interests reasons.

Motions to disqualify counsel, and entire law firms for which the disqualified lawyer works, have become a favored tactical device in litigation, effectively denying an opposing party her counsel of choice and preserving the integrity of the justice system from the threat of conflicts of interest.

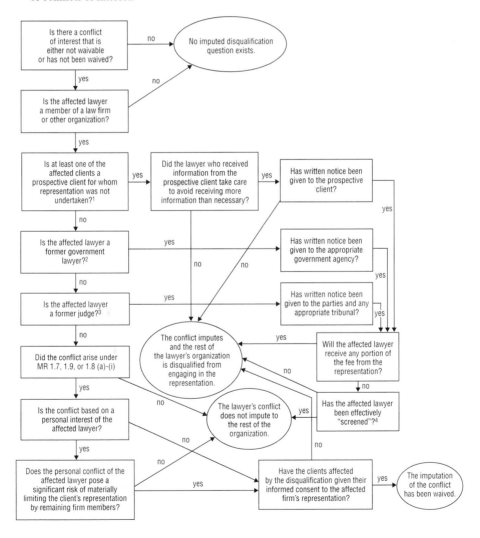

NOTES TO FIGURE 16

IMUPTED DISQUALIFICATION

[1] Less restrictive imputed disqualification rules apply when one of the clients in a multiple client conflict is either a former client or a prospective one. MR 1.9 and 1.18.

[2] Special, more relaxed, imputed disqualification rules apply when former government lawyers are the law firm lawyers who have a conflict. The government would have a difficult time recruiting qualified lawyers if those lawyers knew that their firms would be disqualified from doing virtually all of the type of work they did in government practice. *Example:* Lawyer was employed at the IRS. As an IRS lawyer, Lawyer represented the IRS or more generally the federal government as a client. Lawyer left government service for private practice. If the conflict rules applied strictly in this instance, Lawyer could not represent anyone against the IRS (a former client) without IRS consent. Further, as a general proposition, Lawyer's disqualification would be imputed to Lawyer's law firm, thus preventing both Lawyer and her law firm from doing federal tax practice. The conflict rules relax slightly for former government lawyers. MR 1.11.

The imputed disqualification rules relax with respect to former government lawyers' law firms.
Example: The SEC investigated and prosecuted Defendants for misappropriating money and property from a group of investment companies. Following a default judgment against Defendants, Judge appointed Receiver to recover the judgment from Defendant. Receiver retained Firm to assist in litigation against Defendants. However, Firm employed Lawyer, a former SEC official who had had supervisory authority over the original prosecution of Defendants. Although Lawyer had not participated on daily basis, he was generally aware of the facts of the case and the status of the litigation. Receiver learned of Lawyer's employment with Firm during his initial meetings with Firm, and Receiver and Firm agreed to screen Lawyer from the litigation against Defendants. Both the SEC and Judge authorized this plan.

Although Lawyer may not participate in the representation of the Receiver absent agency consent, Firm is not disqualified because (1) the SEC had turned over its files to Receiver before he retained Firm, (2) Lawyer was properly screened from the case, (3) disqualification would hamper government efforts to recruit qualified attorneys by limiting their future employment opportunities, and (4) disqualification would delay and perhaps thwart Receiver's attempts to redress the wrongs committed by Defendants. Armstrong v. McAlpin, 625 F.2d 433 (2d Cir. 1980), *vacated,* 449 U.S. 1106 (1981).

[3] To prevent a hand-cuffing of former judges' efforts to obtain private law firm employment after judicial service and because former judge conflicts do not implicate the same sort of loyalty and confidentiality abuse as do multiple client lawyer conflicts, special, more relaxed imputed disqualification rules apply to the law firms for which former judges work. Effective screening procedures and notice to the judge's former court permit a former judge's law firm to continue with representation in which the former judge is disqualified from participating. MR 1.12(c).

[4] Effective **screening procedures** will prevent the application of the imputed disqualification rules. Some courts have labeled these screening procedures the "Chinese Wall" defense, because the affected lawyer is walled off. Under such procedures, the conflicted lawyer is isolated from other lawyers in the organization by various devices including, for example, the following: moving the affected lawyer's office, issuing instructions to all lawyers to refrain from discussion of the matter with the affected lawyer, and preventing the affected lawyer from profiting from the matter.

FIGURE 17

IN COURT ACTIVITIES (MISCELLANEOUS)
p. 1

When functioning in court, a lawyer is not only subject to the professional supervision of the organized bar, but of the presiding court as well. As a result, it is not uncommon for a single act of lawyer misconduct to simultaneously produce potential liability for discipline and various court sanctions. This chart therefore includes multiple result targets for various individual lawyer actions.

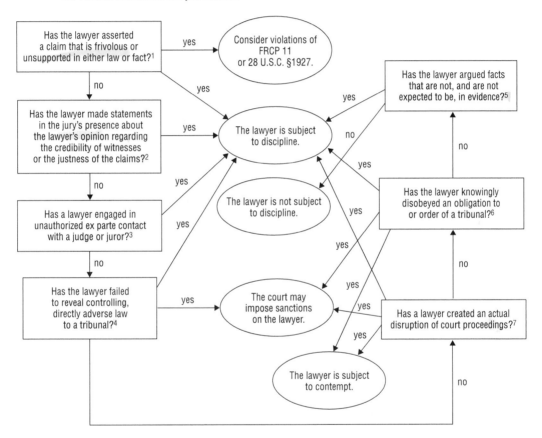

FIGURE 17 (cont'd)

IN COURT ACTIVITIES (MISCELLANEOUS)
p. 2

When functioning in court, a lawyer is not only subject to the professional supervision of the organized bar, but of the presiding court as well. As a result, it is not uncommon for a single act of lawyer misconduct to simultaneously produce potential liability for discipline and various court sanctions. This chart therefore includes multiple result targets for various individual lawyer actions.

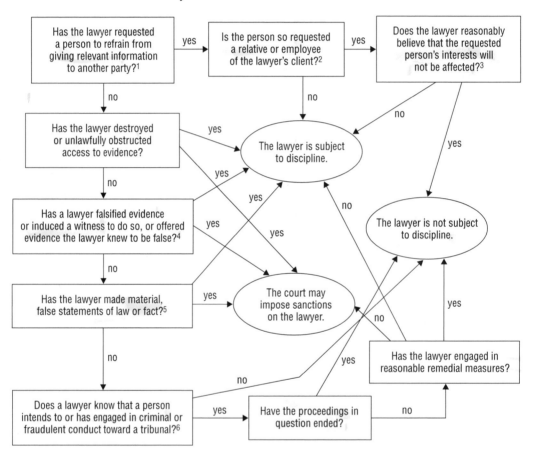

IN COURT ACTIVITIES (MISCELLANEOUS) p. 1

[1] By both ethics code provisions and by litigation sanctions rules, lawyers are prohibited from bringing actions or taking positions in litigation that are frivolous. In several forms, the Model Rules restrict lawyers' behavior regarding frivolous positions. Model Rule 3.1, in most respects tracking Federal Rule of Civil Procedure 11, prohibits lawyers from bringing or defending claims on a frivolous basis.

Frivolous claims or positions may be so because they lack legal or factual merit or because they are taken primarily to harass or maliciously injure a third party.

A claim or position is not frivolous merely because it loses the day. To be frivolous, an argument must be one that a reasonable lawyer would regard as having no legal or factual merit.

Under the analogous Model Code provision, a claim was frivolous when it was brought merely to harass or injure. DR 7-102(A)(1). That standard is found in the Model Rules in both MR 4.4 and in the Comment to MR 3.1. Such conduct is subject to discipline.

Beyond the ethics code limitations that create disciplinary liability for filing frivolous claims and taking frivolous positions in litigation, Federal Rule of Civil Procedure 11 and its state law counterparts create sanctions liability for similar conduct. A court may consider a motion for sanctions even though the proceedings have ended.

Example: Client, a clothing retailer, brought an antitrust action against Manufacturers A and B, alleging a nationwide conspiracy to fix prices and engage in unfair competition. Firm filed Client's Complaint after phoning clothing retailers in New York City, Philadelphia, Baltimore, and Washington, D.C. From this research, Firm inferred that only one store in each major metropolitan area nationwide sold Manufacturer A's product. Later, Firm voluntarily dismissed the claim, and Manufacturers A and B moved for Rule 11 sanctions. The district court awarded sanctions to the Manufacturers, the appellate court affirmed that ruling, and the district court imposed appellate costs on Firm.

District courts may enforce Rule 11 even after the plaintiff has filed a notice of voluntary dismissal because the harm triggering the Rule's application—needless expense and delay—has already occurred. A Rule 11 violation is complete when the baseless claim is filed. Federal courts may consider many such collateral issues after an action is no longer pending. The court correctly sanctioned Firm, but the imposition of appellate costs is appropriate only when the sanctioned party files a frivolous appeal, not when the appellate court has simply upheld the original award. Cooter & Gell v. Hartmarx Corp., 496 U.S. 384 (1990).

[2] Lawyers are prohibited from expressing their personal opinion to jurors about the justness of the client's cause, the credibility of a witness, or the culpability, guilt or innocence of a party. MR 3.4(e). This rule only applies to personal opinion statements. It does not prohibit vigorous argument that attempts to persuade the jury about any of the prohibited personal opinion subject matters.

Example: In closing argument, Lawyer says at various points, "In my 15 years of lawyering, I have never seen so clear a case of a witness lying"; "when a witness says one thing one day and another thing the next, that witness is not worthy of belief"; "my client has every reason to tell you the truth about this matter. She has told you everything she knows about this controversy"; and "I wouldn't represent this client if I didn't believe her story. You see me here today and you know what that means." The first and fourth statements are prohibited; the second and third are appropriate argument.

[3] Our judicial system is built upon the premise that adversaries can make their best arguments to the judge and the judge can then decide the matter. That premise requires that the adversaries' arguments be made in the presence of one another so that each side's response can be heard. **Ex parte** (without the other party) **communications** seriously undermine the prospect of fair process in the justice system. As such, ex parte communication with decisionmakers, both judges and jurors, is strictly regulated.

If lawyers were permitted to have ex parte communications with judges, then litigated matters would be resolved on the basis of a series of one-at-a-time advocacy episodes rather than the give and take of opposing sides presenting evidence in open court and contesting one another's arguments. The justice system would be seriously undermined. As such, except in very limited circumstances, lawyers are prohibited from communicating ex parte with a judge. MR 3.5(b). Some ex parte communications are permitted because of their subject matter.

Communications between lawyers and judges about matters unrelated to pending or impending litigation are not restricted by the rule. Such communications are not truly "ex parte" because they do not involve other parties at all.

Example: Lawyer has various matters pending in Judge's court. Lawyer goes to Judge's garage sale and discusses the purchase of Judge's used wrought-iron dinette set. This discussion is not an ex parte communication between Judge and Lawyer and is therefore not prohibited.

Ex parte communications regarding so-called housekeeping matters that relate to a pending case are permitted. Most such communications will actually occur between the lawyer or her agents and the judge's agents, such as clerks and docket personnel. Housekeeping matters are those that are unrelated to the way in which the judge will ultimately rule on the matter, such as inquiries about available dates for hearings or trial.

Example: Lawyer plans to file an evidentiary motion in Judge's court regarding a pending matter. To schedule the motion hearing efficiently, Lawyer speaks to Judge's Clerk about possible available hearing dates and times without first contacting Opposing Party's Lawyer. As a housekeeping matter, this communication is not prohibited.

Even innocently intended ex parte communications are prohibited.

Questions often place a lawyer in an innocently intended ex parte communication position. Such an ex parte communication is subject to discipline even though no harm is intended and none results.

When authorized by law, lawyers are permitted to engage in ex parte communications. Such authorizations are typically found in rules governing requests for emergency restraining orders, for example. When such communication is authorized, a lawyer is under heightened candor-to-the-court requirements.

Lawyers are strictly prohibited from communicating with jurors outside the courtroom before and during jurors' duties. This restriction applies to both grand jurors and trial jurors. Lawyers are prohibited from communicating with jurors after the jurors' duty ends, with some exceptions. Lawyers are prohibited from harassing jurors at any time. MR 3.5.

Communication outside of open court with jurors during and prior to their duty is strictly prohibited.

Any contact between lawyers and jurors may have an effect on the proceedings. The jurors have a sensitive role to play in the justice system, and all of the influences on their decision should come in the form of evidence and argument in open court.

Even communication about matters other than the current proceedings is prohibited. Lawyers must refrain from even innocent communication with sitting jurors.

Example: Lawyer finds himself in an elevator with two of the jurors on his case's jury panel. One juror comments on the favorable weather and the outcome of a recent baseball game. Lawyer agrees with the juror about the weather and the game. Lawyer is subject to discipline. See, e.g., Florida Bar v. Peterson, 418 So. 2d 246 (Fla. 1982). Rather than be responsive to the juror, Lawyer should have refrained from communicating. Upon returning to court, Lawyer should inform the judge about the incident and request an instruction that the lawyers are not permitted to talk to jurors outside of open court, and that lawyers' silence during encounters such as occurred in the elevator are not rudeness but rather compliance with ethics rules.

Once proceedings have ended, lawyers may have very limited contact with jurors for benign purposes, such as to determine whether the lawyer's presentation manner is effective. Even after proceedings end, however, lawyers must refrain from engaging in harassing contacts with jurors and from conduct that would tend to undermine the jurors' confidence in their verdict and the justice system.

[4] Lawyers are obligated to disclose to the court controlling, directly **adverse legal authority.** MR 3.3 (a)(2).

Lawyers have no obligation to disclose adverse authority to opposing parties. Naturally, when a disclosure of directly adverse, controlling authority is made to a court, it will not ordinarily be done ex parte. As a result, when the disclosure is made to the court, it will ordinarily and coincidentally also be made to the opposing party. The attendant disclosure to opposing counsel is merely the result of the disclosure to the court. It is not mandated on its own strength. Lawyers are required to disclose controlling, directly adverse authority to the court. Such disclosures may take the form of oral statements in open court during a motion or appellate argument or written statements in briefs or other legal argument papers filed with the court.

Example: Lawyer failed to cite adverse, controlling precedent in support of his application for a temporary restraining order and preliminary injunction.

Lawyer is not redeemed by the fact that opposing counsel subsequently cited the controlling precedent that Lawyer should have earlier disclosed. Lawyer was legiti-

mately entitled to press his own interpretations of precedent, including interpretations that render particular cases inapplicable, but he had a duty to disclose the directly adverse, controlling precedent to the court and is subject to discipline for failing to do so. See similar fact pattern in the context of FRCP 11 sanctions, Jorgenson v. County of Volusia, 846 F.2d 1350 (11th Cir. 1988).

[5] The rules of evidence are designed to regulate the information that the jury receives at a trial. Lawyers are prohibited from undermining the evidence law policies by alluding to matters that are either irrelevant or will not be supported by admissible evidence. MR 3.4(e).

Matters must not be alluded to if a reasonable lawyer would recognize that those matters will not be supported by admissible evidence.

Example: Lawyer represents Defendant-Client in a personal injury claim. Client has told Lawyer that shortly after the accident, Client overheard Bystander say, "The light was green for Defendant and red for Plaintiff." Lawyer has been unable to discover Bystander's identity and knows of no hearsay exception that would arguably make the hearsay statement admissible. Nonetheless, in his opening statement, Lawyer says to the jury, "A Bystander who had a good look at the accident has said that the light was green for Defendant and red for Plaintiff." Lawyer is subject to discipline.

Once the court has ruled a piece of evidence inadmissible, a lawyer is prohibited from referring to it to the jury. *Example:* Lawyer represents Client in an auto accident case. Lawyer offers a witness who would testify that Lawyer's Client is a safe driver. Judge rules that the witness's testimony is inadmissible character bolstering evidence. Nonetheless, Lawyer tells the jury in the closing argument that people who have driven with Client regard her as a safe driver. No such evidence was admitted at the trial. Lawyer is subject to discipline.

[6] Lawyers must obey court orders. Even when a lawyer knows that a judge is mistaken in making an order or ruling, the lawyer must obey the order, but may make reasonable efforts to preserve the record for later challenge on appeal.

Example: Lawyer represents Client at trial. Lawyer asks Witness to describe Opposing Party's demeanor at the time of the incident in litigation. Lawyer regards this information as crucial to the case. Opposing Lawyer objects without stating grounds and Judge sustains the objection. Lawyer asks, "Your Honor, may I be heard on this point?" Judge responds, "No, get on to your next question." Lawyer is certain that Judge is wrong. Lawyer tells Witness to answer despite Judge's ruling. Lawyer is subject to discipline and may also be held in contempt of court.

[7] Judges' **contempt** power is a considerable control on lawyer conduct in the litigation setting. The contempt power is meant to give judges reasonable control over the courtroom and to enforce standards of courtroom behavior among litigants.

The contempt power is meant to be used as a last resort to police lawyer in-court conduct when all other means of instruction, persuasion, and command by the court have failed to produce restraint in the wayward lawyer. The contempt power should only be exercised when the lawyer's conduct has an actual disruptive effect on the proceedings. See Taylor v. Hayes, 418 U.S. 488 (1974).

NOTES TO FIGURE 17

IN COURT ACTIVITIES (MISCELLANEOUS) p. 2

[1] In general, a lawyer may not instruct a witness to cooperate only if subpoenaed. MR 3.4(f).

Example: Prosecuting Attorney interviews Eyewitness. Eyewitness tells Prosecuting Attorney that he is nervous about meeting with Defense Counsel. Prosecuting Attorney may offer to be available to accompany Eyewitness any time Defense Counsel wishes to talk with Eyewitness. However, Prosecuting Attorney must not encourage Eyewitness to refrain from speaking with Defense Lawyer until trial.

Although a witness's testimony may favor one side in litigation over another, witnesses do not belong to particular litigants. As such, lawyers are prohibited generally from requesting or advising a witness to refrain from voluntarily cooperating with another litigant. MR 3.4(f). Under no circumstances may a lawyer dissuade a witness from appearing at a hearing or persuade a witness to secrete himself so that the witness will be unavailable. MR 3.4(a).

Example: Lawyer knows that Witness can identify Lawyer's Client, a criminal defendant. Lawyer knows that Witness is hesitant about appearing at trial. Lawyer suggests that if Witness could take an extended vacation to Costa Rica during the trial dates, Witness could avoid the embarrassment that would inevitably come during cross-examination. Lawyer is subject to discipline.

[2] The witness must be a relative, employee or agent of the client. A client, through his lawyer, may ask his mother, brother, or employee, for example, to refrain from being voluntarily cooperative with the opposing litigant if the lack of cooperation will not harm the witness. MR 3.4(f)(1).

[3] The lawyer must reasonably believe that the request will not harm the witness. MR 3.4(f)(2).

Example: Lawyer represents Employer-Client. Employer has been named defendant in a negligence action; Employee's actions may have caused the Plaintiff's damages. Lawyer could not reasonably conclude that Employee's interest would not be adversely affected by Employee's refusal of cooperation with Plaintiff's counsel. Lawyer must not request that Employee refrain from voluntarily giving information to Plaintiff's counsel.

[4] A lawyer is prohibited from offering evidence the lawyer knows to be false. MR 3.3(a)(34).

[5] A lawyer is prohibited from knowingly making false statements of material fact to the court and from otherwise engaging in acts or omissions that amount to fraud. MR 3.3(a).

Lawyers must simultaneously serve the interests of their clients and comply with candor obligations to the court. The rules in this area are an attempt at balance between these competing responsibilities.

Example: Lawyer represents Criminal Defendant. Criminal Defendant has been convicted of assault and is about to be sentenced. Judge asks Lawyer to comment on Criminal Defendant's sentencing. Lawyer, who knows that Criminal Defendant has two prior convictions for assault from another jurisdiction, says, "Criminal Defendant has a heretofore clean record and should be sentenced with leniency." Lawyer has made a material, false statement of fact to the court and is subject to discipline.

[6] When the lawyer knows of the client's intention to commit perjury, the lawyer must attempt to dissuade, attempt to withdraw, and finally, if the perjury occurs, take reasonable remedial measures.

The lawyer must attempt to persuade the client to refrain from offering false testimony. If unsuccessful, the lawyer should request the court's permission to withdraw from the representation. When such a request occurs during or on the eve of trial, courts are unlikely to grant it because of the inevitable delay that will result and the lack of assurance that the same scenario simply will not unfold with the next lawyer to represent the client. The lawyer must attempt to withdraw without breaching a client's confidences.

If the perjury has occurred despite the lawyer's efforts, the lawyer must take reasonable remedial measures. What constitute reasonable remedial measures following perjury is the subject of considerable and unresolved debate. Some argue persuasively that the duty a lawyer owes the client should prevent the lawyer from revealing the perjury; others argue persuasively that the lawyer's duty to the court supersedes the duty to the client and that in any event, lawyers do not owe clients a duty to help them perpetrate frauds on courts. Current law does not effectively resolve this dispute. In either event, although Model Rule 3.3's language requires a lawyer to engage in reasonable remedial measures whether the perjury has come from a client or another witness, what may be reasonable as a remedial measure may well depend on whether the client or another witness has committed the perjury. The Model Rule Comment indicates that whether the client or other witness has committed the perjury, reasonable remedial measures include disclosure of the perjury to the court.

FIGURE 18

ADVERTISING AND SOLICITATION

The ethics rules distinguish between **advertising** and **solicitation.** Categorizing a particular client-getting activity as one or the other is the first step to analyzing whether the activity is permitted.

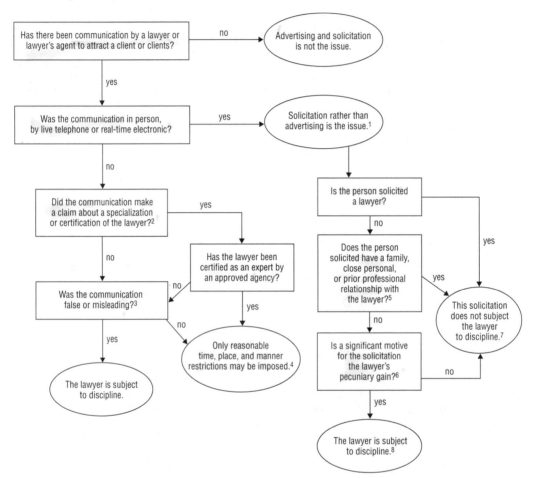

Notes to Figure 18

ADVERTISING AND SOLICITATION

[1] The term **solicitation** has traditionally referred to narrower communications directed at one or a small group of identified recipients who are known to need a particular service. *Examples:* In-person proposals of professional employment to accident victims [Ohralik v. Ohio State Bar Ass'n, 436 U.S. 447 (1978)], lectures to community groups that are accompanied by proposals of professional employment of the speaker, in-person solicitation of professional employment on the fourth tee during a round of golf.

The term **advertising** has traditionally referred to widely distributed, public statements about the services available from a particular lawyer or law organization. *Examples:* Yellow Pages listings, general newspaper advertisements, television or radio broadcast advertisements.

[2] Until the 1970s, state bars were quite restrictive in their regulation of lawyers' indications of practice concentration, **specialization** or certification in areas of practice.

As long as the words used by the lawyer to designate areas in which the lawyer practices fairly communicate those areas, they will be protected commercial speech and will not subject the lawyer to discipline. Whether the lawyer chooses to designate areas of practice as "torts" or "personal injury," "contracts" or "commercial litigation," "property" or "real estate transfers" will not matter for disciplinary purposes. All are permitted. In re R.M.J., 455 U.S. 191 (1982). Claiming a certification in a particular area presents additional concerns. An unqualified statement of certification may mislead the reader into thinking that the state has certified the lawyer in a particular area. However, a state may not impose a blanket prohibition on statements of certification. Peel v. Illinois Attorney Registration and Disciplinary Comm'n, 496 U.S. 91 (1990). *Example:* In her advertising and communication with the public, Lawyer referred to her status as a licensed CPA and Certified Financial Planner (CFP). The Board that licensed Lawyer as a CPA reprimanded her for engaging in false, deceptive, and misleading advertising. In particular, the Board disapproved of her including the unapproved CFP designation in her ads. Lawyer's advertisements constituted commercial speech. Because she did in fact hold a valid CPA license, her advertisements were truthful in that regard, could not mislead the public, and thus deserved constitutional protection. Without evidence of specific harm resulting from Lawyer's use of the CFP designation, that portion of the advertisements also fell within the First Amendment's safeguards. Ibanez v. Florida Dep't of Business & Professional Regulation, 512 U.S. 136 (1994).

[3] Advertising and solicitation are speech. As such, some First Amendment protection is provided to these activities, effectively limiting the states' authority to prohibit and regulate them. Commercial speech, such as advertising, is given some protection under the First Amendment. Virginia Bd. of Pharmacy v. Virginia Citizens Consumer Council, Inc., 425 U.S. 748 (1976). Lawyer client-getting speech is protected commercial speech under the First Amendment. Bates v. State Bar of Arizona, 433 U.S. 350 (1977). The public's right to receive information is a key underpinning of the First Amendment commercial speech analysis. Central Hudson Gas & Electric Co. v. Public Service Comm'n of New York, 447 U.S. 557, 563 (1980).

As such, there are limits on the client-getting restrictions that a bar association and the state may enforce. Restrictions on commercial speech must further a substantial government interest and must be no broader than necessary.

The government has a substantial interest in protecting the public from being misled or coerced by lawyer communications.

To pass constitutional muster, restrictions must be focused on the substantial government interest and must be narrowly drawn.

Regulating commercial speech based on its "dignity" or "taste" is constitutionally **impermissible.** Despite the constitutional limitations on its power to restrict lawyer commercial speech, a state may prohibit lawyer client-getting that is false or misleading, that is coercive, or that promotes transactions that are themselves illegal. In re Primus, 436 U.S. 412 (1978); Zauderer v. Office of Disciplinary Counsel of Supreme Court of Ohio, 471 U.S. 626 (1985); *Bates,* 433 U.S. 350 (1977).

False or misleading statements in lawyer client-getting communication are subject to discipline. MR 7.1. *Examples:* Lawyer advertises that he is "experienced in sports law" when in fact he is a recent law graduate who took a sports law course and was once a college athlete. Such a statement is false and subject to discipline.

Personal injury Lawyer advertises in the Yellow Pages, "Recovery is guaranteed! If you don't recover, you don't pay me a fee!" Such a statement is not false but is misleading and subject to discipline. Although the contingent fee arrangement that Lawyer proposes in the ad will result in no fee to the lawyer unless there is a recovery from which to draw the fee, the statement implies that the client will have no liability if the Lawyer fails to obtain recovery when in fact the client may be liable for litigation costs. *Zauderer.*

Law Firm uses television advertisement depicting lawyers in courtroom jury trial scene even though none of the Law Firm's lawyers had tried a case to conclusion before a jury. Such an ad is misleading and subject to discipline. In re Zang, 154 Ariz. 134 (1987).

Firm names may be misleading when they untruthfully imply a relationship to a government or other institution. MR 7.5. *Examples:* "The Ohio Law Firm," "Social Security Legal Services," or "New York Legal Aid," when used by a private law firm, would be regarded as false or misleading.

Since *Bates,* lawyer's statements about fees have been constitutionally protected. Like other advertising statements, they may be restricted only when they are false or misleading. *Examples:* "Reasonable" and "moderate" are adjectives that may be used to describe fees; "the low cost alternative," "give-away prices," or "below cost" are adjectives that have been held to be misleading. See, e.g., Bishop v. Committee on Professional Ethics and Conduct of the Iowa State Bar Ass'n, 521 F. Supp. 1219 (S.D. Iowa 1981); D.C. Bar Op. 172-9 (1986).

[4] Some restrictions have particular applicability to advertising.

Lawyers, of course, may pay reasonable costs associated with advertising. MR 7.2(c). This rule states what may seem to be the obvious because outside of the advertising context, lawyers may not pay others for recommending the lawyer.

All advertisements must include the name of at least one lawyer or law firm responsible for the advertisement's content. MR 7.2(d).

[5] Subject only to the general limitations on client-getting speech, lawyers may solicit people with whom the lawyer has a family or prior professional relationship. MR 7.3(a). *Example:* Lawyer had a conversation with Bank President. Lawyer had formerly done legal work for Bank, and Lawyer and Bank President were social acquaintances. Lawyer told Bank President that Lawyer's cousin, a friend of Bank President, was near death. Lawyer suggested to Bank President that if the Bank was named executor of Cousin's estate and if estate work needed to be done after Cousin's impending death, Lawyer could be retained to do it. Although this act would otherwise be in-person solicitation and subject to discipline, the personal and family relationships in this case fall within the exception to Model Rule 7.3's restriction. Goldwaithe v. Disciplinary Board, 408 So. 2d 504 (Ala. 1982).

[6] The specific restrictions on in-person and live telephone solicitation apply only when a significant motive for the solicitation is pecuniary gain for the lawyer. MR 7.3(a).

[7] There are additional restrictions on solicitation of specific prospective clients or those known to be in need of specific services.

Once a prospective client makes known her desire not to be contacted by the lawyer, the lawyer may not contact that prospective client. MR 7.3(b)(1).

Written or recorded communications to those known to be in need of specific services must include the words "Advertising Material" on the outside of any envelope used and at the beginning and end of any recorded communication. MR 7.3(c).

[8] In-person and live telephone solicitation are subject to prophylactic rules that are much more restrictive than the advertising rules.

Although all client-getting communication is subject to discipline if it involves duress or coercion, restrictions on in-person and live telephone client solicitation are meant to protect prospective clients from special dangers of lawyer coercion and duress that attend such communications.

FIGURE 19

SUPERVISOR-SUBORDINATE LAWYERS p. 1

More frequently than ever before, lawyers practice in settings that involve employer-employee relationships. Within those relationships, some lawyers supervise the work of other lawyers, and lawyers frequently supervise the work of non-lawyer subordinates. Under certain circumstances, **supervising lawyers** will be ethically responsible for the acts of their **subordinates,** both lawyer and non-lawyer. Under certain circumstances, subordinate lawyers will be relieved of ethical responsibility for their actions.

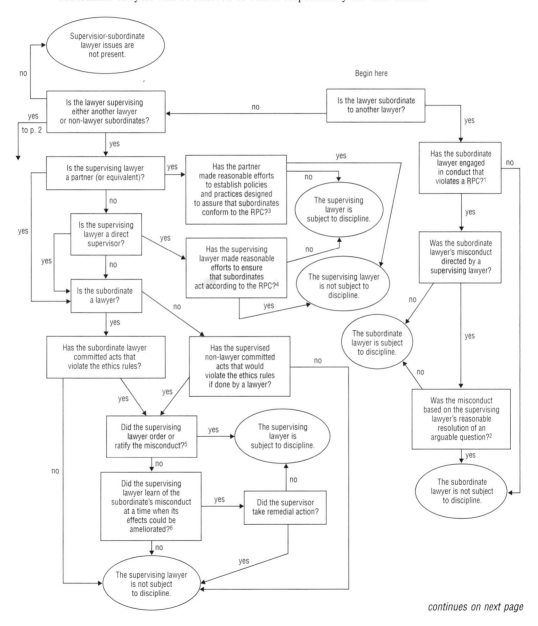

continues on next page

FIGURE 19 (cont'd)

SUPERVISOR-SUBORDINATE LAWYERS p. 2

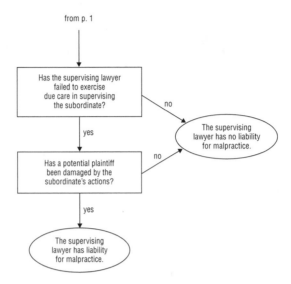

NOTES TO FIGURE 19

SUPERVISOR-SUBORDINATE LAWYERS

[1] Subordinate lawyers are not relieved of the duty to follow the rules of professional conduct merely because they are supervised, nor for that matter merely because the misconduct in which they might engage is ordered by the supervising lawyer. MR 5.2.

Example: Supervising Lawyer instructs Subordinate Lawyer to impersonate Client and swear out a Complaint in Client's name, thereby saving Client a trip to the courthouse to sign the Complaint himself. If Subordinate Lawyer complies with Supervisor's instruction and commits this fraud, Subordinate Lawyer will be subject to discipline. MR 5.2(a).

Example: Same facts as example above except that Supervisor threatens to fire Subordinate Lawyer if Subordinate Lawyer refuses to commit the fraud. If Subordinate Lawyer complies with Supervisor's instruction under threat and commits this fraud, Subordinate Lawyer will still be subject to discipline. Threat of job loss does not excuse a subordinate lawyer from complying with the rules of professional conduct.

[2] A subordinate lawyer is not subject to discipline when she "acts in accordance with a supervisory lawyer's reasonable resolution of an arguable question of professional duty." MR 5.2(b). When close questions arise about which supervisors and subordinates disagree, someone's view of the matter must ultimately control the actions of the lawyer. Under this provision, subordinate lawyers may safely defer **on close questions and close questions alone** to the judgment of supervisory, usually senior, lawyers.

Example: Subordinate Lawyer produces a draft Complaint for a client. The Complaint attempts to state a type of claim that State Supreme Court has rejected. Other states' courts have intimated in dicta that they may recognize the claim, but none have as yet. Subordinate Lawyer is concerned about pleading a frivolous claim under FRCP 11 and MR 3.1. Supervisory Lawyer examines the Complaint and assures Subordinate Lawyer that the Complaint's claim is not frivolous. Supervisory Lawyer's resolution of this arguable question is reasonable. If a court later determines that the Complaint's claim was frivolous and violative of MR 3.1, Supervisory Lawyer and not Subordinate Lawyer will be subject to discipline. Ironically, under the pre-1991 FRCP 11, in the same situation, Subordinate Lawyer (the pleading's signer) and not Supervisory Lawyer would be liable for the FRCP 11 monetary sanctions.

The exception requires that the ethics question being resolved be an arguable one. There must exist reasonable arguments on various sides of the question being resolved.

Close questions may often be resolved in a variety of ways. The exception requires that the supervisory lawyer's resolution of the arguable question be a reasonable one. A subordinate lawyer is not protected if he follows a supervisory lawyer's unreasonable resolution of a close question.

[3] Separate from the acts of lawyer subordinates, supervising lawyers are subject to discipline if they fail to provide adequate supervision.

Law firm partners must make reasonable efforts to establish systems that will give reasonable assurance that the firm's lawyers will not engage in conduct that would violate the rules of professional conduct for lawyers. Notice the double use of the word "reasonable." Partners are responsible for taking reasonable efforts to set up systems; if the subordinate lawyers engage in violative conduct despite those systems, the partner is not subject to discipline. MR 5.1(a). Typical systems include file maintenance systems, conflict-of-interest check procedures, standard forms for fee agreements and engagement letters, and confidentiality requirements systems. Supervising lawyers, whether partners or not, who directly supervise other lawyers must make reasonable efforts to ensure that the subordinate lawyers comply with the rules of professional conduct. MR 5.1(b).

[4] Supervisory lawyers are responsible for providing reasonable supervision of lawyer subordinates. MR 5.1.

Example: Subordinate Lawyer goes to work for Firm. Firm assigns Supervisory Lawyer to work with Subordinate Lawyer on a complex project. Supervisory Lawyer leaves town for a long weekend, instructing Subordinate Lawyer to file the Complaint on Monday, no matter what. When Subordinate Lawyer asks whether she might have a telephone number where she can reach Supervisory Lawyer over the weekend, Supervisory Lawyer says, "No, I won't be back until Tuesday; I don't expect to hear from anyone here. Just have the Complaint filed before I return." When Subordinate asks whether anyone else in Firm is sufficiently familiar with the matter to answer a question for her while Supervisory Lawyer is away, Supervisory Lawyer says, "Don't you dare ask anyone else. You'll embarrass me. I am supposed to get this job done and I'm instructing you to do it." Supervisory Lawyer is subject to discipline for failing to make reasonable efforts to supervise Subordinate Lawyer. "[L]eaving new lawyers to 'sink or swim' will not be tolerated." In re Yacavino, 494 A.2d 801, 803 (N.J. 1985).

[5] The supervisory lawyer has disciplinary liability for the subordinate's violation when the supervisor orders the subordinate lawyer to engage in the misconduct or ratifies the misconduct. MR 5.1(c)(1).

Example: Supervising Lawyer instructs Subordinate Lawyer to impersonate Client and swear out a Complaint in Client's name, thereby saving Client a trip to the courthouse to sign the Complaint himself. If Subordinate Lawyer complies with Supervisor's instruction and commits this fraud, Supervisory Lawyer will be subject to discipline.

The supervisory lawyer ratifies the subordinate lawyer's misconduct. MR 5.1(c)(1).

Example: Subordinate Lawyer impersonates Client and swears out a Complaint in Client's name, thereby saving Client a trip to the courthouse to sign the Complaint himself. Supervisory Lawyer learns of Subordinate Lawyer's conduct and says, "Well done. Client will be pleased." Supervisory Lawyer is subject to discipline.

[6] The supervisory lawyer has disciplinary liability for the subordinate's violation when the supervisor is a lawyer who is either a partner or the subordinate's direct supervisor learns of the misconduct at a time when its effect

could be avoided or mitigated and yet fails to take reasonable remedial action. MR 5.1(c)(2).

Example: Subordinate Lawyer impersonates Client and swears out a Complaint in Client's name, thereby saving Client a trip to the courthouse to sign the Complaint himself. Supervisory Lawyer and Partner learn of Subordinate Lawyer's conduct on the day of its occurrence, before service of the Complaint on the defendant. Supervisory Lawyer or Partner could easily have instructed Subordinate Lawyer to dismiss the Complaint immediately and avoid further harm. Instead Supervisory Lawyer and Partner do nothing, except enjoy a long lunch together. Supervisory Lawyer and Partner are both subject to discipline.

CAPSULE SUMMARY

SUMMARY OF CONTENTS

CHAPTER 1

INTRODUCTION AND THE ROLE OF LAWYER

I. COURSES CALLED PROFESSIONAL RESPONSIBILITY, LEGAL ETHICS, AND LEGAL PROFESSION

The law of professional responsibility and, therefore, the course in which it is studied are about the relationships of lawyers to their clients, their peers, the justice system, the profession, and the public.

II. MORAL PHILOSOPHY, RIGHT AND WRONG, AND THE LAW GOVERNING LAWYERS

A. Moral philosophy: *Moral philosophy* informs the study of professional responsibility law, but moral philosophy does not replace legal analysis as the tool for determining the application of professional responsibility law.

B. Right and wrong: There is a great deal more to the law governing lawyers than the difference between right and wrong. The law governing lawyers must be studied and mastered like any other law field.

C. The law governing lawyers: The *law governing lawyers* is a complicated mix of many different areas of substantive law from many different sources.

D. Role morality: Important to an understanding of lawyer ethics is the concept of *role morality.* Lawyers' moral decision-making involves a balancing process. Lawyers owe many duties, not all of which point in a single direction at any given moment. Lawyers owe duties to clients, the justice system, third parties generally, opposing parties, the society, and the profession.

III. THE ROLE OF LAWYER

The professional responsibility codes are an attempted expression of the limits of conduct by people acting in *the role of lawyer.*

A. Differing conceptions of the lawyer's role: Different lawyers perceive themselves and the appropriate role of lawyer in differing ways.

B. Differences between lawyers' litigation and planning roles

　　1. Litigation context: In a litigation context, most of the lawyer's work is backward looking. The litigation seeks to assess legal responsibility for the client's and the opposing party's past conduct. The lawyer's work involves the operation of the justice system on the client's behalf.

2. **Planning context:** In the planning context, most of the lawyer's work is forward looking. The planning seeks to predict the consequences of proposed future conduct.

3. **Responsibility for clients' acts:** A lawyer bears more responsibility for a client's acts in the planning context than in the litigation context. The lawyer's planning work, advice, and assistance in execution help shape future client conduct.

C. **Practice setting:** A lawyer's practice setting affects the law governing that lawyer in a variety of ways. Essentially, lawyers in different practice settings have different lawyer-client relationships. The differences on those lawyer-client relationships drive a variety of adjustments in the law governing lawyers. Aside from the private law firm representing a natural person as a client in civil matters, lawyers practice as, for example, prosecuting attorneys, other government lawyers, criminal defense lawyers including public defenders, and in-house and external corporate counsel. Some practice settings trigger the application of practice-setting-specific rules; others create adjustments by implication of attributes of the lawyer-client relationship.

1. **Prosecutors:** Prosecuting attorneys represent the government or the people of their jurisdiction in the prosecution of crimes. As such, prosecutors have no individual client with whom to consult. With this lawyer-client relationship comes substantial freedom and responsibility. Prosecutors are expected to seek justice and have obligations of fairness to the opposing party (a criminal defendant) that exceed those of other lawyers.

2. **Other government lawyers:** Like prosecutors, government lawyers represent the government or the people of their jurisdiction. The government obviously has public-abiding obligations that private citizens do not, and as a representative of government as a client, government lawyers are obligated to reflect their clients' public-abiding obligations.

3. **Criminal defense:** Some criminal defense lawyers' fees are paid at public expense. For these lawyers, both public defenders and appointed counsel, third party interference conflicts issues are simply a part of the job description. For all criminal defense lawyers, the special relationship with a client who faces loss of liberty and who faces the government as an opposing party creates special responsibilities for the criminal defense lawyer.

4. **Corporate or other organization counsel:** Corporate or other organization counsel represent the entity and not the corporate officers. Such a client cannot communicate with the lawyer, however, except through the living, breathing officers, board members, and designated individuals. Special conflicts rules result from this reality.

5. **Legal aid:** Lawyers working for nonprofit corporations set up to receive government funding to represent low-income individuals must account for third party interference conflicts. In such a setting, a lawyer has an individual client but is paid a salary by the nonprofit entity. Legal aid lawyers also operate under legislative restrictions on their funding, creating difficult-to-navigate constraints on their ability to effectively represent their clients.

CHAPTER 2

REGULATION OF THE LEGAL PROFESSION

The institutional framework within which lawyers and the law of lawyering exist has a significant effect on the interpretation of the law of lawyering.

I. ORGANIZATION OF THE BAR

The legal profession has organized itself in a variety of ways. Membership in some organizations is voluntary, whereas membership in others is required of those who wish to practice law in a particular jurisdiction. See §III.

A. The American Bar Association: The *American Bar Association* (ABA) is a national, *voluntary* association of lawyers.

B. Alternative national bar associations: National organizations of lawyers have been established, in some instances, to express alternative views from those held by the ABA.

C. State bar associations: The ABA does not license lawyers to practice law. States, through their courts and sometimes legislatures, license lawyers to practice law within the relevant jurisdiction.

  1. Voluntary state bar associations: In some states, voluntary bar associations exist that licensed lawyers may or may not join at the individual lawyer's discretion.

  2. The integrated bar: In some states, membership in the state bar association is mandatory. This mandatory membership establishes what is called an "integrated bar," of which all the lawyers licensed to practice in the state are members.

II. SOURCES OF LAW GOVERNING LAWYERS

The law that governs lawyers comes from a variety of sources and exists in a variety of forms.

A. Ethics codes: Every state has an adopted code of ethics for lawyers that operates as a set of mandatory legal rules governing lawyer conduct.

  1. ABA models and their organization: Beginning in 1908, the ABA adopted a series of three model ethics codes that have served as models for state adoption.

  a. The 1908 Canons of Ethics: The 1908 Canons of Ethics (Canons) were adopted by the ABA but were not initially expected to be routinely enforced as rules by courts and bar authorities.

  b. The 1969 Model Code of Professional Responsibility: The Model Code was the ABA's first effort to influence the setting of mandatory, national standards for lawyer conduct.

  c. **The 1983 Model Rules of Professional Conduct:** The Model Rules was drafted in the late 1970s and early 1980s and then adopted in 1983. Extensive amendments were adopted in 2002.

  2. **State-adopted codes:** The states have adopted ethics codes. Although all but one of the state-adopted codes are based on the ABA models, it is the state-adopted code, not the ABA model, that actually controls in the particular jurisdiction.

B. **Case authority:** In several ways, courts make the law governing lawyers.

  1. **Interpretation of codes:** Courts have interpreted the existing ethics codes and, as such, make the law of lawyering in their interpretive activities in the same way as courts make law by interpreting statutes.

  2. **Inherent power to regulate lawyers:** Because courts have inherent power to regulate lawyers (who are officers of the court), a common law of lawyer regulation also exists.

C. **Ethics opinions:** Both the ABA and state bar associations issue nonbinding *ethics opinions* that are frequently relied on by courts in law of lawyering cases.

D. **Restatement:** In 2000, in an exceedingly important development for the law of professional responsibility, the American Law Institute completed work on the Restatement of the Law Governing Lawyers. The Restatement, Third, of the Law Governing Lawyers has already been influential with courts and with the Ethics 2000 Commission revision of the Model Rules.

E. **Constitutional restraints:** Like any other area of state or federal regulation, the law governing lawyers is subject to constitutional limitations.

F. **"Other law":** The law of a wide variety of other substantive areas forms an essential part of the law of lawyering.

III. ADMISSION TO PRACTICE

A license to practice law is a prerequisite to a person's lawful engagement in the activities of lawyering.

A. **Policy:** The state has a need to protect the public from those who are incompetent or who lack integrity.

B. **General requirements:** Education, knowledge, and character requirements are the chief hurdles in the path of the applicant for admission to the practice of law.

  1. **Education:** All states impose educational requirements on applicants for admission to practice law.

  2. **Knowledge:** An examination (the bar exam) is administered in each state.

  3. **Good character:** To be a successful applicant for admission to practice law, one must be found to be of good character.

  4. **Misconduct in the application process:** An applicant to the bar may not make any material false statement and must not "fail to disclose a fact necessary to

correct any misapprehension known by the [applicant] to have arisen in the matter. . . ." MR 8.1(b).

5. **No assistance with admission of unqualified applicant:** Licensed lawyers are duty-bound not to assist in the admission of an unqualified applicant. MR 8.1.

C. **Federal courts:** Each federal court maintains a bar (a list of licensed lawyers), separate from the states in which they sit.

D. **Admission pro hac vice:** When a lawyer who is licensed to practice in one state has an occasional, nonrecurring need to represent a client before the courts of another state, the lawyer requests admission before that state's courts *"pro hac vice"* ("for this turn only"). The application is made by the lawyer filing a motion with the particular court before which the lawyer wants permission to appear.

IV. UNAUTHORIZED PRACTICE

By the nature of the licensing requirements, lawyers licensed to practice in a given state have a monopoly on the practice of law in that state. When a person engages in the *unauthorized practice* of law, civil and sometimes criminal penalties attach.

A. **Attributes of the practice of law:**

1. **Court appearance:** Court appearance constitutes the core of the practice of law for purposes of unauthorized practice analysis.

2. **Legal advice and counsel:** Although giving legal advice is clearly lawyer's work, courts are understandably more reluctant to attempt to monitor and police the unauthorized practice of giving legal advice. If the advice-giving is accompanied by either a fee or document-drafting or both, the activity is seen as more clearly impinging on the lawyer monopoly.

B. **Two forms of unauthorized practice:** Unauthorized practice may occur when a licensed lawyer practices outside the jurisdiction in which the license was granted or when those not licensed engage in the practice of law.

1. **Extraterritorial practice of licensed lawyers:** Lawyers licensed in one jurisdiction commit unauthorized practice violations when they practice in another jurisdiction without obtaining permission from the second jurisdiction's courts. See §III.D.

2. **Practice by the unlicensed:** Professionals and others whose business borders the law may not engage in the legal work that borders their other professional duties. Real estate agents, bankers, and insurance professionals are the usual examples.

V. SELF-GOVERNANCE AND THE DUTY TO REPORT MISCONDUCT

Among the chief features of the legal profession's claim to be *self-governing* is the requirement of reporting a fellow lawyer's or a judge's serious misconduct to the appropriate professional authority. MR 8.3. In re Himmel, 533 N.E.2d 790 (Ill. 1988).

A. Knowledge of misconduct: Before a duty to report misconduct can arise, the lawyer must have "knowledge that another lawyer has committed" the *misconduct.* MR 8.3(a); Model Rules, 1.0(f).

B. Level or type of misconduct: The rule requires a lawyer to report misconduct "that raises a substantial question as to that lawyer's honesty, trustworthiness or fitness as a lawyer in other respects. . . ." MR 8.3(a). "Substantial" means a "material matter of clear and weighty importance." Model Rules, 1.0(l).

C. Confidentiality limitation on duty to report: The rule does not require a report of misconduct when the lawyer has learned of the misconduct through confidential communications that would be protected by the ethical duty of confidentiality under Model Rule 1.6. MR 8.3(c). See Chapter 5. But it must also be remembered that the exceptions to the duty of confidentiality (e.g., the future crime exception) continue to apply with equal force in this setting as in any other.

D. Defamation privilege: When a lawyer reports another lawyer's misconduct, the potential exists for a defamation action to be filed by the reported-on lawyer against the reporting lawyer.

CHAPTER 3

CONTROLS ON LAWYER CONDUCT

I. DISCIPLINE

Discipline imposed at the hands of the organized bar is the most often referred to and studied, but much less often actually imposed, control on lawyer conduct. *Discipline* by the bar and then the court system operates by authority of the licensing of lawyers. See Chapter 2, §III.

A. Discipline versus malpractice: Discipline is imposed for the protection of the public generally and for the benefit of the profession, whereas malpractice is a tort- or contract-based civil action that is meant to compensate victims of a lawyer's negligence or contract breach. Although a single act of negligence will support a malpractice action, unless that single act is sufficiently gross to indicate a substantial likelihood that the lawyer is unfit to practice, that single act will not subject the lawyer to bar discipline.

B. Grounds for discipline: Discipline may be based on an incredibly wide range of conduct, both within and without the lawyer's role. It may be imposed for violations of the ethics code rules; for acts involving moral turpitude; for criminal conduct; for dishonesty, fraud, and deceit; and for acts that are prejudicial to the administration of justice.

C. Forms of discipline: Discipline generally comes in the form of disbarment, suspension, or reprimand, either public or private. Courts may also require disciplined lawyers to engage in professional responsibility educational programs.

1. **Disbarment:** Disbarment is an indefinite dismissal from the rolls of lawyers licensed to practice in the particular jurisdiction.

2. **Suspension:** Suspension is a fixed-period revocation of the license to practice law.

3. **Reprimand:** Reprimand is a statement of reproach issued by the bar to the disciplined lawyer. Reprimands may be either private or public. When a reprimand is public, the reprimand is published in a newspaper.

D. **Disciplinary procedure:** The formal disciplinary procedure is designed around the goals of bar discipline. It is intended to protect the public from lawyers who have committed serious misconduct, rather than to benefit the particular complaining party, usually a client. When a complaint is dismissed, the complaining party has no right of appeal.

II. MALPRACTICE

Malpractice is a civil claim for relief intended to remedy a wrong done by a professional (in this case a lawyer) to an individual client or a group of clients.

A. **Contract theories:** Contract theory malpractice actions have the common contract elements of agreement, breach, and damage. Damage measurement under contract theories is more limited than that under tort theories.

B. **Tort theories:** Under tort theories, the most frequently used of the malpractice theories, the elements are the familiar negligence elements of duty, breach, causation, and damages.

1. **Duty:** The lawyer's duty to the client is measured by the skill and knowledge of ordinary lawyers in the community, unless the lawyer is an expert in a specialized field. An expert is held to the standard of the reasonable expert in that field.

2. **Breach:** Breach of the duty owed is a required element of a malpractice action. Lawyers are not guarantors of particular results. Often, a variety of reasonable strategies will be available from which to choose. When a lawyer chooses a reasonable course of action and that course later produces bad results, the lawyer has not breached the duty of care owed to the client.

3. **Causation:** For a malpractice claim to exist, the lawyer's breach of duty must cause the client's damages. Often, this means that the client will have to prove that she would have prevailed in the matter had the lawyer not breached the duty of care. This requirement is called the "*case within a case.*" The malpractice plaintiff must prove the value of the underlying case in order to prevail in the malpractice case.

4. **Damages:** As with any tort action, the wrong is insufficient to create a claim for relief in the absence of damages.

C. **Fiduciary duty:** As a *fiduciary,* a lawyer owes duties to clients beyond the tort and contract duties. Fiduciary duties modify contract principles. These special duties can be the basis for a malpractice action that might not otherwise lie under contract or tort theories. See Chapter 4, §III.

D. Necessity of expert testimony: As with other forms of professional malpractice, expert testimony is usually needed to establish the nature of the professional duty and the existence of a breach of that duty.

E. Prospective limitation on malpractice liability: The Model Code prohibited lawyers from any prospective limitation on their malpractice liability to clients. DR 6-102. The Model Rules restrict the lawyer's ability to prospectively limit malpractice liability to clients to those occasions when such agreements are permitted by law in the relevant state and a client is represented by other counsel in making the limitation of liability agreement. MR 1.8(h).

F. Liability to third parties for malpractice: Under limited circumstances, a lawyer may be liable for malpractice to a nonclient. See Chapter 6, §VI.

III. LIABILITY FOR CLIENT CONDUCT

Lawyers are prohibited under the Model Rules from "counselling a client to engage or assisting a client in conduct that the lawyer knows is criminal or fraudulent." MR 1.2(d). While this provision sets up the disciplinary exposure of a lawyer who violates the rule, a lawyer may also be criminally and civilly liable for the wrongs of their clients that the lawyer assists.

IV. CONTEMPT OF COURT

Judges' *contempt* power is a considerable control on lawyer conduct in the litigation setting. The contempt power is meant to give judges reasonable control over the courtroom and to enforce standards of courtroom behavior among litigants.

V. DISQUALIFICATION MOTIONS AND OTHER LITIGATION-DRIVEN CONTROLS

Powerful constraints on lawyer conduct exist in the form of various litigation motions. These motions, when granted, have an immediate and significant impact on the lawyer against whom they were filed.

A. Disqualification for conflict of interest: When a lawyer perceives that an opposing lawyer may have a conflict of interest in litigation, the lawyer may request that the court *disqualify* opposing counsel from further participation in the case.

   1. Substantive standards: The standards for when a disqualification motion should be granted are substantially the same as the underlying conflict of interest standards, including the shield or "Chinese Wall" defense. See Chapter 6.

   2. Other interests: Because litigation consequences are at stake instead of lawyer disciplinary consequences, courts take into account interests such as delay caused by granting the motion; wrongful conduct of the moving party, especially as it relates to the timing of the motion; and the nonmoving party's legitimate interest in retaining counsel of her choice, in addition to the typical conflicts of interest concerns.

B. FRCP 11 and its state law counterparts: Money sanctions are available against an offending lawyer under various *frivolous claim* prohibition rules, especially Federal Rule of Civil Procedure (FRCP) 11. See Chapter 8, §III.A.

1. **Analogous to frivolous claims ethics code provisions:** Ethics code rules exist that are analogous to FRCP 11. See MR 3.1.

2. **Claims that lack a basis in law or fact:** To avoid frivolous claim liability, a claim must have a basis in fact and a basis in law.

3. **Safe harbor:** Under the 1993 amendments to Rule 11, a safe harbor provision exists. Before one may file a Rule 11 motion, notice must be given to the alleged offending lawyer.

4. **Sanctions against signer and firm:** Under the 1993 amendments to FRCP 11, sanctions may be imposed by the court on both the lawyer who signed the frivolous court paper and the lawyer's firm.

C. Other sanctions: A few other sanctions provisions that are similar to FRCP 11 exist to govern the frivolous argument conduct of lawyers, especially on appeal. See, e.g., 28 U.S.C. §1927.

CHAPTER 4

FORMAL ASPECTS OF THE LAWYER-CLIENT RELATIONSHIP

I. UNDERTAKING REPRESENTATION

Before a lawyer has formally undertaken representation, a limited set of lawyer-to-client duties exist, including the confidentiality duty that is owed to prospective clients. See Chapter 5, §II.A.2. *Undertaking representation* signifies the beginning of the formal lawyer-client relationship. Once a lawyer has undertaken representation, the full range of duties from lawyer to client exist.

A. Duty to undertake representation:

1. **General:** In general, lawyers have no duty to undertake a particular representation.

2. **Limited duty to accept representation:** Lawyers have a limited duty to undertake a fair share of pro bono work and to accept court appointments unless good cause exists to decline the appointment. For more on pro bono, see Chapter 8, §VII.

B. Duty to reject representation: Unlike the general rule that a lawyer has no duty to accept every client's matter, lawyers are prohibited from accepting (i.e., lawyers must reject) representation when the representation will violate ethics rules or other law. MR 1.16(a). See also §VI.B.

C. **Lawyer-client contracts and the beginning of the lawyer-client relationship:** The lawyer-client relationship is governed by the particular contract entered into by the lawyer and client and by general contract principles, modified by the various duties that lawyers owe clients. See §§II, III. See Chapters 4, 5, 6. The lawyer-client relationship formally begins when a client reasonably believes that the lawyer has undertaken to provide the client with legal service. The relationship does not depend for its onset on the existence of a written contract or a fee payment. Togtad v. Vesely, Otto, Miller & Keefe, 291 N.W.2d 686 (Minn. 1980).

II. FEES

Although the regulation of lawyer's fees is relatively light and rarely enforced, it does exist. MR 1.5. Fees are regulated for their amount and their nature.

A. **Reasonableness standard:** A lawyer's fee must be reasonable. MR 1.5. A range of factors may be considered in setting a reasonable fee. MR 1.5(a).

B. **Writing and timing:** In general, a written contract setting the fee is preferred but not required. But see §C regarding contingent fees.

C. **Contingent fees:** With a few exceptions and restrictions, a lawyer is permitted to charge a fee that is contingent on the outcome of the matter. Generally, cases that produce a *res,* a pool of recovery money from which the contingent fee may be paid, are appropriate for contingent fees. There are two exceptions: criminal cases and certain domestic relations cases. When contingent fees are permitted, additional restrictions apply. MR 1.5(c).

1. **Writing and terms:** Although ordinarily a fee agreement need not be in writing, a contingent fee agreement must be in writing and must be signed by the client. The written agreement must explain the way in which the fee will be calculated and, in particular, the way in which deductions for expenses will be calculated. MR 1.5(c).

2. **Ending statement:** The lawyer must provide an ending statement in writing to the client explaining the outcome of the matter and providing the calculation of the fee and expenses. MR 1.5(c).

D. **Fee splitting:** Lawyers in the same firm routinely share fees with one another. However, when lawyers who are not members of a firm share fees or when lawyers seek to share fees with non-lawyers, special problems arise.

1. **Among lawyers:** Fee splitting among lawyers not in the same firm, in particular the "forwarding fee," has been thought to be offensive to lawyer ethics. A forwarding fee is a fee charged by a lawyer who does no more than send a prospective client to another lawyer who actually provides the legal service.

2. **The modern rule governing lawyer fee splitting:** Rather than prohibit all fee splitting among lawyers from different firms, the Model Rule drafters crafted a rule to regulate the practice. The fee splitting practice is permitted if the total fee

is reasonable, the client agrees to the arrangement, and either the fee is shared in proportion to the work done or the lawyers accept joint responsibility for the representation. The agreement must be confirmed in writing. MR 1.5(e).

3. **With former partners:** If a profit sharing, separation agreement, or retirement plan calls for it, fees may be shared with former partners and associates of the primary lawyer in the matter.

4. **With non-lawyers:** Fees may not be shared with non-lawyers except under quite limited circumstances.

E. **Court awarded fees:** Lawyers receive court awarded attorney's fees pursuant to both court appointment to representation and various statutes that allow for collection of attorney's fees.

F. **Minimum fee schedules:** At one time, the organized bar typically imposed *minimum fee schedules* on lawyers and their clients. Such schedules are unlawful and therefore no longer enforceable. Goldfarb v. Virginia State Bar, 421 U.S. 773 (1975).

G. **Fee forfeiture:** Modern fee forfeiture statutes provide that attorney's fees that are paid by clients from crime proceeds may be forfeited to the government. See, e.g., 21 U.S.C. §§848-853 and 12 U.S.C. §§1961-1968.

III. FIDUCIARY DUTIES

In addition to contractual duties and tort duties, lawyers owe their clients fiduciary duties.

A. **General role of a fiduciary:** A *fiduciary* is one in whom a special trust is placed. A fiduciary owes to the beneficiary scrupulous good faith, candor, and care in the management of the beneficiary's interests.

B. **Handling clients' money:** Lawyer fiduciary duties, beyond the general care owed to client interests and confidences that the relationship implies, are usually thought of in terms of the lawyer's handling of clients' money and property.

1. **Violations a most serious matter:** Violations of the lawyer's duty to properly handle client property have been among the most frequent grounds for lawyer discipline because such violations are easy to verify, because they present a significant opportunity for continued abuse of clients by the offending lawyer, because the rules governing property-handling are per se rules that require no intentional wrongdoing on the part of the lawyer, and because these rules involve no balancing of competing duties.

2. **Client trust accounts:** Lawyers must maintain client trust accounts and safety deposit boxes for the safekeeping of client property. Lawyers must maintain the account in the state in which they practice, they must maintain records of the account for later examination, and they must keep client property and funds separate from lawyer property and funds. MR 1.15(a).

3. **Commingling funds:** Only client money may be in the trust account. The lawyer must maintain a separate office operating account. When a lawyer commingles his funds with a client's, the lawyer is subject to discipline. MR 1.15(a).

4. **Prompt delivery and accounting:** Unless the client agrees to another arrangement, when a lawyer receives property of another, the lawyer must promptly deliver that property and provide an accounting on request. MR 1.15(d).

IV. COMPETENCE AND DILIGENCE

Competence and diligence are core lawyer duties. MR 1.1, 1.3.

A. Competence: *Competence* requires that the lawyer possess and exercise on the client's behalf "the legal knowledge, skill, thoroughness, and preparation reasonably necessary for the representation." MR 1.1.

1. **Distinct from malpractice:** While the competence standard is similar to descriptions of the tort duty for malpractice purposes, they operate differently.

2. **Does not require possession of expertise at the beginning of representation:** A lawyer is not required to know the law that governs the client's legal claim before undertaking representation, provided the lawyer will be able to acquire the necessary knowledge with reasonable diligence.

3. **But basic, cross-cutting skills and knowledge are always required:** Virtually all practicing lawyers in all areas of expertise must have certain basic skills, such as an understanding of the use of precedent, legal research skills, ability to identify and evaluate a client's problem, and writing or drafting skill. MR 1.1 Comment.

4. **Emergency:** In an emergency situation, a lawyer may provide limited assistance to a client in a matter on which the lawyer would ordinarily require further study or research before service is rendered. But the lawyer must limit this service to that which is necessary under the circumstances. MR 1.1 Comment.

B. Diligence: *Diligence* is the timeliness aspect of competence. Lawyers are obligated to be diligent in their clients' behalf. MR 1.3.

1. **Expediting matters:** The duty of diligence is related to the lawyer's duty to expedite matters consistent with client interests. MR 3.2.

2. **Starting and stopping:** The most common pattern in a diligence duty violation involves a lawyer who begins work on a client's matter, perhaps even by filing a civil complaint, but then does little or nothing to pursue the matter to a conclusion.

3. **Misleading about diligence:** Most of the cases that have produced lawyer discipline for diligence failures have also involved a lawyer who then misleads the client about the progress being made.

4. **Inadequate excuses:** Several excuses have been offered for lack of diligence and rejected by the courts.

V. COMMUNICATION AND SHARED DECISION-MAKING

Lawyers owe clients a duty to communicate with clients and to meaningfully share decision-making responsibilities with them. MR 1.2 and 1.4.

A. **Communication:** The communication duty is critical to maintaining a quality lawyer-client relationship. It is related to the duties regarding shared decision-making, competence, and diligence and forms the underpinning of every duty that requires client consent and consultation. MR 1.4. A lawyer must keep a client informed of the status of the client's matter and must respond to a client's reasonable requests for information. MR 1.4(a).

B. **Shared decision-making:** Lawyers and clients must share decision-making responsibility.

1. **Scope of representation:** Because the scope of their relationship is generally set by contract, lawyers and their clients may negotiate and settle on the lawyer's *scope of representation.*

   a. **Duration of representation:** Lawyer and client can negotiate over the lengths to which the lawyer is committed to proceed in the matter.

   b. **Subject matter:** The lawyer and client may negotiate the breadth of the lawyer's service.

2. **Means and ends:** As a general proposition, clients set the goals or ends of the representation, whereas lawyers are generally empowered to determine the best means to use to achieve those ends. MR 1.2(a) Comment.

3. **Lawyer independence from client views:** A lawyer's representation of a client does not implicate the lawyer's sharing of or responsibility for the client's cause or views regarding matters relevant to the representation. MR 1.2(b).

4. **Counseling crimes or frauds:** As an underpinning to the scope of decision-making between lawyer and client, lawyers are prohibited from counseling or assisting their clients in the commission of crimes or frauds. MR 1.2(d).

   a. **In general:** When a lawyer does so advise or assist, the lawyer is not only subject to discipline but is liable criminally or civilly as the case may be.

   b. **Exceptions:** This prohibition does not prevent a lawyer from either discussing proposed courses of action with a client or assisting a client in the pursuit of a test case.

5. **The client under a disability:** When a lawyer represents a client whose capacity to make decisions regarding the representation is diminished, the lawyer must attempt to maintain an ordinary lawyer-client relationship to the extent possible. In seeking protective action for a client, a lawyer may reveal confidential information to the extent reasonably necessary to protect the client's interests. MR 1.14.

VI. TERMINATING REPRESENTATION

The formal lawyer-client relationship ends when representation terminates. Despite termination, many lawyer duties to clients continue, such as confidentiality and a limited conflict avoidance duty. ***Withdrawal*** from representation is a critically important device for the lawyer who is faced with the prospect that continued representation of the client will result in a violation of the ethics code or other law.

A. Rejection of representation: In a way, rejection of representation is a form of termination of representation. See §I.B.

B. Mandatory withdrawal: Under some circumstances, lawyers are required to withdraw from representation, thereby terminating the lawyer-client relationship. Failure to withdraw under these circumstances subjects the lawyer to discipline. MR 1.16(a).

   1. Continued representation will violate the ethics rules: MR 1.16(a)(1).

   2. Continued representation will violate other law: MR 1.16(a)(1).

   3. Lawyer's physical or mental health is impaired: MR 1.16(a)(2).

   4. Lawyer is discharged: MR 1.16(a)(3).

C. Permissive withdrawal: In some instances lawyers are permitted but not required to withdraw. The practical effect of this rule is to allow lawyers to withdraw from representation in the enumerated circumstances without breaching a duty of continued representation to the client. MR 1.16(b).

   1. No harm to client: Without regard to any cause for withdrawal, a lawyer may withdraw if it can be done without material adverse effect to the client. MR 1.16(b)(1).

   2. Causes that will excuse some material harm to the client: Even if some harm may come to the client from the withdrawal, a lawyer may withdraw when any of the following causes exist.

      a. Lawyer's reasonable belief that client is acting criminally or fraudulently: MR 1.16(b)(2).

      b. Past use of service for crime or fraud: MR 1.16(b)(3).

      c. Client actions that are repugnant or imprudent: MR 1.16(b)(4).

      d. Client failure to meet obligations: MR 1.16(b)(5).

      e. Unreasonable financial burden: MR 1.16(b)(6).

      f. Client unreasonably difficult to work with: MR 1.16(b)(6).

      g. Other good cause: MR 1.16(b)(7).

D. Court order to continue: Even when a lawyer has good cause to withdraw, a court may order the lawyer to continue the representation. MR 1.16(c).

E. Procedural requirements for withdrawal: Without regard to what cause a lawyer has for the withdrawal, certain procedural requirements must be met.

   1. Notice: Clients must be given reasonable notice before the withdrawal is effected. MR 1.16(d).

   2. Court approval: When litigation is pending, a lawyer must obtain the court's permission to withdraw from representation. MR 1.16(d) Comment.

F. **Duties upon termination of the lawyer-client relationship:** In addition to the duties that continue beyond the end of the lawyer-client relationship, such as confidentiality and conflicts avoidance, lawyers owe clients certain specific duties that arise upon termination of representation. In general, a lawyer is obliged to take reasonable measures to minimize the harm to the client upon termination of representation. MR 1.16(d).

   1. **Fee refund:** Any fees that have been paid to the lawyer but not yet earned must be refunded to the client upon withdrawal.

   2. **Client's papers and property:** Papers and property of the client that are in the lawyer's possession must be promptly returned upon withdrawal. The lawyer may desire to retain the client's materials in an effort to persuade the client to pay any remaining fee that is owed the lawyer. A lawyer may not do so, however, unless the law of the lawyer's jurisdiction gives the lawyer a lien that may be secured by such materials.

G. **Fee liability upon termination:** Although a client may discharge a lawyer without cause, the client will continue to have an obligation to pay fees to the lawyer that have already been earned. MR 1.16(d).

   1. **Fixed or hourly fees:** When a fee is a fixed amount for a particular service or is based on hours of service, the fee upon discharge will be calculated as the value of the services rendered. Such a recovery theory is called *quantum meruit*.

   2. **Contingent fee:** Contingent fee arrangements have presented a challenge to courts trying to determine the measure of compensation owed the discharged lawyer. Some courts have ruled that a contingent fee lawyer who is discharged without cause is entitled to no fee. Others have ruled that a contingent fee lawyer who is discharged without cause is entitled to the full benefit of the contingency if, indeed, the client eventually recovers in the matter. Still others have ruled that the discharged contingent fee lawyer is entitled to the reasonable value of the services actually rendered (a quantum meruit theory), limited by the amount that the lawyer would have earned had the contingency occurred and the lawyer had recovered the agreed-on percentage.

CHAPTER 5

CONFIDENTIALITY

I. THE DUTY OF CONFIDENTIALITY AND THE ATTORNEY-CLIENT EVIDENTIARY PRIVILEGE

This section covers the overlap between the evidentiary privilege and the duty of *confidentiality*.

A. **Secrets and confidences:** The Model Code duty of confidentiality provision (DR 4-101) defines the scope of the duty as the sum of the material protected by the evidentiary ***attorney-client privilege*** (called *"confidences"* in DR 4-101) and the material that, although not included in the attorney-client evidentiary privilege, would be embarrassing or detrimental to the client if revealed or that the client has expressly requested be held in confidence (called *"secrets"* in DR 4-101). The Model Rules provision abandons the "confidences" + "secrets" = duty of confidentiality formula in favor of a more general and inclusive definition, "information relating to representation of a client. . . ." MR 1.6(a).

B. **Scope of the attorney-client privilege:** Despite the change of terminology, the scope of the attorney-client evidentiary privilege remains critical to defining what is ultimately protected by the duty of confidentiality. When information is within the ethical duty of confidentiality, but outside the protection of the evidentiary privilege, a judge may order the lawyer to speak in the form of testimony or otherwise. See §IV.F. Thus, although the lawyer would not be free to speak absent court compulsion, the coverage of the evidentiary privilege largely determines whether compulsion will be well founded.

C. **Parameters of the evidentiary privilege:** In general, the evidentiary privilege is created when a client or prospective client communicates in confidence to a lawyer (or a person the client reasonably believes to be a lawyer) who is being consulted as a lawyer.

    1. **Clients or prospective clients:** The privilege applies to communication from a client or a prospective client.

    2. **Desire for confidentiality required:** The privilege is not created when the communication is made in circumstances that do not indicate a desire for confidentiality by the client.

        a. **Eavesdroppers:** Most modern authority indicates that if the client exercises reasonable care to avoid being overheard (or intercepted when speaking on the telephone), the court should rule an eavesdropper's testimony inadmissible upon assertion of the privilege.

        b. **Multiple clients:** When multiple prospective clients consult a lawyer together, each holds a privilege that can be asserted against third parties, but none of them can prevent others among the prospective clients from testifying or otherwise waiving the privilege. Their collective communication indicates an absence of desire for confidentiality within the group.

    3. **Communication, not knowledge:** The privilege covers the client's communication, not the client's knowledge that was communicated.

    4. **Lawyer observations:** The privilege may also protect lawyer observations that result directly from the client's protected communications, as long as the lawyer does nothing to prevent other interested parties from making the same observation.

    5. **Physical evidence:** Although the observations of a lawyer that result directly from client communication may sometimes be privileged, items collected by the lawyer are not privileged.

6. **Exceptions:** Many of the exceptions to the duty of confidentiality are paralleled by exceptions to the evidentiary privilege.

   a. **Client holds privilege:** The client holds (controls the assertion of) the evidentiary privilege. Client waiver eviscerates the privilege.

   b. **Future crimes and frauds:** Communications that further future crimes or frauds are excepted from protection by the evidentiary privilege. This is called the *crime-fraud exception.*

II. TO WHOM IS THE DUTY OWED?

This section focuses on the ethical duty of confidentiality and, in particular, to whom the duty is owed.

A. **Generally:** The duty of confidentiality is owed to current clients, former clients, and prospective clients.

   1. **Former clients:** Former clients are owed the duty of confidentiality.

   2. **Prospective clients:** Prospective clients are owed a measure of confidentiality.

   3. **No fee necessary:** It is not necessary for a fee to be charged for the duty of confidentiality and the evidentiary privilege to be effective.

B. **Organizational clients:** In addition to representing people, lawyers represent organizations as clients. See MR 1.13 Comments 3, 6.

   1. **Agents of the organizational client:** Communications from agents of an *organizational client* are within the evidentiary privilege and, therefore, within the duty of confidentiality if two conditions are met: the information communicated is treated as confidential within the organization, and it is communicated to the lawyer so that the lawyer can give advice or counsel to the organization. Upjohn v. United States, 499 U.S. 383 (1981).

   2. **Government agency client:** Because of the special public responsibilities of government agencies, government lawyers may strike a confidentiality balance somewhat more toward the public interest in disclosure of government wrongdoing.

C. **Client and lawyer agents:** Both lawyers and clients routinely use agents for communicating with each other.

   1. **Lawyer agents:** For purposes of the duty of confidentiality, client communication to a lawyer through a lawyer's agent is treated as if it were made directly to the lawyer. In addition, protected client information may be shared with other lawyers within the law firm or organization that represents the client.

   2. **Client agents:** Communications from clients through agents to lawyers are treated as if they were made directly by the client to the lawyer.

III. TO WHAT DOES THE DUTY APPLY?

The duty of confidentiality applies to "information relating to representation of a client. . . ." MR 1.6(a). The Model Code definition is the "confidences" + "secrets" formula referred to in §I.A.

A. **Duty of confidentiality or evidentiary privilege:** To be protected by the evidentiary privilege, the information must come from the client or a client's agent. Information that the lawyer learns from third parties is protected by the duty of confidentiality but not the privilege. To be protected by the duty of confidentiality, the information need merely "relat[e] to representation of a client." MR 1.6(a).

B. **Duty of confidentiality broader than evidentiary privilege:** The duty of confidentiality applies to all information relating to the representation, not merely communications from client to lawyer.

   1. **Lawyer observations:** Lawyer observations are protected by the duty of confidentiality.

   2. **Communications from third parties:** Communications from third parties about the representation are protected by the duty of confidentiality.

   3. **Work product:** Lawyer thoughts and strategies about the representation are protected by the duty of confidentiality. They are also protected by the related discovery doctrine called the work product doctrine.

IV. EXCEPTIONS TO THE DUTY OF CONFIDENTIALITY

A. **Consent:** A client may give informed consent to disclosure of information that would otherwise be protected by the duty of confidentiality. MR 1.6(a).

B. **Implied authorization:** In order to carry out the purposes of the representation, some information that would be subject to the duty of confidentiality must be disclosed.

C. **Self-defense disclosures:** Under certain circumstances, lawyers may reveal client confidences to defend themselves or to pursue claims against former clients.

   1. **The three categories of self-defense permitted disclosure:**

      a. **"[T]o establish a claim or defense on behalf of the lawyer in a controversy between the lawyer and the client."** This exception usually means a fee dispute between lawyer and client, but it applies beyond fee disputes to any controversy between lawyer and client, such as a lawyer malpractice claim.

      b. **"[T]o establish a defense to a criminal charge or a civil claim against the lawyer based upon conduct in which the client was involved."** When a lawyer is the defendant in a criminal or civil action based on conduct of the client or is otherwise accused of misconduct that relates to a client's conduct, the lawyer may respond, using confidential information as necessary. MR 1.6 Comment 8.

      c. **"[T]o respond to allegations in any proceeding concerning the lawyer's representation of the client."** This exception extends the type of proceedings in which the lawyer may use confidential information in self-defense to include, for example, bar disciplinary proceedings, government agency investigatory proceedings, or criminal collateral review claims of ineffective assistance of counsel.

2. **Limit disclosure to facts necessary to defend:** With respect to any of the three categories of permitted disclosure, the lawyer must limit disclosure to those facts necessary to self-defend.

3. **Limit disclosure to individuals who need to know:** Lawyers must also limit their self-defense disclosures to those who need to know for the lawyer's self-defense or fee collection purpose.

D. **Future crimes, frauds, and harms:** In certain circumstances, lawyers may reveal confidential information to prevent *future crimes*, frauds, or harms by clients. The circumstances defined by the Model Code and Model Rules are quite different from one another. MR 1.6(b)(1), DR 4-101(C)(3).

1. **Distinction with past crimes or frauds:** As long as all other requirements are satisfied, when a client reveals a *past* crime or fraud, that information is protected by the duty of confidentiality and the attorney-client privilege.

2. **Policy rationale:** When a client has committed a crime or fraud, the lawyer's representation of the client is what the legal system expects the client to be afforded. When the lawyer knows the client intends to commit a future crime or fraud, and *the lawyer's services are used to commit the crime or fraud,* the lawyer will share both the moral and legal responsibility for the wrong. See Chapter 3, §III.

3. **Model Code:** The Model Code exception for future crimes or frauds is broad but permissive. Under the Code, a lawyer "*may* reveal the intention of his client to commit a crime and the information necessary to prevent the crime." DR 4-101(C)(3).

4. **Model Rules:** Prior to the 2002 amendments, the Model Rules' exception for future crimes had retained the permissive language of the Model Code but restricted the type of future crime that may permit revelation of confidential information. The exception prior to February 2002 read, "A lawyer *may* reveal . . . information [relating to representation of a client] to the extent the lawyer reasonably believes necessary to prevent the client from committing a criminal act that the lawyer believes is *likely to result in imminent death or substantial bodily harm.*" Former MR 1.6(b)(1). Model Rule 1.6 was amended in a significant way in February 2002. The new language for the future crime exception to the duty of confidentiality allows the lawyer to reveal confidences "to the extent the lawyer reasonably believes necessary to prevent reasonably certain death or substantial bodily harm." MR 1.6(b)(1). Following the amendment to MR 1.6(b)(1), this exception to the confidentiality duty might better be referred to as the "future harm" exception rather than the future crime exception because it requires no criminal act by the client for a trigger. See also sections on perjury and noisy withdrawal, §III.D.4 and Chapter 8, §I.C.

E. Other professional responsibility rules: Some ethics rules, such as MR 2.3, 2.4, and 3.3, require or permit lawyers to disclose information that would otherwise be protected by the duty of confidentiality.

F. "Other law" or orders of court: Lawyers may reveal confidences when required to do so by other law or by order of court.

G. Information generally known: Even when some others in addition to the lawyer and client know the protected client information, the duty of confidentiality continues to protect the information. When the information *is generally known,* however, its continued protection by the lawyer will in some cases serve little purpose, and most would say that the duty of confidentiality is lost as well.

V. OTHER PROFESSIONAL DUTIES THAT ARE SUBJECT TO THE DUTY OF CONFIDENTIALITY

A wide range of lawyer duties impose requirements on lawyers only when the duty does not offend the duty of confidentiality.

A. MR 8.3: This rule requires a lawyer to report certain misconduct of other lawyers, but not if such reporting would "require disclosure of information otherwise protected by Rule 1.6." MR 8.3(c). See Chapter 3, §V.

B. MR 1.9(c)(2): This rule defines the nature of conflict of interests with former clients and restricts the use of information from the former client's representation "except as [Rule 1.6] . . . would permit or require."

C. MR 1.13 Comment 5: This rule sets out the special duties and roles of lawyers whose clients are organizations. See Chapter 6, §IV.A.2.a. The Comment indicates that Rule 1.13 "does not limit or expand the lawyer's responsibilities under Rule 1.6. . . ."

D. MR 2.3(c): This rule permits lawyers to prepare materials on a client's behalf for the evaluation by third parties. In doing so, "[e]xcept as authorized in connection with a report of an evaluation, information relating to the evaluation is otherwise protected by Rule 1.6."

E. MR 4.1: This rule requires lawyers to disclose certain facts to "avoid assisting a criminal or fraudulent act by a client, unless disclosure is prohibited by Rule 1.6."

VI. USE OF CONFIDENTIAL INFORMATION FOR THE LAWYER'S BENEFIT

As a client's agent, a lawyer is generally restricted from using confidential information of the client, either for the lawyer's benefit or to the client's detriment.

A. Model Code: The Model Code expressly prohibits a lawyer from using confidential information of the client, either for the lawyer's benefit or to the client's detriment. DR 4-101(B)(2), 4-101(B)(3).

B. **Model Rules:** The Model Rules drafters kept only the explicit restriction on using client information to the client's detriment. MR 1.8(b).

C. **A meaningless distinction:** Technically, the distinction is important because, on its face, the Model Rules provision permits lawyer use of client confidences for the lawyer's or a third person's gain, as long as the client is not disadvantaged. As a practical matter, the distinction matters little because disadvantage to client will almost always occur when there is advantage to the lawyer and because the law of agency prohibits the lawyer from profiting by using the client's confidences.

CHAPTER 6

CONFLICT OF INTERESTS

I. LOYALTY AND OTHER GENERAL PRINCIPLES

A variety of central principles are at play in analyzing ***conflict of interests*** questions.

A. **Loyalty:** Basic to the lawyer-client relationship is the premise that lawyers owe clients a duty of ***loyalty.***

B. **Independence of professional judgment:** Lawyers owe clients a duty of ***independent professional judgment.*** When the independence is threatened by some interest other than the client's, a conflicts question is present and requires analysis.

C. **Implications of confidentiality:** Many conflicts questions are primarily about breaches of confidentiality. See Chapter 5.

D. **Direct adversity:** Relatively easy cases of conflict of interest analysis occur when the lawyer attempts to represent directly adverse interests.

E. **Material limitations on representation:** The application of many of the conflicts rules is triggered by a determination of whether the conflict "will materially limit[] the [lawyer's representation of the client]." See, e.g., MR 1.7(b). This standard is objective.

II. ORGANIZATION OF THE MODEL RULES PROVISIONS ON CONFLICTS

The Model Rules conflicts provisions are found in MR 1.7 through 1.13, and 1.18.

A. **General rule:** Model Rule 1.7 sets out the general standards for conflict of interests analysis.

B. **Specific transactions:** Model Rule 1.8 sets out a series of specific conflicts rules that apply to particular lawyer-client transactions.

C. **Special problems of former clients:** Model Rule 1.9 applies to multiple client conflicts when one of the clients is a former client.

D. **Prospective clients:** A new rule adopted in February 2002, MR 1.18, defines and identifies duties owed to prospective clients.

E. **Role-relevant rules:** Conflict rules that apply to lawyers in particular lawyer roles are found in MR 1.11, 1.12, and 1.13.

F. **Imputed disqualification:** Model Rule 1.10 provides the general imputed disqualification rules. More specific imputed disqualification rules are found in MR 1.9, 1.11, and 1.12.

III. WAIVER OF CONFLICTS

A. **Rationale:** Because most conflicts put client interests at risk and because client autonomy and decision-making are values worthy of some respect, clients are empowered to *waive* most conflicts of interest.

  1. **The gross conflict exception:** The general rationale of honoring client autonomy does not apply when the conflict is sufficiently gross to make any client waiver suspect. See MR 1.7(b).

  2. **The interest-other-than-the-client's exception:** The general rationale of honoring client autonomy does not apply when the conflicts rule is less about the risk to client interests than it is about risks to justice system interests.

B. **Elements of waiver:** At a minimum, conflict of interests waiver requires informed consent by the client. Some of the conflicts rules that allow waiver require more than informed consent. See, e.g., MR 1.8(a), MR 1.8(f).

IV. SOURCES OF CONFLICTS

There are three primary sources of conflict of interests: third party interference, lawyer interests, and multiple client interests.

A. **Third party interference:** *Third party interference* conflicts occur when someone who is not a party to the lawyer-client relationship seeks to affect or becomes positioned to affect the independence of the lawyer's judgment on behalf of the client. See MR 1.7(a)(2) for the general rule. Such conflicts may be waived if the client consents after consultation.

B. **Lawyer-client conflicts:** The second major source of conflicts is lawyer interests that conflict with client interests.

  1. **General principles**

    a. **Material limitation:** As a general matter, a conflict of interest exists when a lawyer's "representation of a client will be materially limited by the lawyer's . . . personal interests." MR 1.7(a)(2).

    b. Waiver: Waiver of this general conflict is possible if "the lawyer reasonably believes that the lawyer will be able to provide competent and diligent representation to [the client] and [the client] gives informed consent, confirmed in writing." MR 1.7(b). See §III.

2. Particular transactions: A variety of particular transactions between lawyers and clients is governed by specific conflicts rules.

    a. Business transactions with clients: Model Rule 1.8(a), which addresses business transactions between lawyer and client, requires that the client's consent be in writing, that the client be "advised in writing of the desirability of seeking and is given a reasonable opportunity to seek the advice of independent counsel," that the transaction be objectively reasonable, and that the transaction itself be in writing and in terms that can be understood by the client. The business transactions restrictions of MR 1.8(a) apply only when the client expects the lawyer to exercise legal judgment regarding the transaction.

    b. Literary rights: Lawyers are prohibited from negotiating for literary or media rights based on their clients' stories until the conclusion of representation. MR 1.8(d). No waiver of this conflict is permitted.

    c. Drafting instruments that benefit the lawyer: A lawyer is prohibited from drafting a document that makes a substantial gift to the lawyer or the lawyer's close relatives. This restriction does not apply when the donee is related to the donor. MR 1.8(c).

    d. Sexual or amorous relations with clients: Because of the complicated mixture of interests that can develop when a professional lawyer-client relationship is mingled with an amorous one, lawyers are well-advised to avoid amorous relationships with current clients. A new Model Rule adopted in February 2002, 1.8(j), prohibits most sexual relationships between lawyers and clients. The rule does not prohibit sexual relationships that predated the beginning of the lawyer-client relationship.

    e. Agreements limiting the lawyer's liability: A lawyer is prohibited from entering into a contract with a client that prospectively limits the lawyer's liability for malpractice, unless state law permits and the client is represented by independent counsel with respect to the agreement. MR 1.8(h).

    f. Settling claims with unrepresented clients: A lawyer is prohibited from settling malpractice claims with unrepresented clients or former clients, unless the lawyer first advises the client or former client that independent counsel is advisable. MR 1.8(h).

3. Lawyer-client conflicts and champerty, barratry, and maintenance: Various restrictions on lawyer conduct, often interrelated with lawyer-client conflicts issues, are based on the doctrines of champerty, barratry, and maintenance.

    a. Champerty, barratry, and maintenance: These three doctrines together are concerned with prohibiting the stirring up and maintaining of litigation. See definitions of champerty, barratry, and maintenance in Chapter 10, §VIII.

b. **Advancing funds to clients:** Lawyers are prohibited from advancing financial assistance to clients when there is pending or contemplated litigation, except that the lawyer may advance court costs. Client waiver of this "conflict" is not permitted. MR 1.8(e).

c. **Acquiring an interest in the litigation or its subject matter:** A lawyer is prohibited from acquiring an interest in litigation or its subject matter, whether that interest is consistent or inconsistent with the client's interests. This prohibition is not a restriction on the lawyer's contract with a client for a reasonable contingent fee. Client waiver of a violation of this rule is not permitted. MR 1.8(i).

4. **Miscellaneous lawyer-client conflicts rules:**

a. **Using confidential information to the client's detriment:** A lawyer is prohibited from using information learned in the lawyer-client relationship to the detriment of the client. MR 1.8(b).

C. **Multiple client conflicts:** The third major source of conflicts is the interaction of *multiple clients'* interests. Multiple client conflicts can implicate not only concurrent representation of multiple clients but also conflicts between former and current clients, prospective and current clients, or prospective and former clients.

1. **Concurrent clients:** Even when the conflicts involve only concurrent clients, a variety of different configurations may present themselves.

a. **Directly adverse:** The easiest cases involve multiple representation of clients whose interests are in direct conflict. Such a direct conflict cannot be effectively waived by the clients on the theory that it is too gross a conflict. MR 1.7(a). But see exceptions in intermediary role, Chapter 9 §III.

b. **Adverse in unrelated actions:** A lawyer may also find herself representing one client against a second client in a matter unrelated to the representation of the second client. In general, such a conflict may not be waived, but when the adversity is general, waiver has been permitted.

c. **Same side multiple client representation:** Even multiple representation of clients who are at least initially on the same side of litigation or a transaction implicates conflicts analysis.

2. **Prospective and current clients:** Lawyers owe prospective clients a limited loyalty duty and the duty of confidentiality. MR 1.18. Because confidentiality breaches are a primary consideration in multiple client conflicts analysis, conflicts analysis must be done on potential conflicts between prospective and current or former clients.

3. **Former and current clients—The substantial relationship test:** Because lawyers owe clients a continued measure of loyalty after representation ends and because lawyers owe clients a full measure of the duty of confidentiality after representation ends, conflicts between former and current clients arise when their interests are directly adverse or when there is a *substantial relationship* between the two representations. Such a conflict may be waived by both clients by informed consent. MR 1.9.

4. **Lawyer for an organization:** A lawyer who represents an organization, such as a corporation, a labor union, or a public interest organization, represents the organization, not its officers. At times, the interests of the organization and its officers may converge. Under such circumstances, a lawyer may represent both the organization and its officers, but the lawyer must withdraw if the interests of the organization and the officers diverge. MR 1.13.

5. **Positional conflicts of interest:** When a lawyer represents two clients in unrelated matters for whom the lawyer must argue opposite sides of the same legal issue, a potential positional conflict of interests exists. Although "[o]rdinarily a lawyer may take inconsistent legal positions in different tribunals at different times on behalf of different clients, . . . a conflict of interest exists . . . [when] there is a significant risk that the lawyer's action on behalf of one client will materially limit the lawyer's effectiveness in representing another client in a different case. . . ." MR 1.7 Comment 24. Especially when these opposite positions are argued before the same court, however, the lawyer is effectively arguing for a precedent in one case that harms the client in the other case. This would "adversely affect" one of the clients while benefitting the other.

V. IMPUTED CONFLICTS

As a general rule, when a lawyer has a conflict of interest, that conflict imputes to (transfers to, extends to) all of the lawyers in the law organization (usually a law firm) in which the lawyer works. MR 1.10.

A. **Basic issues:** This *imputed disqualification* rule is mainly based on the notion that confidential information possessed by one lawyer is effectively possessed by all lawyers in the same firm.

B. **Motions to disqualify:** *Motions to disqualify* counsel and entire law firms for which the disqualified lawyer works have become a favored tactical device in litigation, effectively denying an opposing party her counsel of choice and preserving the integrity of the justice system from the threat of conflicts of interest.

C. **The ambulatory lawyer:** The increasing movement of lawyers from one practice setting to another, from one law firm to another, has dramatically increased the frequency and impact of imputed disqualification rules.

D. **Screening defenses:** An increasing number of courts, supported by Model Rules 1.10, 1.11, and 1.12, have ruled that effective *screening procedures* will prevent the application of the imputed disqualification rules. Some courts have labeled these screening procedures the "Chinese Wall" defense, because of the walling off of the affected lawyer. Under such procedures, the conflicted lawyer is isolated from other lawyers in the organization by various devices. Haagen-Dazs Co. v. Perche No! Gelato, 639 F. Supp. 282 (N.D. Cal. 1986).

E. **Other interests at play in the motion to disqualify setting:** When a court is considering a motion to disqualify, several factors may be considered in addition to the conflicts principles that are relevant in the disciplinary context. See examples in §§V.F.1-4.

1. **Client choice of lawyer:** Clients have a limited interest in having their lawyer of choice. This interest weighs against granting of motions to disqualify.

2. **Timing of screening procedures and motion to disqualify:** Effective screening procedures instituted *after* the conflicted lawyer has been in the law firm for some time or, worse yet, *after* the motion to disqualify is filed, make the screening procedures less likely to excuse imputed disqualification. By contrast, a motion to disqualify filed well after the moving party had reason to know of the presence of the conflicted lawyer or, worse yet, close to the date of trial when the presence of the conflicted lawyer had been known to the moving party for some time, make the motion to disqualify less likely to be successful.

3. **Intentional creation of conflicts by the moving party:** Some institutional clients (banks, hospitals, insurance companies, etc.) have spread their legal work among a variety of law firms so that all such firms will be arguably disqualified from representing clients against the institution. At least one court has indicated that such tactics will make such an institution's motions to disqualify less likely to be successful. SWS Financial Fund A v. Salomon Brothers, Inc., 790 F. Supp. 1392 (N.D. Ill. 1992).

4. **Judicial economy:** When a motion to disqualify is granted, litigation is set back while replacement counsel becomes familiar with the matter. Notions of judicial economy favor the denial of motions to disqualify.

F. **Special role-related imputed disqualification rules:** Special rules regarding imputed disqualification apply to former government lawyers and former judges. See §VI. Armstrong v. McCalpin, 625 F.2d 433 (2d Cir. 1980).

VI. SPECIAL ROLE-RELATED CONFLICTS RULES

Lawyers who find themselves in special roles find that special conflicts rules apply.

A. **Former judge:** Former judges' conflicts differ from those of lawyers who move from one practice setting to another, and they require special conflicts rules. MR 1.12. A former judge shall not engage in private representation in a matter in which the judge participated personally and substantially as a judge, unless all parties to the matter consent after consultation. MR 1.12.

1. **Negotiating for employment:** Judges are prohibited from negotiating for employment with lawyers who are currently representing parties before the judge's court if the judge is personally and substantially participating in the matter before the court. Similar, but waivable, restrictions apply to judicial law clerks. MR 1.12(b).

2. **Special imputed disqualification rules:** Special, more relaxed imputed disqualification rules apply to the law firms for which former judges work. Effective screening procedures and notice to the parties and the judge's former court permit a former judge's law firm to continue with representation in which the former judge is disqualified from participating. MR 1.12(c).

B. **Former government lawyer:** Special conflicts rules apply to lawyers who move from government practice to private practice. MR 1.11.

1. **General:** A former government "lawyer shall not represent a client in connection with a matter in which the lawyer participated personally and substantially" as a government lawyer. MR 1.11. Notice that this conflict rule applies without regard to whether the lawyer has effectively changed sides in the matter.

2. **Exceptions:** Three exceptions allow the former government lawyer to engage in the later private representation even when his participation in the government employment was personal and substantial.

   a. **Law otherwise permits:** The conflicts rule excepts from its reach cases in which the law otherwise expressly permits the private representation to occur.

   b. **Not a "matter":** The rule defines what it means by a "matter." It is only later private representation in connection with a government service "matter" that triggers a conflict of interest analysis. A matter includes a wide variety of instances and actions that engage the agency with a particular party or parties. The definition excludes rule drafting and other agency actions that have more general application.

   c. **Consent:** The agency may waive the conflict by giving its informed consent.

3. **Use of confidential government information:** Except when law otherwise expressly permits such representation, a former government lawyer is also prohibited from representing private parties who are adverse to parties about whom the lawyer has confidential information gained in the government practice that could be used against the adverse party. MR 1.11(c). The private party's interests are the ones at risk in such a case. As such, it is the private party and not the agency that must waive the conflict if the lawyer is to be permitted to proceed.

4. **Special imputed disqualification rules:** Special, more relaxed, imputed disqualification rules apply when former government lawyers are the law firm lawyers who have a conflict.

C. **Lawyer as witness:** Special conflict problems are associated with the occasion on which a lawyer is to be called as a witness. MR 3.7. See §VI.C.

CHAPTER 7

DUTIES TO THIRD PARTIES

The duties owed to third parties operate as limits on the primary duty the lawyer owes to a client. In other words, they operate to form boundaries around acceptable, client-favoring actions by lawyers.

I. TRUTH-TELLING OUTSIDE THE COURT CONTEXT

Rules governing lawyers' truth-telling duties outside the court context contrast with those that apply inside the court context. See Chapter 8, §I. The outside the court truth-telling rules apply in a lawyer's dealings with opposing lawyers, opposing parties (but also see the special communications with opposing parties rules in §§IV and V), witnesses (but also see special communication with witnesses rules in §§IV.E.1 and V), and anyone else with whom the lawyer communicates as a lawyer.

A. **False statements of material law or fact:** For a statement to a third party to subject a lawyer to discipline, it must be both false and material.

B. **Fraudulent statements and silences:** Lawyers are prohibited from making statements that are fraudulent or remaining silent when the statement or silence would amount to fraud under applicable tort principles. See MR 1.0(d).

C. **The negotiation setting:** The negotiation setting presents a special circumstance within which the nature and effect of misleading statements must be analyzed. By its nature, an element of misleading is present in the negotiation process. The rules prohibit only certain forms of misleading. MR 4.1 Comment.

   1. **The parties to the negotiation:** Statements made to other lawyers in negotiations (and arguably to very sophisticated non-lawyers) are regarded much differently from statements made to non-lawyers.

   2. **What is a fact?** Some statements made in the negotiation setting are not regarded as statements of fact because they are simply too nebulous to be called "statements of fact," or they are accepted parts of the negotiation game that ought to be evaluated for what they are worth by the other side.

   3. **Reducing agreements to writing:** The process of reducing an oral agreement to writing poses special truthfulness problems.

II. HARASSMENT AND OTHER ABUSIVE CONDUCT

A. **In general:**

   1. **Unlawful acts by lawyers:** Lawyers are prohibited from engaging in (or using agents to engage in) unlawful acts on behalf of clients.

   2. **Assisting clients in committing unlawful or fraudulent acts:** Although a lawyer may counsel a client about the legal consequences of a course of conduct proposed by the client, a lawyer is prohibited from counseling a client to engage (or assisting a client engaged) in criminal or fraudulent conduct. MR 1.2(d). See Chapter 4, §V.B.

   3. **Harassing conduct:** Model Rule 4.4(a) prohibits a lawyer from using "means that have no substantial purpose other than to embarrass, delay, or burden a third person. . . ." The rule prohibits only actions that serve no substantial, legitimate purpose but are merely done to embarrass, delay, or burden the third person.

B. Opposing parties: Opposing parties are a special category of third party. Their interests are most directly contrary to those of the lawyer's client. Opposing parties are, therefore, routinely the object of a lawyer's client-favoring activities.

C. Witnesses: A great deal of lawyer conduct toward witnesses may be perceived by the witness as harassing. (For other witness-lawyer relationship rules that affect the trial process, such as payment limitation rules, see Chapter 8.)

1. **In general:** Conduct will violate the law of professional responsibility only when the lawyer has no "substantial purpose other than to embarrass, delay, or burden" the witness. MR 4.4(a).

2. **Investigation:** Lawyers may not use unlawful means to gather evidence from witnesses. MR 4.4(a).

D. Jurors: Lawyers are prohibited from engaging in live contact investigations of jurors and from other harassing conduct. (For other, "duty to the justice system" rules that relate to lawyers and jurors, see Chapter 8, §VI.B.)

1. **Investigation:** Lawyers may investigate jurors' backgrounds by means of public records such as deeds, judgments, available voting records, and so on. Lawyers may not contact jurors either in person or through agents. MR 4.4(a).

2. **Post-verdict harassing conduct:** Lawyers may not engage in conduct that will cause jurors to question the justice system's use of their verdict. See Chapter 8, §VI.B.

III. THREATENING CRIMINAL PROSECUTION

The Model Code includes a specific provision prohibiting threats of criminal prosecution "solely to obtain advantage in a civil matter." DR 7-105. Threatening criminal prosecution for reasons other than gaining an advantage in a civil matter is not prohibited by this rule. The Model Rules drafters did not include a specific provision on this subject in the Model Rules. Rather, they relied on the general, "rights of third parties" rule to cover the use of inappropriate threats. MR 4.4. In effect, when a threat would amount to extortion, it is a prohibited threat under MR 4.4(a).

IV. COMMUNICATING WITH REPRESENTED PERSONS

Lawyers are prohibited from communicating about the subject matter of a dispute with represented opposing parties without first obtaining permission from the opposing party's lawyer. MR 4.2. Opposing parties, however, may communicate with one another without offending MR 4.2, provided that the lawyer has not instructed the client to do so as a means of circumventing the rule.

A. Parties and persons: The rule includes represented persons, even if they are not formally parties to active litigation.

B. Who is an opposing party or person?

1. **Mere witnesses:** No matter how much a particular witness's testimony is expected to favor one side in a dispute, a mere witness is not a represented party. Model Rule 4.2 does not apply to communication with mere witnesses.

2. **Organizational parties:** Organizations speak and function through individuals who are not in and of themselves the organization. When dealing with a represented organization, Model Rule 4.2 prohibits unauthorized communication between an opposing lawyer and employees with managerial responsibilities for the subject of the matter, employees whose acts or omissions may be imputed to the organization with respect to the matter, and employees whose statements may constitute an admission attributable to the organization. MR 4.2 Comment 7.

3. **Former employees:** Whether former employees may be considered as parties for purposes of MR 4.2 has been a controversial question. Both the ABA and the majority of decisions say that former employees are not parties under MR 4.2. Other courts have ruled to the contrary. The better approach is probably to distinguish cases based on the category of employee at issue and that employee's relationship to the matter.

4. **Class action members:** Members of a class are treated as parties for purposes of MR 4.2.

C. Obtaining permission: A lawyer may communicate with an opposing party about the subject matter of the representation if the opposing party's lawyer has given consent.

D. Authorized by law: A lawyer may communicate with an opposing party about the subject matter of the representation if the lawyer is "authorized by law" to so communicate.

E. Authorized by court order: The February 2002 amendments to MR 4.2 added a provision permitting unconsented contact when authorized by court order. The amendment to Model Rule 4.2 creates an unstated link to the former "Reno Rule," which replaced the former Thornburgh Memorandum on the subject of federal government lawyers' compliance with MR 4.2 and other state ethics rules. Though its effects remain murky, the McDade Amendment (28 U.S.C. sec. 530B) and DOJ regulations adopted pursuant to it [28 C.F.R. sec. 77.1 *et seq.*] have also affected the analysis in this area.

F. Special criminal practice concerns: In criminal practice, of course, the opposing party of the prosecutor is a criminal defendant. Two different aspects of this special configuration are worthy of note.

1. **Added constitutional limitations:** Fifth and Fourteenth Amendment due process rights and Sixth Amendment right to counsel protection restrain prosecutors' contact with criminal defendants in ways that go beyond the professional responsibility law constraints of Model Rule 4.2.

2. **Investigation of crime:** Prosecutors, especially federal prosecutors invoking not only Model Rule 4.2's "authorized by law" language but also the Supremacy Clause of the United States Constitution, have argued that their crime investigation

activities are not restricted by Model Rule 4.2's requirements of consent by an opposing party's lawyer prior to communication.

V. COMMUNICATING WITH UNREPRESENTED PERSONS

Although not prohibited from communicating with unrepresented persons who are involved in a client's matter, lawyers are restricted in what they may say to such a person. MR 4.3.

A. Avoid misleading about the lawyer's interest:

1. **Affirmative duty:** A lawyer is under an affirmative obligation to refrain from stating or implying that the lawyer is disinterested in the matter about which the lawyer is communicating. Any effort to mislead an unrepresented person about the lawyer's interest subjects the lawyer to discipline.

2. **Clarifying duty:** When a lawyer "reasonably should know" that an unrepresented person misunderstands the lawyer's interest in the matter, the lawyer is obliged to make reasonable efforts to clarify his role.

B. Giving advice: Lawyers are prohibited from giving legal advice to the unrepresented persons with whom they inevitably come into contact, except to advise unrepresented persons to obtain counsel.

C. Fact gathering: Model Rule 4.3 does not prohibit fact gathering, provided the lawyer does so without giving advice (other than advice to obtain counsel) to the unrepresented person.

VI. CIVIL LIABILITY TO THIRD PERSONS

In limited circumstances, a lawyer may have civil liability for wrongful or negligent lawyering activity to those outside the lawyer-client relationship.

A. General: As a general rule, lawyers do not owe a duty to third persons that supports a negligence action.

B. Intended beneficiaries of the lawyer's work for a client: When a lawyer's work for a client is intended to benefit a third person, the lawyer owes a duty of care to that third person.

C. Invited reliance: When a lawyer's work for a client specifically invites the reliance of a third person, the lawyer owes a duty of care to that third person.

D. Assisting clients in breaching fiduciary duties: When a lawyer does work for a client who is a fiduciary (such as a trustee of a trust for the benefit of a beneficiary), the lawyer owes a duty to the beneficiary requiring the lawyer to refrain from engaging in acts that assist the client in breaching the client's fiduciary duties.

E. Preventing client harm to a third person: Lawyers who know that a client will harm a third person and fail to engage in reasonable steps to prevent the harm may have liability to the third person who is harmed by the client. This duty is highly controversial and not widely accepted.

CHAPTER 8

DUTIES TO THE LEGAL SYSTEM AND SOCIETY

Many of the lawyer's duties to the legal system or the public generally conflict with duties to the client, and the discussion in this Chapter covers rules that set the lines across which client-favoring actions become unacceptably harmful to the legal system or the public.

I. TRUTH-TELLING INSIDE THE COURT CONTEXT

Truth-telling inside the court context carries implications not present in out-of-court contexts, such as negotiation. When a lawyer misleads in court, the court itself is misled in addition to the opposing party.

  A. Statements to opposing parties: Lawyers' out-of-court obligations of candor to opposing parties continue in like form in the litigation context. See Chapter 7, §I.

  B. Fact statements to the court: A lawyer is prohibited from knowingly making false statements of material fact to the court and from otherwise engaging in acts or omissions that amount to fraud. MR 3.3(a).

   1. Generally: Despite the duty of candor to the court, a lawyer is under no general obligation to reveal unfavorable facts to the court. Although a lawyer is under no general obligation to reveal unfavorable facts to the court, a lawyer must disclose material facts "when disclosure is necessary to avoid assisting a criminal or fraudulent act by the client." MR 3.3(a)(1).

   2. Ex parte proceedings: On those occasions when a lawyer is permitted by law to engage in ex parte communications with the court (see §VI.A), the lawyer must disclose to the court both favorable and unfavorable material facts. MR 3.3(d).

  C. Perjury: The perjury problem presents extraordinary difficulties for the lawyer, especially when the person committing the perjury is the lawyer's client. Perjury's affront to the justice system is great, as is the harm that comes to the client when the lawyer reveals the client's perjury. Nix v. Whiteside, 475 U.S. 157 (1985).

   1. General duty to refrain from offering false evidence: A lawyer is prohibited from offering evidence the lawyer knows to be false. MR 3.3(a)(3).

   2. Discretion to refuse to offer some evidence: Further, a lawyer "may refuse to offer evidence that the lawyer reasonably believes is false." MR 3.3(a)(3).

   3. Perjury by a witness: When a lawyer knows that a witness other than the client has offered perjured testimony, the lawyer must promptly reveal the perjury to the court. MR 3.3(a)(3).

4. Perjury by a client: Unlike the Model Code approach, which explicitly distinguished between client perjury and other witness perjury, the Model Rules' language requires the same answer to both. MR 3.3(a)(3); DR 7-102(B).

    a. Knowledge before the perjury: When the lawyer knows of the client's intention to commit perjury, the lawyer must attempt to dissuade, attempt to withdraw and, finally if the perjury occurs, take reasonable remedial measures. The Model Rule indicates that whether the client or another witness has committed the perjury, reasonable remedial measures include disclosure of the perjury to the court.

    b. Knowledge gained after the perjury: When the lawyer learns that the client's testimony was perjurious after the perjury occurs but before proceedings end, the lawyer must first attempt to persuade the client to rectify the matter by revealing the fraud and then testifying truthfully. If that effort fails, the lawyer has only the reasonable remedial measures option and, according to the Model Rules Comment, must reveal the perjury if the lawyer learns of the perjury before the proceedings conclude. If the lawyer does not learn of the perjury until after the conclusion of the proceedings, then the lawyer has no obligation to reveal it. MR 3.3(c).

    c. Duty applies despite confidentiality: The Model Rule duty to rectify the perjury applies even if doing so would otherwise violate the duty of confidentiality under Model Rule 1.6. MR 3.3(c).

    d. Distinctions between criminal and civil representation: Perjury issues in criminal representation present special problems because of the criminal defendant's right to testify in his own behalf, the obligation on the state to prove the defendant guilty beyond a reasonable doubt, the privilege against self-incrimination, and the right to counsel. MR 3.3(a)(3).

    e. Other suggested options: Although not accepted in all circles, suggested options for counsel faced with a perjurious client in a criminal case include allowing the client to give a narrative as testimony, refusing to call the client as a witness, and exempting of criminal defense counsel from the general requirement to remedy a client's perjury.

D. Law statements to the court: A lawyer is prohibited from making false statements of law to the court. MR 3.3(a). As an advocate, the lawyer need not reveal his objective analysis of the law to the court but may make any nonfrivolous, client-favoring arguments regarding the law to the court.

E. Disclosing adverse legal authority: Lawyers are obligated to disclose to the court controlling, directly *adverse legal authority.* MR 3.3(a)(2).

    1. To opposing parties: Lawyers have no obligation to disclose adverse authority to opposing parties.

    2. To the court: Lawyers are required to disclose controlling, directly adverse authority to the court.

        a. Controlling: Only controlling authority, that is, mandatory authority that is controlling on the court currently making the decision, must be disclosed.

b. Directly adverse: Only directly adverse authority must be disclosed under this rule. Authority is directly adverse when it is applicable to the present case without extended analogy.

c. Contesting the disclosed authority: The requirement of disclosing the controlling directly adverse authority does not prevent the disclosing lawyer from arguing that the authority does not apply or is wrong and should not be followed.

II. SUPPRESSING EVIDENCE AND WITNESS PAYMENT

A lawyer is limited in the ways in which witnesses may be compensated and in instructing witnesses about whether to make themselves available for testimony or interview by the opposing side.

A. Suppressing witness availability: Lawyers are prohibited generally from requesting or advising a witness to refrain from voluntarily cooperating with another litigant. MR 3.4(f).

1. Procuring witness unavailability: Under no circumstances may a lawyer dissuade a witness from appearing at a hearing or persuade a witness to secrete himself so that the witness will be unavailable. MR 3.4(a).

2. Instructing a witness to cooperate only if subpoenaed: In general, a lawyer may not instruct a witness to cooperate only if subpoenaed. MR 3.4(f).

3. Exception: A lawyer is permitted to request that a witness not cooperate voluntarily if the witness is a relative, employee, or agent of the client and the lawyer reasonably believes that the request will not harm the witness. MR 3.4(f)(2).

B. Witness payment rules:

1. Lay witnesses: Lawyers may pay nonexpert witnesses only a statutory fee and reasonable expenses incurred by the witness in attending the trial or hearing. MR 3.4 Comment 3.

2. Expert witnesses: Expert witnesses may be paid the professional fee that someone in the expert's field charges for his or her time and reasonable expenses incurred by the witness in attending the trial or hearing. However, an expert may not be paid a fee that is contingent on the outcome of the matter. MR 3.4 Comment 3.

III. LIMITATIONS ON PRESENTATIONS TO A COURT

A. Frivolous claims and litigation positions: Lawyers are prohibited from bringing actions or taking positions in litigation that are frivolous.

1. Ethics code limits: In several forms, the Model Rules restrict lawyers' behavior regarding frivolous litigation positions.

a. The frivolous claims rule: Model Rule 3.1, in most respects tracking Federal Rule of Civil Procedure 11, prohibits lawyers from bringing or defending claims on a frivolous basis.

      i. What is frivolous? Frivolous claims or positions may be so because they lack legal or factual merit or because they are taken primarily to harass or maliciously injure a third party.

      ii. Difference between civil and criminal cases: In a criminal case, unlike a civil case, a defendant has a due process right to plead "not guilty" and require the government to be put to its proof. Model Rule 3.1 is not intended to prevent a lawyer from assisting a criminal defendant in the process of putting the government to its proof. Prosecuting lawyers have special obligations regarding the prosecution of charges that lack merit. See Chapter 9, §I.B.

   b. Discovery and other pretrial conduct: Frivolous discovery requests and those intended merely to delay are prohibited. MR 3.4(d).

   c. Expediting litigation: In general, lawyers are obliged to expedite litigation to the extent that such activity is consistent with the client's interests. MR 3.2.

 2. FRCP 11 and other sanctions: Beyond the ethics code limitations that create disciplinary liability for filing frivolous claims and taking frivolous positions in litigation, Federal Rule of Civil Procedure 11 and its state law counterparts create sanctions liability for similar conduct. See also Chapter 3, §V.B.

B. Personal opinion: Lawyers are prohibited from expressing their personal opinion to jurors about the justness of the client's cause, the credibility of a witness, or the culpability, guilt, or innocence of a party. MR 3.4(e).

C. Alluding to matters outside the record: Lawyers are prohibited from undermining the evidence law policies by alluding to matters that are either irrelevant or will not be supported by admissible evidence. MR 3.4(e).

 1. Reasonable lawyer standard: Matters must not be alluded to if a reasonable lawyer would recognize that those matters will not be supported by admissible evidence.

 2. Certainty not required: The lawyer need not be certain that the evidence will be admitted. If the lawyer reasonably believes that the evidence will be admitted, then the lawyer may freely allude to the evidence.

 3. Outside the lawyer's control: If evidence will be admissible only on a condition over which the lawyer in question has no control, the lawyer must not allude to that matter until the evidence is admitted.

 4. Matters already ruled inadmissible: Once the court has ruled a piece of evidence inadmissible, a lawyer is prohibited from referring to it to the jury.

D. Obey court orders: Lawyers must obey court orders. Even when a lawyer knows that a judge is mistaken in making an order or ruling, the lawyer must obey the order but may make reasonable efforts to preserve the record for later challenge on appeal.

E. Intemperate remarks: Although the First Amendment protects most lawyer expression, lawyers are subject to discipline for intemperate remarks that serve no useful purpose.

IV. OBLIGATION TO IMPROVE THE LEGAL SYSTEM

Lawyers have a responsibility to make efforts to improve the legal system. MR, Preamble; Model Code, Canon 8.

V. LIMITATIONS ON LITIGATION PUBLICITY

Lawyers generally and especially prosecutors are limited in what they may say to the media regarding pending litigation and criminal investigations. MR 3.6, MR 3.8(g).

A. Constitutional challenge: The original Model Rule 3.6 was held void for vagueness in Gentile v. State Bar of Nevada, 501 U.S. 1030 (1991).

B. General standard: Because of such statements' possible effects on the judicial process, lawyers are prohibited from making out-of-court statements that a reasonable lawyer would expect to be disseminated by public communication and that the lawyer knows or should know will have a substantial likelihood of materially prejudicing the matter. MR 3.6(a).

  1. Out of court: Only statements made out of court are restricted by this rule.

  2. Likely to be disseminated by public communication: Only statements that a reasonable statement-maker would expect to be disseminated by means of public communication are restricted by MR 3.6.

  3. Materially prejudice a matter: Statements that subject the lawyer to discipline are those that a lawyer knows or reasonably should know will be likely to materially prejudice the matter.

C. Permitted statements: Notwithstanding the general prohibition, statements in several distinct categories may safely be made without the risk of discipline. MR 3.6(b).

D. Exception for statements that are necessary to protect the client: When a lawyer reasonably believes that making a statement is necessary to counter the effects of a public statement made by the other side in the matter, the lawyer may make such a statement without being subject to discipline. MR 3.6(c).

E. Prosecutors' supervision of subordinates' statements: All lawyers have a general obligation to provide reasonable supervision of subordinates in an effort to avoid their breaches of the lawyer's ethics code, but prosecutors have a specially identified duty in the case of extrajudicial statements to exercise reasonable care to prevent violative extrajudicial statements by investigators, police, and others under the supervision of the prosecutor. MR 3.8(f).

VI. EX PARTE CONTACT WITH JUDGES AND JURORS

Ex parte (without the other party) *communications* seriously undermine the prospect of fair process in the justice system. As such, ex parte communication with decision-makers, both judges and jurors, is strictly regulated. MR 3.5.

A. Judges: Except in very limited circumstances, lawyers are prohibited from communicating ex parte with a judge. MR 3.5(b).

1. **Subject matter:** Some ex parte communications are permitted because of their subject matter.

   a. **Unrelated matters:** Communications between lawyers and judges about matters unrelated to pending or impending litigation are not restricted by the rule. Such communications are not truly "ex parte" because they do not involve other parties at all.

   b. **Housekeeping matters:** Ex parte communications regarding so-called housekeeping matters that relate to a pending case are permitted.

2. **No intent requirement:** Even innocently intended ex parte communications are prohibited.

3. **Authorized by law:** When authorized by law, lawyers are permitted to engage in ex parte communications. Such authorizations are typically found in rules governing requests for emergency restraining orders, for example. When such communication is authorized, a lawyer is under heightened candor-to-the-court requirements. See §I.B.2.

4. **Oral or written communications covered:** All forms of communication are covered by this rule. A lawyer who sends a letter to the judge or files a paper with the court without serving a copy on opposing counsel is engaging in prohibited ex parte communications with the judge.

5. **Prohibited even if judge initiates:** A lawyer is subject to discipline if he engages in even judge-initiated ex parte communication.

B. **Jurors:** Lawyers are strictly prohibited from communicating with jurors outside the courtroom before and during jurors' duties. This restriction applies to both grand jurors and trial jurors. Lawyers are prohibited from communicating with jurors after the jurors' duty ends, with some exceptions. Lawyers are prohibited from harassing jurors at any time. MR 3.5(c). See Chapter 7, §II.D.

   1. **Before and during proceedings:** Communication outside of open court with jurors during and prior to their duty is strictly prohibited. Even communication about matters other than the current proceedings is prohibited. Lawyers must refrain from even innocent communication with sitting jurors.

   2. **After proceedings end:** Once proceedings have ended, lawyers may have very limited contact with jurors for benign purposes, such as to determine whether the lawyer's presentation manner is effective. See Chapter 7, §II.D.

   3. **Reporting juror misconduct:** A lawyer is under an affirmative obligation to report to the court in which the proceedings are being held juror misconduct or others' misconduct with respect to jurors. Failure to do so subjects the lawyer to discipline.

VII. PRO BONO PUBLICO

The ethics rules encourage lawyers to engage in pro bono activities.

A. **Organized legal services for the poor:** Through the organized bar and public agencies, legal services are provided for a portion of the population that would otherwise be unable to afford to retain a lawyer.

B. Individual lawyer's duty: Amendments in 1993 and 2002 to Model Rule 6.1 have come as close as the organized bar has to imposing a requirement on individual lawyers to render pro bono service. Nonetheless, even the 1993 version of MR 6.1 remains aspirational and not mandatory. A lawyer is not subject to discipline for failing to render pro bono service.

CHAPTER 9

SPECIAL ROLE-RELATED DUTIES

I. SPECIAL DUTIES OF PROSECUTORS

Criminal prosecutors have ethical responsibilities in addition to those of other lawyers. Prosecutors do not represent the crime victim or a complaining witness. Charged with representing the public's interests rather than those of an individual litigant, prosecutors are required to seek justice rather than mere victory in their work.

A. Avoid conflicts with private interests represented: Prosecutors, often part-time prosecutors, also represent private clients. Prosecutors must avoid conflicts between the representation of private clients and the prosecutor's duty to seek justice on behalf of the public.

B. Dismissal of charges not supported by probable cause: Prosecutors are prohibited from prosecuting charges that the prosecutor knows are not supported by probable cause, the usual standard below which judges will not issue warrants and will dismiss charges at preliminary hearings. MR 3.8(a).

C. Advising defendants of their right to counsel: Prosecutors are charged with the responsibility to make reasonable efforts to assure that defendants are advised of their right to counsel. MR 3.8(b).

D. Fair treatment of unrepresented accused: Prosecutors must not unfairly extract waivers of important pretrial rights, such as right to a jury trial, right to counsel, and privilege against self-incrimination, from the unrepresented accused. MR 3.8(c).

E. Disclosure of exculpatory evidence: Prosecutors must timely disclose **exculpatory evidence** and mitigating circumstances regarding sentencing. MR 3.8(d).

F. Afford respect to lawyer-client relationships: Prosecutors are required to respect the lawyer-client relationship by refraining from unnecessarily issuing subpoenas that call on lawyers to give evidence about past or present clients. MR 3.8(e).

G. Fairness in investigation: A prosecutor is obliged to pursue investigative leads evenhandedly, without regard to whether they might favor or damage her case.

H. Grand jury fact fairness: All lawyers are obligated to reveal unfavorable facts in ex parte settings, such as hearings on emergency temporary restraining orders. MR 3.3(d). See Chapter 8, §I.B. Prosecutors are in such settings regularly in the grand jury context. Thus prosecutors have a regular duty in grand jury settings to present adverse material facts.

II. SPECIAL DUTIES OF SUPERVISING AND SUBORDINATE LAWYERS

Under certain circumstances, *supervising lawyers* will be ethically responsible for the acts of their *subordinates,* both lawyer and non-lawyer. Under certain circumstances, subordinate lawyers will be relieved of ethical responsibility for their actions.

A. Lawyers subordinate to other lawyers:

    1. General: Subordinate lawyers are not relieved of the duty to follow the rules of professional conduct merely because they are supervised or, for that matter, merely because the misconduct in which they might engage is ordered by the supervising lawyer. MR 5.2.

    2. Exception: A subordinate lawyer is not subject to discipline when she "acts in accordance with a supervisory lawyer's reasonable resolution of an arguable question of professional duty." MR 5.2(b).

B. Lawyers supervising lawyers: Supervisory lawyers are responsible for providing reasonable supervision of lawyer subordinates. MR 5.1.

    1. Providing supervision: Separate from the acts of lawyer subordinates, supervising lawyers are subject to discipline if they fail to provide adequate supervision.

    2. Responsibility for lawyer subordinates' misconduct: Supervisory lawyers are subject to discipline for the conduct of lawyer subordinates that violates the rules of lawyer conduct when the supervisory lawyer orders the subordinate lawyer to engage in the misconduct, when the supervisory lawyer ratifies the subordinate lawyer's misconduct, or when a lawyer who is either a partner or the subordinate's direct supervisor learns of the misconduct at a time when its effect could be avoided or mitigated and yet fails to take reasonable remedial action.

C. Lawyers supervising non-lawyers: Lawyers are responsible for providing reasonable supervision of non-lawyer subordinates on the same terms as they are responsible for supervising lawyer subordinates. MR 5.3.

III. LAWYERS AS INTERMEDIARIES

Contrary to the ordinary picture of the lawyer as a partisan, representing one party against the interests of another, lawyers may in limited circumstances act in the role of *intermediary.* Former MR 2.2. As an intermediary, a lawyer attempts to achieve the goals and interests of multiple parties with potentially adverse interests. Such a role is inappropriate when litigation is pending or contemplated.

A. Requirements: In order to pursue a matter for multiple clients as an intermediary, the clients must consent after consultation, the intermediary form of representation must be in the clients' best interest, and the lawyer must believe that she can represent the clients impartially.

B. Confidentiality: The evidentiary privilege and the duty of confidentiality do not apply as between the parties commonly represented.

C. Withdrawal: If any of the requirements ceases to be met during the representation, the lawyer must withdraw from the representation of all of the clients. Former MR 2.2(c).

IV. ANCILLARY BUSINESSES

Some lawyers maintain *ancillary,* associated *businesses* along with their law practice. MR 5.7.

A. General rule: Lawyers are subject to the rules of professional conduct for lawyers while providing ancillary services when either of the following two conditions is present.

    1. Not distinct: When the services provided are not distinct from the lawyer's legal services. MR 5.7(a)(1).

    2. Failure to communicate to client: When the services are provided by an entity controlled either by the lawyer or by the lawyer with others, and the lawyer fails to communicate clearly to the client that the services are not legal services and are not subject to the normal protections in the lawyer-client relationship. MR 5.7(a)(2).

B. What are ancillary services? Ancillary or "law-related" services are services that are related to legal services and are not prohibited as unauthorized practice of law when performed by a non-lawyer. MR 5.7(b). Side businesses of lawyers that are entirely unrelated to law practice are not ancillary businesses.

CHAPTER **10**

ADVERTISING AND SOLICITATION

Warning: The Model Code advertising and solicitation provisions are misleading. DR 2-101, 2-102, 2-103, 2-104, 2-105. The Code was amended during the 1970s to reflect some of the earliest constitutional limitations on the regulation of client-getting. But because the Model Code has not been updated and amended by the ABA since the Model Rules' adoption in 1983, many of its provisions do not reflect recent court decisions that render enforcement of some of its provisions unconstitutional.

I. TRADITIONAL DISTINCTIONS BETWEEN ADVERTISING AND SOLICITATION

The ethics rules distinguish between *advertising* and *solicitation.* Categorizing a particular client-getting activity as one or the other is the first step to analyzing whether or not the activity is permitted.

A. Advertising: The term *advertising* has traditionally referred to widely distributed, public statements about the services available from a particular lawyer or law organization.

B. Solicitation: The term *solicitation* has traditionally referred to narrower communications directed at one or a small group of identified recipients who are known to need a particular service.

C. Blurring of the traditional distinctions: Direct, personal, but form, mail to people known to have particular legal needs partakes of some of the attributes of both advertising and solicitation.

D. Model Rules: The Model Rules treat advertising and solicitation in separate rules (MR 7.2 for advertising and MR 7.3 for solicitation). See §§IV and V. They also create general restrictions that apply to both advertising and solicitation in MR 7.1, 7.4, and 7.5. See §III.

II. CONSTITUTIONAL LIMITATIONS ON DISCIPLINARY AUTHORITY

Advertising and solicitation are speech. As such, some First Amendment protection is provided to these activities, effectively limiting the states' authority to prohibit and regulate them.

A. Commercial speech: Commercial speech, such as advertising, is given some protection under the First Amendment. Virginia Bd. of Pharmacy v. Virginia Citizens Consumer Council, Inc., 425 U.S. 748 (1976).

B. No broader restrictions than necessary: Restrictions on commercial speech must further a substantial government interest and must be no broader than necessary.

    1. Government interest in truthful advertising: The government has a substantial interest in protecting the public from being misled or coerced by lawyer communications.

    2. Narrowly drawn: To pass constitutional muster, restrictions must be focussed on the substantial government interest and must be narrowly drawn.

    3. No accounting for matters of taste: Regulating commercial speech based on its "dignity" or "taste" is constitutionally *impermissible.*

C. Permissible regulation: Despite the constitutional limitations on its power to restrict lawyer commercial speech, a state may prohibit lawyer client-getting that is false or misleading, that is coercive, or that promotes transactions that are themselves illegal. In re Primus, 436 U.S. 412 (1978); Zauderer v. Office of Disciplinary Counsel of

Supreme Court of Ohio, 471 U.S. 626 (1985); Bates v. State Bar of Arizona, 433 U.S. 350 (1977).

III. GENERAL CONSTRAINTS ON ALL COMMUNICATION REGARDING SERVICES

Some restrictions apply equally to all forms of client-getting, whether denominated as advertising or solicitation.

A. **False and misleading statements, generally:** False or misleading statements in lawyer client-getting communication are subject to discipline. MR 7.1. In re RMJ, 455 U.S. 191 (1982).

   1. **Testimonials:** Courts in some states have held that lawyer ads that use client testimonials are inherently misleading by focusing the viewer's attention on selected, favorable client examples and excluding unfavorable examples.

   2. **Self-laudation:** Self-laudation that is either unverifiable or misleading-but-true is subject to discipline as false or misleading.

      a. **Unverifiable:** Statements that are unverifiable are deemed misleading.

      b. **Misleading but true:** Self-laudation is subject to discipline as being misleading-but-true when, although verifiable and true, the statement misleads the reader or viewer usually because it appears to be more important than it would be if it could be put into a full context.

   3. **Firm names:** Firm names may be misleading when they untruthfully imply a relationship to a government or other institution. MR 7.5.

   4. **Information about fees:** Since *Bates,* lawyers' statements about fees have been constitutionally protected. Like other advertising statements, they may be restricted only when they are false or misleading.

B. **Specialization and certification:** Until the 1970s, state bars were quite restrictive in their regulation of lawyers' indications of practice concentration, specialization, or certification in areas of practice.

   1. **Areas of practice:** As long as the words used by the lawyer to designate areas in which the lawyer practices fairly communicate those areas, they will be protected commercial speech and will not subject the lawyer to discipline.

   2. **Certification:** An unqualified statement of certification may mislead the reader into thinking that the state has certified the lawyer in a particular area. However, a state may not impose a blanket prohibition on statements of certification. Peel v. Illinois Attorney Registration and Disciplinary Commission, 496 U.S. 91 (1990). To make Model Rule 7.4 consistent with Peel v. Attorney Registration and Disciplinary Commission of Illinois, 496 U.S. 91 (1990), the rule was amended in February 2002 to permit statements of certification by clearly identified organizations approved by the ABA or the appropriate state bar. See §II.D.5.

C. **Post-event waiting periods:** In an effort to guard against the potential for lawyer overreaching of accident victims and their families, some states have imposed waiting periods before any targeted communications may be made. Narrowly drawn waiting period restrictions are constitutional. Florida Bar v. Went For It, Inc., 115 S. Ct. 2371 (1995).

IV. CONSTRAINTS PARTICULAR TO ADVERTISING

Some restrictions have particular applicability to advertising.

A. **Record keeping:** A lawyer is required to retain a copy of any advertisement, including the text of any broadcast advertisement, for two years after its last publication. Although still in effect in most states, the language requiring lawyers to maintain a two-year record of advertisements was deleted from Model Rule 7.2 in the February 2002 amendments.

B. **Payment for advertising:** Lawyers, of course, may pay reasonable costs associated with advertising. MR 7.2(b). This rule states what may seem to be the obvious because, outside of the advertising context, lawyers may not pay others for recommending the lawyer.

C. **Name of the lawyer:** All advertisements must include the name and address of at least one lawyer or law firm who is responsible for the advertisement's content. MR 7.2(c).

V. CONSTRAINTS ON IN-PERSON AND LIVE TELEPHONE SOLICITATION

In-person and live telephone solicitation are subject to prophylactic rules that are much more restrictive than the advertising rules. Ohralik v. Ohio State Bar Assoc., 436 U.S. 447 (1978).

A. **Duress, coercion, and harassment:** Although all client-getting communication is subject to discipline if it involves duress or coercion, restrictions on in-person and live telephone client solicitation are meant to protect prospective clients from special dangers of lawyer coercion and duress that attend such communications.

B. **Exceptions to the restrictions:**

1. **Non-live telephone:** Computer, autodial, and recorded telephone solicitations are restricted only by the advertising rules and by the general, false and misleading and actual duress or coercion limitations.

2. **Relationship with the prospective client:** Subject only to the general limitations on client-getting speech, lawyers may solicit other lawyers or people with whom the lawyer has a family, close personal, or prior professional relationship. MR 7.3(a).

3. Pecuniary gain: The specific restrictions on in-person and live telephone solicitation apply only when a significant motive for the solicitation is pecuniary gain for the lawyer. MR 7.3(a).

VI. OTHER RESTRICTIONS ON SPECIFIC SOLICITATION

There are additional restrictions on solicitation of specific prospective clients or those known to be in need of specific services.

A. "We don't want any!": Once a prospective client makes known her desire not to be contacted by the lawyer, the lawyer may not contact that prospective client. MR 7.3(b)(1).

B. Disclaimer: Written or recorded communications to those known to be in need of specific services must include the words "Advertising Material" on the outside of any envelope used and at the beginning and end of any recorded communication. MR 7.3(c).

VII. CLIENT-GETTING ON THE INTERNET

An emerging problem relates to the application of the client-getting rules to internet communications regarding lawyer services.

A. General: In general, it seems likely that internet advertising ought to be treated largely as direct mail advertising is treated now.

B. Territorial difficulties: The Model Code restricts a lawyer's advertising to an area where the lawyer resides or maintains an office or where a significant portion of the lawyer's clients resides. DR 2-101(B). The Model Rules has no such territorial restriction. When a message is sent out on the internet, it obviously violates the Model Code provision for any lawyer or firm that does not have a truly global practice. It seems likely that these territorial restrictions will go the way of the states' failed efforts to impose residency requirements for admission to practice. See Chapter 2, §III.

VIII. CLIENT-GETTING'S RELATIONSHIP TO BARRATRY, MAINTENANCE, AND CHAMPERTY

Lawyers have long been restrained by both ethics rules and criminal statutes from engaging in barratry, maintenance, and champerty.

A. Barratry: Barratry is a term that refers to stirring up controversy and thereby litigation. Its relationship to client-getting activities is the connection between soliciting clients and generating the prospective clients' interest in pursuing litigation.

B. Maintenance: Lawyers are limited in the ways in which they may maintain, that is, financially support, their clients. In terms of client-getting, a lawyer is prohibited from using offers of financial support of a client to induce the client to retain the lawyer.

C. **Champerty:** Champerty law restricts lawyers from acquiring an interest in the subject matter of litigation. In terms of client-getting, champerty law restricts lawyers from buying into client claims for the purpose of attracting the client to retain the lawyer. See also Chapter 6, §IV.B.

IX. LAWYER'S CLIENT-GETTING AGENTS

A. **Runners and cappers:** Runners and cappers monitor accidents and other events likely to produce legal work and then direct potential clients to the lawyer for whom the runner or capper works.

   1. **Discipline:** Lawyers who employ runners or cappers are subject to discipline. MR 5.3(c).

   2. **Criminal violation:** In many states, employment of runners or cappers is also a criminal violation.

B. **Payment for client referrals:** In general, lawyers may not give anything of value to anyone who refers a client to the lawyer.

CHAPTER 11

JUDICIAL CONDUCT

Judicial conduct law is fundamentally different from lawyer conduct law because the judge and lawyer roles are fundamentally different. For example, judges are neutrals and not partisans, so the lawyer's duty of loyalty to a client is simply not a part of a judicial conduct discussion. Likewise, judges are not confided in by either of the parties, so the lawyer confidentiality discussion drops out of judicial conduct discussions.

I. SOURCES OF JUDICIAL CONDUCT LAW

The law governing judges comes from a wide range of sources.

A. **ABA Model Code of Judicial Conduct:** The American Bar Association has adopted a *Model Code of Judicial Conduct* (CJC). Like its lawyer conduct models, the CJC is not directly applicable to anyone. Rather, it becomes so when adopted by a state's legislature or court system as the applicable rules of judicial conduct for the particular jurisdiction.

B. **Federal statutes:** A few federal statutes modify the CJC in federal court, particularly as it relates to judicial disqualification procedures and standards.

C. **Lawyer ethics rules:** Most judges are also lawyers, and to the extent they remain relevant to the judge's role, the professional ethics rules governing lawyers apply to judges as well.

D. Other sources: The constitution, case law, and bar ethics opinions are also important sources of judicial conduct law.

II. WHO IS A JUDGE?

The CJC defines what it means to be a judge and also expressly identifies special rules and exemptions from the rules that apply to various categories of part-time judges. CJC, Application of the CJC. Judges are officers of judicial systems who perform judicial functions, that is, decide cases. CJC, Application of CJC §I.

III. GENERAL JUDICIAL ATTRIBUTES

A. Independence: Our system of justice requires that judges and the judiciary be independent of outside influences, including those of the legislative and executive branches.

B. Integrity: Although a lack of integrity is rarely the sole ground for imposing judicial discipline, a fundamental expectation of judges is that they have integrity. CJC Canon 1.

C. Impartiality: Most of the assumptions underlying our judicial system hinge on the impartiality of judges. See §V.A.

IV. PERSONAL CONDUCT AND ACTIVITY OUTSIDE THE JUDICIAL ROLE

Public perception of judges has a significant effect on the public confidence in the justice system. As such, the notion of avoiding even the appearance of impropriety has greater force in judicial conduct law than it does in lawyer conduct law. CJC §2A Comment.

A. Avoid impropriety and appearance of impropriety: The CJC cautions judges about engaging in conduct that "would create in reasonable minds a perception that the judge's ability to carry out judicial responsibilities with integrity, impartiality and competence is impaired." CJC §2A Comment 2. This standard is an objective one.

B. Comply with the law: Judges' misconduct that violates law violates the "comply with law" standard of the CJC. CJC §2A.

    1. No conviction necessary: A judge's contrary to law conduct need not result in a conviction before judicial discipline is imposed.

    2. Intentional or bad faith refusal to follow precedent and other mandatory authority: A judge can be subject to discipline for repeatedly failing to follow the law in his own decisions.

C. Preserving the prestige of the judicial office: Judges are prohibited from lending the prestige of their offices to private interests.

D. Judges as witnesses: Because of the judge's potentially excessive influence on a fact finder, there are some limitations on the use of judges as witnesses. The limitations in fact, however, are minimal.

1. **As fact witness:** As long as the judge is not presiding over the proceeding, a judge may be called as a fact witness.

2. **As character witness:** A judge is prohibited from voluntarily testifying as a character witness. CJC §2. A judge must be subpoenaed in order to obtain her presence and testimony as a character witness.

E. **Organizational membership:** A judge is not permitted to be a member of an organization that "practices invidious discrimination on the basis of race, sex, religion or national origin." CJC §2C.

F. **Speaking, writing, and teaching:** Within certain constraints, judges are permitted to teach, speak, and write about the law, the legal profession, and the justice system. CJC §3B.

1. **Pending cases:** Judges are required to be cautious in their discussion of pending cases. They must refrain from making either public or nonpublic comments that risk the fairness of the proceedings.

2. **Judicial duties take precedence:** Speaking, teaching, and writing activities must be secondary in importance to the judge's judicial responsibilities.

3. **Appearance of bias:** A judge must be careful to avoid creation of an appearance that the judge would not enforce the law or decide cases fairly.

G. **Government activities:** Judges are permitted to engage in legislative and public hearings and to consult about legal matters with the executive or legislative branches.

H. **Civic and charitable activities:** Judges may serve as directors, board members, or trustees of not-for-profit organizations unless the organization would be likely to come before the judge's court or will regularly be involved in litigation in any court. CJC §4C. Judges may not engage in direct fundraising for such organizations. CJC §4C(3)(b).

I. **Financial activities:** Except for closely held family businesses, judges may not be director, officer, manager, partner, advisor, or employee of a business. CJC §4D(3).

J. **Fiduciary activities:** Except for such services performed for family members, a judge is prohibited from serving as executor, administrator, trustee, guardian, or other fiduciary. CJC §4E.

K. **Practicing law:** Except for serving interests of herself or her family members, full-time judges are not permitted to practice law. CJC §4G.

L. **Outside income limitations and reporting requirements:** When judges are permitted to earn outside income (from teaching, writing, speaking, etc.), such income must be limited to reasonable amounts for the services rendered and must not appear to compromise the judge's integrity and impartiality.

1. **Gifts and favors:** Judges may not accept gifts or favors from a person whose interests are or are likely to be before the judge. Gifts that are appropriate to special occasions (wedding or anniversary, for example), are permitted.

2. **Reporting of income:** Judges must file annually as a public document a statement of the nature and amount of compensation received. CJC §4H(2).

V. JUDICIAL DUTIES

The defining characteristic of the judge is the performance of judicial duties, that is, deciding cases.

A. **Impartiality:** Perhaps the most central attribute of the judge's role in our justice system is impartiality. All of the other rules and assumptions flow from this central notion. See, for example, ex parte communication rules in §V.G and disqualification rules in §V.L.

B. **Diligence:** Judges are required to be diligent in the discharge of their duties. CJC §3A(5).

C. **Competence:** Judges must also have and maintain competence in the law and decision-making. CJC §3B(2).

D. **Maintain courtroom decorum:** Judges are authorized and required to maintain courtroom decorum. CJC §3B(3).

E. **Patience:** Even while maintaining courtroom decorum and disposing of the court's business diligently, a judge must exhibit patience. CJC §3B(4).

F. **Avoid bias and prejudice:** In order to remain impartial, a judge must avoid bias and prejudice. CJC §3B(5).

   1. **In judicial functions:** In addition to racial, sexist, and ethnic biases, judges must avoid bias in favor of friends and associates and against particular causes or groups of lawyers.

   2. **Restraining lawyer bias:** In maintaining courtroom decorum and conduct, judges are required to restrain lawyer bias, though not to the extent of prohibiting legitimate argument. CJC §3B(6).

G. **Ex parte communications:** Except in limited circumstances, judges may not engage in ex parte communications. See Chapter 8, §VI.A.

   1. **Rationale:** Our adversarial justice system is undermined when some parties have opportunities to influence the judge's decision-making in the absence of other parties.

   2. **Good faith is no excuse:** Even when a judge engages in ex parte communications for good but not authorized-by-law reasons, the judge is subject to discipline.

   3. **Pending matter discussion presumed:** In the absence of evidence to the contrary, a private communication between a judge and a lawyer with a matter pending before the judge will be presumed to have been about the pending matter.

   4. **Timing:** A case continues to be a pending matter until its final disposition. As such, even after a trial judge has ruled, the judge is not permitted to have ex parte communications with counsel while appeals are pending.

   5. **Exceptions:** The CJC permits ex parte communications in a few distinct situations.

      a. **Housekeeping matters:** Communications for scheduling or administrative purposes do not violate the ex parte communication rules, provided the judge "reasonably believes that no party will gain [an] advantage [from the communication] and the judge promptly notifies all parties and affords them an opportunity to respond." CJC §3B(7)(a).

    b. Disinterested experts: Judges may consult with other judges and with disinterested experts on the law if the judge identifies the person consulted to the parties and affords the parties an opportunity to respond. CJC §3B(7)(b).

    c. Court clerks: Judges may consult with clerks about the law in the absence of the parties without restriction. Even judicial clerks, however, may not do independent fact investigation and then communicate the results to the judge. CJC §3B(7)(c).

    d. Authorized by law: Other law authorizes ex parte communications in various, limited circumstances, such as requests for emergency temporary restraining orders.

H. Public comments: Judges are prohibited from making public or private comments regarding pending matters that risk the fair outcome of the matter. CJC §3B(9).

I. Criticism of jurors: Aside from expressing appreciation of jurors' service, judges may neither compliment nor criticize jurors' decisions. CJC §3B(10).

J. Making appointments: Judges are required to make appointments that their office permits on the basis of merit and not based on nepotism or favoritism. CJC §3C(4).

K. Reporting others' misconduct: Judges have duties to report misconduct of other judges and of lawyers under certain circumstances. CJC §3D.

    1. Other judges: Judges have an obligation to report other judges' misconduct under certain circumstances. CJC §3D(1).

        a. Permissive reporting: Judges "should take appropriate action" (which may, in the judge's discretion, mean reporting misconduct) when a judge receives information that raises a "substantial likelihood that another judge" has violated the CJC. CJC §3D(1).

        b. Mandatory reporting: A judge "shall inform the appropriate authority" when the judge "has knowledge" that another judge has committed misconduct "that raises a substantial question" about that judge's fitness for office. CJC §3D(1).

    2. Lawyers: Judges are required to report certain lawyer misconduct as well. CJC §3D(2).

        a. Permissive reporting: Judges "should take appropriate action" (which may, in the judge's discretion, mean reporting misconduct) when a judge receives information that raises a "substantial likelihood that a lawyer" has violated her state's professional ethics rules.

        b. Mandatory reporting: A judge "shall inform the appropriate authority" when the judge "has knowledge" that a lawyer has committed misconduct "that raises a substantial question" about the lawyer's honesty, trustworthiness, or fitness as a lawyer in other respects.

3. **Privilege:** A judge's report of misconduct is absolutely privileged from civil actions for damages.

L. **Disqualification and waiver:** Disqualification is among the most important and most litigated areas of judicial conduct. Both CJC Canon 3E and federal statutes govern this topic. A judge who voluntarily removes herself from hearing a matter is said to have *recused* herself. 28 U.S.C. §§47, 144, 455.

1. **Objective and subjective test:** The basic standard for judicial disqualification is an objective one. "A judge shall disqualify himself or herself [when] the judge's impartiality might reasonably be questioned. . . ." CJC §3E(1). The central federal statute is similar. 28 U.S.C. §455. A judge must also, however, be subjectively free from bias.

2. **Rule of necessity:** Occasionally, an issue arises that would disqualify every judge that is sitting on a court with jurisdiction to resolve the issue. When this phenomenon occurs, the "rule of necessity" says that judges are not disqualified.

3. **Grounds for disqualification:** Beyond the general standard, a wide variety of specific categories of reasons may cause a reasonable person to question a judge's impartiality.

   a. **Bias in general:** Naturally, a judge's bias may be reason to question her impartiality. Bias, however, will be grounds for disqualification only when the bias is against a party, as opposed to the legal rules governing the case, and when the bias against a party arises from a source outside the present litigation.

   b. **Judge's relationship to party, witness, or lawyer:** A wide variety of personal and professional relationships may cause a question to be raised regarding the judge's impartiality.

   c. **Judge's prior relationship to the matter:** Judges may have prior relationships to the matter before them as well as to the parties and lawyers.

      i. **Judge was the lawyer:** When the judge was formerly a lawyer on the same or a substantially related matter, the judge is disqualified.

      ii. **Judge formerly associated with the lawyer:** When the judge was associated with one of the lawyers while the lawyer was representing the party in the same or a substantially related matter, the judge is disqualified. CJC §3E(1)(b).

      iii. **Judge is a material witness:** When a judge has been a material witness in a matter, the judge is disqualified. CJC §3E(1)(b).

      iv. **Prior personal knowledge of disputed facts:** When a judge has prior personal knowledge of disputed evidentiary facts regarding the matter, the judge is disqualified. CJC §3E(1)(a).

   d. **Economic interest:** A judge is disqualified from hearing the matter when she has more than a de minimis (very small) economic interest in the outcome of the matter.

i. **Type of interest:** The disqualifying interest under this rule must be economic; it may be in either the subject matter of the controversy or a party to the proceeding. CJC §3E(1)(c).

ii. **By whom and in what capacity held:** The disqualifying interest may be held by the judge personally or as a fiduciary, by a member of the judge's family residing in the judge's household, or by the judge's spouse or a person within the third degree of relationship to the judge.

iii. **How affected:** The interest must be one that "could be substantially affected by the proceeding." However large the interest might be, minor or highly speculative effects on it are not disqualifying. CJC §§3E(1)(c), 3E(1)(d).

iv. **Magnitude of interest:** A de minimis (very small) interest in the subject matter or a party to the proceeding is not disqualifying. CJC §§3E(1)(c), 3E(1)(d).

v. **Knowledge:** Only those interests that are known to the judge are disqualifying, but a judge has a duty to keep informed about the judge's and his or her spouse's and minor children's economic interests. CJC §§3E(1)(c), 3E(1)(d), 3E(2). The judge also has a duty to make reasonable efforts to be informed of the economic interests of family members.

4. **Remittal (waiver) of disqualification:** Most sources of disqualification can be waived by the parties, permitting the judge to continue in the matter, provided the appropriate procedures are followed. CJC §3F; 28 U.S.C. §455.

   a. **CJC:** Under the CJC, parties may not waive the judge's personal bias regarding a party. They may waive any other form of disqualification.

   b. **Federal law:** Under 28 U.S.C. §455, the parties may waive disqualification only when it follows from the general standard, that is, when the judge's "impartiality might reasonably be questioned." They may not waive any of the more specific reasons for disqualification.

   c. **Procedure:** For the waiver to be effective, the judge must disclose the nature of the disqualifying interest on the record, and the parties must all agree on the record, without the participation of the judge, that the judge should continue in the matter. CJC §3F.

VI. POLITICAL ACTIVITIES

Judges must maintain a separation from the give and take of politics. As a result, a variety of restrictions on the political activities of judges and judicial candidates exists. CJC Canon 5.

A. **In general:** Because states have so many varied systems for selecting judges, the CJC provisions are in some respects internally inconsistent. Some general points may be made nonetheless.

B. Restrictions on judges and candidates of all types: Both judges and candidates are prohibited from political party leadership, from making public statements endorsing or opposing political candidates, and from solicitation of campaign funds.

C. Restrictions on judges: A judge is required to resign from judicial office when the judge becomes a candidate for a nonjudicial office.

D. Restrictions on candidates: Candidates must maintain the dignity of the judicial office they seek and refrain from making promises or pledges other than to faithfully and impartially discharge the judicial function. This provision's constitutional status is in doubt. Although not specifically addressing the "pledges and promises" clause, the Supreme Court, in Republican Party of Minnesota v. White (2002), held that Minnesota's CJC violated the First Amendment by prohibiting judicial candidates from speaking publicly about their views on legal and political issues.

VII. LIABILITY FOR CIVIL WRONGS COMMITTED

When judges engage in the core judicial function of deciding cases, they are absolutely immune from civil damage suits.

A. Immunity for judicial action: Even when a judge errs in judicial decision-making, the judge is immune from damage actions. Pierson v. Ray, 386 U.S. 547 (1967). The immunity does not extend beyond the judicial function. For example, judges may be liable for negligence in driving their automobiles, for breach of contract when they fail to make the installment payments on their CD players, and so on.

B. Administrative actions: Administrative actions by judges also fall outside the protection of absolute judicial immunity.

EXAM TIPS

SUMMARY OF CONTENTS

Exam Tips on
INTRODUCTION AND THE ROLE OF LAWYER

The law of professional responsibility, and therefore the course in which it is studied, is about the relationships of lawyers to their clients, their peers, the justice system, the profession, and the public.

☛ Some essay questions may call on you to discuss moral philosophy. But remember, *moral philosophy* informs the study of professional responsibility law, but does not replace legal analysis as the tool for determining the application of professional responsibility law.

☛ There is a great deal more to the law governing lawyers than the difference between right and wrong. The law governing lawyers is *law.* It must be studied and mastered like any other law field.

Role Morality

☛ The concept of *role morality* plays an important role in analyzing lawyer ethics. Lawyers' moral decision-making involves a balancing process. Lawyers owe many duties not all of which point in a single direction at any given moment. Lawyers owe duties to clients, the justice system, third parties generally, opposing parties, the society, and the profession. Balancing among those competing duties is the mark of a thoughtful essay exam answer.

Practice Setting

☛ Watch for the context of the lawyer's representation:

　☞ In a litigation context, most of the lawyer's work will be backward-looking. The litigation will seek to assess legal responsibility for the client's and the opposing party's past conduct. The lawyer's work will involve the operation of the justice system on the client's behalf.

　☞ In the planning context, most of the lawyer's work will be forward-looking. The planning will seek to predict the consequences of proposed future conduct. The lawyer bears more responsibility for a client's acts in the planning context than in the litigation context. The lawyer's planning work, advice, and assistance in execution will help shape future client conduct.

　☞ A lawyer's practice setting can have significant effects on the law governing that lawyer's conduct.

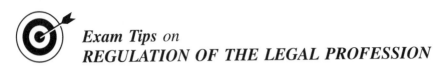

Exam Tips on
REGULATION OF THE LEGAL PROFESSION

Do not assume that every answer to an exam question will be found in the ethics codes. Some topics are simply not addressed in the ethics codes, and others require an examination of the overlap between the ethics code provisions and other law.

The institutional framework within which the law of lawyering, and lawyers, exist has a significant effect on the interpretation of the law of lawyering. Note the institutions that are involved in your exam question: Are they courts? A state bar association? The ABA?

The **American Bar Association** (ABA) is a national, **voluntary** association of lawyers that plays a critical role in the creation of the law governing lawyers. But remember, the ABA does not license lawyers to practice law, nor does it impose discipline. States, through their courts, bar associations, and sometimes legislatures, license lawyers to practice law within the relevant jurisdiction and impose discipline on lawyers who violate the adopted rules. Federal courts both admit lawyers to practice before them and impose discipline.

The law that governs lawyers comes from a variety of sources and exists in a variety of forms including state adopted ethics code, ABA model codes, case law, lawyer ethics opinions, the Restatement of the Law Governing Lawyers, constitutional provisions, and other law. Consider a range of sources of law in your essay answers, while recognizing that the Model Rules, as adopted by particular states, still dominate analysis of most topics.

Admission to Practice

A license to practice law is a prerequisite to a person's lawful engagement in the activities of lawyering. The state has a need to protect the public from those who are incompetent or who lack integrity.

☞ To become licensed, one must satisfy education, knowledge, and character requirements.

☞ An applicant to the bar may not make any material false statement and must not "fail to disclose a fact necessary to correct misapprehension known by the [applicant] to have arisen in the matter . . . ." MR 8.1(b). The number of cases of denied applications based on misrepresentation in the application process outnumbers cases of denied applications based on prior misconduct. Particularly because of its immediate relevance to law students, misconduct in the bar application process is a fruitful area for exam questions.

☞ Licensed lawyers are duty bound not to assist in the admission of an unqualified applicant. MR 8.1.

Unauthorized Practice

By the nature of the licensing requirements, lawyers licensed to practice in a given state have a monopoly on the practice of law in that state. When a person engages in the **unauthorized practice** of law, civil and sometimes criminal penalties attach. Unauthorized practice may occur when a licensed lawyer practices outside the jurisdiction in which the license was granted or when those not licensed engage in the practice of law.

☞ When a lawyer who is licensed to practice in one state has an occasional, nonrecurring need to represent a client before the courts of another state, the lawyer requests admission before that state's courts "***pro hac vice,***" "for this turn only." Don't immediately conclude that a lawyer has engaged in unauthorized practice when she appears in court in a state in which she is not licensed.

Reporting Misconduct

Among the chief features of the legal profession's claim to be ***self-governing*** is the requirement of reporting fellow lawyers' or a judge's serious misconduct to the appropriate professional authority. MR 8.3.

☞ The topic of reporting misconduct makes an ideal subject area for an exam question because of the difficult mixture of competing values that is implicated. Duties to the public and the profession compete with confidentiality duties to clients when a nonlawyer client reveals the misconduct of a former lawyer to her current lawyer.

☞ Before a duty to report misconduct can arise, the lawyer must "know that another lawyer has committed" the ***misconduct.*** MR 8.3(a).

☞ The rule requires a lawyer to report misconduct "that raises a substantial question as to that lawyer's honesty, trustworthiness or fitness as a lawyer in other respects . . . ." MR 8.3(a). "Substantial" means a "material matter of clear and weighty importance." Trivial misconduct need not be reported.

☞ The rule does not require a report of misconduct when the lawyer has learned of the misconduct through confidential communications that would be protected by the ethical duty of confidentiality under Model Rule 1.6. MR 8.3(c). But it also must be remembered that the exceptions to the duty of confidentiality (such as, e.g., the future crime exception) continue to apply with equal force in this setting as in any other.

☞ When a lawyer reports another lawyer's misconduct, the potential exists for a defamation action to be filed by the reported-on lawyer against the reporting lawyer. A privilege applies to required reporting of another lawyer's misconduct.

Exam Tips on
CONTROLS ON LAWYER CONDUCT

Most exam questions ask whether the lawyer is subject to discipline. For such a purpose, you should disregard the form of discipline that you think might be appropriate to the conduct and any mitigating circumstances that might be likely to reduce the punishment. You also should disregard the likelihood that the conduct by the lawyer would be discovered and the likelihood that the bar disciplinary authorities might choose not to pursue charges against the lawyer. Such a question simply asks whether the lawyer's conduct has violated the rules (i.e., whether the lawyer is subject to discipline).

Discipline

Many questions test the differences between discipline and malpractice. Usually, the discipline involved in such questions is for competence. *Discipline* by the bar and then the court system operate by the courts' authority over the licensing of lawyers.

- ☞ Discipline is imposed for the protection of the public generally and for the benefit of the profession, while malpractice is a tort or contract-based civil action that is meant to compensate victims of a lawyer's negligence or contract breach.

- ☞ While a single act of negligence will support a malpractice action, unless that single act is sufficiently gross to indicate a substantial likelihood that the lawyer is unfit to practice, that single act will not subject the lawyer to bar discipline. Be careful with fact patterns in which the lawyer has engaged in a careless lapse that has harmed a client. Given the same conduct by the lawyer, an isolated incident will support a malpractice claim by the client but not a disciplinary action by the bar. A repeated series of lapses will support both malpractice claims and bar discipline.

Malpractice

- ☞ Contract theory malpractice actions have the common contract elements of agreement, breach, and damage. Damage measurement under contract theories is more limited than that of tort theories.

- ☞ Under tort theories, the most used of the malpractice theories, the elements are the familiar negligence elements of duty, breach, causation, and damages. Watch for questions that say that the lawyer acted "reasonably" or "with due care." Such language means by definition that the lawyer has not breached the tort duty and is therefore not liable for malpractice.

- ☞ The lawyer's tort duty to the client is measured by the skill and knowledge of ordinary lawyers in the community, unless the lawyer is an expert in a specialized field. An expert is held to the standard of the reasonable expert in that field.

- ☞ Breach of the duty owed is a required element of a malpractice action. Lawyers are not guarantors of particular results. Often, a variety of reasonable strategies will be available from which to choose. When a lawyer chooses a reasonable course of action, and that course later produces bad results, the lawyer has not breached the duty of care owed to the client.

- ☞ For a malpractice claim to exist, the lawyer's breach of duty must cause the client's damages. Often, this means that the client will have to prove that she would have prevailed in the matter had the lawyer not breached the duty of care. This requirement is called the *"case within a case."* The malpractice plaintiff must prove the value of the underlying case in order to prevail in the malpractice case.

- ☞ As with any tort action, the wrong is insufficient to create a claim for relief in the absence of damages.

Fiduciary Duties

As a *fiduciary,* a lawyer owes duties to clients beyond the tort and contract duties. Fiduciary duties modify contract principles. These special duties can be the basis for a malpractice action that might not otherwise lie under contract or tort theories. Many test questions focus on lawyer-client contracts. Remember that the lawyer's fiduciary duties enhance the lawyer's obligations to the client beyond the terms of their contract.

Lawyers are prohibited under the Model Rules from "counselling a client to engage or assisting a client in conduct that the lawyer knows is criminal or fraudulent." MR 1.2(d). While this provision sets up the disciplinary exposure of a lawyer who violates the rule, a lawyer also may be criminally and civilly liable for the wrongs of their clients that the lawyer assists. Watch for fact patterns that ask about lawyer criminal or civil liability for actions that further the client's crimes or civil wrongs.

When the question places the lawyer in court, remember to consider the judge's *contempt* power. The contempt power is a considerable control on lawyer conduct in the litigation setting. The contempt power is meant to give judges reasonable control over the courtroom and to enforce standards of courtroom behavior among litigants.

Litigation Sanctions

Powerful constraints on lawyer conduct exist in the form of various litigation motions. These motions, when granted, have an immediate and significant impact on the lawyer against whom they were filed.

☞ When a lawyer perceives that an opposing lawyer may have a conflict of interest in litigation, the lawyer may request that the court *disqualify* opposing counsel from further participation in the case.

☞ The standards for when a disqualification motion should be granted are substantially the same as the underlying conflict of interest standards including the shield or "Chinese Wall" defense. Because litigation consequences are at stake instead of lawyer disciplinary consequences, courts take into account interests such as delay caused by granting the motion, wrongful conduct of the moving party, especially as it relates to the timing of the motion, and the nonmoving party's legitimate interest in retaining counsel of her choice, in addition to the typical conflicts of interest concerns. In the disqualification setting, be sure to discuss these other interests. It is tempting to do no more than discuss the conflicts rules and their application, but such an approach would leave out significant parts of the analysis.

☞ Money sanctions are available against an offending lawyer under various *frivolous claim* prohibition rules, especially Federal Rule of Civil Procedure 11.

Exam Tips on
FORMAL ASPECTS OF THE LAWYER-CLIENT RELATIONSHIP

Before a lawyer has formally undertaken representation, a limited set of lawyer-to-client duties exist including the confidentiality duty that is owed to prospective clients. ***Undertaking representation*** signifies the beginning of the formal lawyer-client relationship. Once a lawyer has undertaken representation, the full range of duties from lawyer to client exist.

In general, lawyers have no duty to undertake a particular representation. Lawyers have a limited duty to undertake a fair share of pro bono work and to accept court appointments unless good cause exists to decline the appointment. Two otherwise identical fact patterns, one with an appointment and one without, will be resolved as opposites.

Unlike the general rule that a lawyer has no duty to accept every client's matter, lawyers are prohibited from accepting (that is, lawyers must reject) representation when the representation will violate ethics rules or other law. MR 1.16(a).

The lawyer-client relationship is governed by the particular contract entered into by the lawyer and client and by general contract principles, modified by the various duties that lawyers owe clients. The lawyer-client relationship formally begins when a client reasonably believes that the lawyer has undertaken to provide the client with legal service. The relationship does not depend for its onset on the existence of a written contract nor a fee payment. Watch for fact patterns involving casual discussions of a prospective client's matter.

Fees

Whenever a fee is mentioned in a fact pattern, some comment is warranted. Although the regulation of lawyers' fees is relatively light and rarely enforced, it does exist. MR 1.5. Fees are regulated for their amount and their nature.

☞ A lawyer's fee must be reasonable. MR 1.5. A range of factors may be considered in setting a reasonable fee. MR 1.5(a).

☞ In general, a written contract setting the fee is preferred but not required.

☞ With a few exceptions and restrictions, a lawyer is permitted to charge a fee that is contingent on the outcome of the matter. There are two exceptions, criminal cases and certain domestic relations cases. When contingent fees are permitted, additional restrictions apply. MR 1.5(c). A contingent fee agreement must be in writing. Because these technical contingent fee restrictions stand in sharp contrast to the lack of such restrictions on fees generally, they are popular, easy-to-isolate exam question topics.

Lawyers in the same firm routinely share fees with one another. However, when lawyers who are not members of a firm share fees, or when lawyers seek to share fees with nonlawyers, special problems arise. ***Fee splitting*** by lawyers not in the same firm is permitted if the total fee is reasonable, the client agrees to the arrangement in writing, and the fee is either shared in proportion to the work done by the lawyers or the lawyers accept joint responsibility for the representation. MR 1.5.

At one time, the organized bar typically imposed ***minimum fee schedules*** on lawyers and their clients. Such schedules are unlawful and therefore no longer enforceable. Goldfarb v. Virginia State Bar, 421 U.S. 773 (1975).

Fiduciary Duties

A ***fiduciary*** is one in whom a special trust is placed. A fiduciary owes to the beneficiary scrupulous good faith, candor, and care in the management of the beneficiary's interests.

☞ Lawyer fiduciary duties, beyond the general care owed to client interests and confidences that the relationship implies, are usually thought of in terms of the lawyer's handling of the client's money and property.

☞ Violations of the lawyer's duty to properly handle client property are per se rules that require no intentional wrongdoing on the part of the lawyer. Remember that not every violation of the lawyer ethics codes is a precise match with distinctions between right and wrong. In this area, in particular, no one need be harmed by the conduct for the conduct to be subject to discipline.

☞ Lawyers must maintain ***client trust accounts*** and safety deposit boxes for the safekeeping of client property. Lawyers must maintain the account in the state in which they practice, they must maintain records of the account for later examination, and they must keep client property and funds separate from lawyer property and funds. MR 1.15(a).

☞ Only client money may be in the trust account. The lawyer must maintain a separate office operating account. When a lawyer ***commingles*** his funds with a client's, the lawyer is subject to discipline. MR 1.15(a).

Competence and Diligence

Competence and diligence are core lawyer duties. MR 1.1 and 1.3. These duties apply to all representations, and as such are appropriate for brief comment in virtually every essay exam.

☞ ***Competence*** requires that the lawyer possess and exercise on the client's behalf "the legal knowledge, skill, thoroughness, and preparation reasonably necessary for the representation." MR 1.1.

☞ Questions often ask about a lawyer undertaking representation in an area that is unfamiliar to the lawyer. A lawyer is not required to know the law that governs the client's legal claim before undertaking representation provided the lawyer will be able to acquire the necessary knowledge with reasonable diligence. But basic, cross-cutting skills such as an understanding of the use of precedent, legal research skills, ability to identify and evaluate a client's problem, and writing or drafting skill and knowledge are always required.

☞ Watch for emergency situations. In an emergency, a lawyer may provide limited assistance to a client in a matter on which the lawyer would ordinarily require further study or research before service was rendered. But the lawyer must limit this service to that which is necessary under the circumstances. MR 1.1 Comment.

☞ *Diligence* is the timeliness aspect of competence. Lawyers are obligated to be diligent in their clients' behalf. MR 1.3. Fact patterns that involve unreasonable delay by the lawyer raise diligence issues.

Decision-making

Lawyers owe clients a duty to communicate with clients and to meaningfully share decision-making responsibilities with them. MR 1.2 and 1.4. A breach of the communication duty rarely stands alone. Such a breach is almost always combined with another breach of duty, such as a failure to explain the basis of a contingent fee calculation or a failure to provide a client with the information necessary to obtain a valid client consent to waive a conflict of interest.

As a general proposition, clients set the goals or ends of the representation while lawyers generally are empowered to determine the best means to use to achieve those ends. MR 1.2(a) Comment.

Lawyers are prohibited from counseling or assisting their clients in the commission of crimes or frauds. MR 1.2(d). When a lawyer does so advise or assist, the lawyer is not only subject to discipline but is liable criminally or civilly as the case may be. This prohibition does not prevent a lawyer from either discussing proposed courses of action with a client or assisting a client in the pursuit of a test case.

☞ Timing is everything. When a lawyer knows that a client will use the lawyer's services to perpetrate a crime or fraud before representation has begun, the lawyer must reject the representation. When the lawyer learns the same during representation, the lawyer must withdraw from the representation. Watch for the timing of the lawyer's knowledge of client misconduct.

Withdrawal

The formal lawyer-client relationship ends when representation terminates. Despite termination, many lawyer duties to clients continue, such as confidentiality and a limited conflict avoidance duty. *Withdrawal* from representation is a critically important device for the lawyer who is faced with the prospect that continued representation of the client will result in a violation of the ethics code or other law.

Under some circumstances, lawyers are required to withdraw from representation, thereby terminating the lawyer-client relationship. Failure to withdraw under these circumstances subjects the lawyer to discipline. MR 1.16(a).

☞ **Continued representation will violate the ethics rules:** MR 1.16(a)(1).

☞ **Continued representation will violate other law:** MR 1.16(a)(1).

☞ **Lawyer's physical or mental health is impaired:** MR 1.16(a)(2).

☞ **Lawyer is discharged:** MR 1.16(a)(3).

In some instances lawyers are permitted but not required to withdraw. The practical effect of this rule is to allow lawyers to withdraw from representation in the enumerated circumstances without breaching a duty of continued representation to the client. MR 1.16(b).

☞ Without regard to any cause for withdrawal, a lawyer may withdraw if it can be done without material adverse effect to the client. MR 1.16(b)(1).

☞ Even if some harm may come to the client from the withdrawal, a lawyer may withdraw when any of the following causes exist.

    ☞ **Lawyer's reasonable belief that client is acting criminally or fraudulently:** MR 1.16(b)(2).

    ☞ **Past use of service for crime or fraud:** MR 1.16(b)(3).

    ☞ **Client actions that are repugnant or imprudent:** MR 1.16(b)(4).

    ☞ **Client failure to meet obligations:** MR 1.16(b)(5).

    ☞ **Unreasonable financial burden:** MR 1.16(b)(6).

    ☞ **Client unreasonably difficult to work with:** MR 1.16(b)(6).

    ☞ **Other good cause:** MR 1.16(b)(7).

Even when a lawyer has good cause to withdraw, a court may order the lawyer to continue the representation. MR 1.16(c).

When litigation is pending, a lawyer must obtain the court's permission to withdraw from representation. MR 1.16(c).

Although a client may discharge a lawyer without cause, the client will continue to have an obligation to pay fees to the lawyer that have already been earned. MR 1.16(d).

When a fee is a fixed amount for a particular service or is based on hours of service, the fee upon discharge will be calculated as the value of the services rendered. Such a recovery theory is called *quantum meruit.*

Contingent fee arrangements and lawyer discharge is an especially tricky combination. Some courts have ruled that a contingent fee lawyer who is discharged without cause is entitled to no fee. Others have ruled that a contingent fee lawyer who is discharged without cause is entitled to the full benefit of the contingency if indeed the client eventually recovers in the matter. Still others have ruled that the discharged contingent fee lawyer is entitled to the reasonable value of the services actually rendered (a quantum meruit theory) limited by the amount that the lawyer would have earned had the contingency occurred and the lawyer had recovered the agreed-upon percentage.

Exam Tips on CONFIDENTIALITY

To determine when the duty of confidentiality restricts the lawyer's revelation of information, these questions must be analyzed.

☞ Is the information of the type that is covered by the duty?

☞ Is the person or entity that communicated the information to the lawyer a client or a client's agent for the purposes of the duty?

☞ Do any of the exceptions to the duty apply?

Answers to these questions will determine the applicability of the duty of confidentiality.
   Before analyzing any exception, first make sure the information is protected by the duty of confidentiality (or the communication protected by the attorney-client privilege).

Evidentiary Privilege

☞ The Model Code duty of confidentiality provision (DR 4-101) defines the scope of the duty as the sum of the material protected by the evidentiary *attorney-client privilege* (called *"confidences"* in DR 4-101) and material that, while not included in the attorney-client evidentiary privilege would be embarrassing or detrimental to the client if revealed or that the client has expressly requested be held in confidence (called *"secrets"* in DR 4-101). The Model Rules provision abandons the "confidences" + "secrets" = duty of confidentiality formula in favor of a more general and inclusive definition, "information relating to representation of a client . . . ." MR 1.6(a).

☞ In general, the evidentiary privilege is created when a client or prospective client communicates in confidence to a lawyer or a person the client reasonably believes to be a lawyer who is being consulted as a lawyer. It is not necessary for a fee to be charged for the duty of confidentiality and the evidentiary privilege to be effective.

☞ The privilege applies to communication from a client or a prospective client and continues beyond the end of the lawyer-client relationship even beyond the client's death.

☞ The privilege is not created when the communication is made in circumstances that do not indicate a desire for confidentiality by the client.

☞ The privilege covers the client's communication, not the client's knowledge that was communicated.

☞ The privilege also may protect lawyer observations that result directly from the client's protected communications, as long as the lawyer does nothing to prevent other interested parties from making the same observation.

☞ Although the observations of a lawyer that result directly from client communication may sometimes be privileged, physical items collected by the lawyer are not privileged.

☞ Many of the exceptions to the duty of confidentiality are paralleled by exceptions to the evidentiary privilege.

   ☞ The client holds (controls the assertion of) the evidentiary privilege; informed client consent to disclosure eviscerates the privilege and waives the duty of confidentiality.

   ☞ In order to carry out the purposes of the representation, some information that would be subject to the duty of confidentiality must be disclosed.

☞ Under certain circumstances, lawyers may reveal client confidences to defend themselves or to pursue claims against former clients.

☞ The lawyer must limit disclosure to those facts necessary to self-defend. Lawyers must also limit their self-defense disclosures to those who need to know for the lawyer's self-defense or fee collection purpose.

Crime, Fraud, and Harm Exception

Communications that further future crimes or frauds are excepted from protection by the evidentiary privilege. This is called the ***crime-fraud exception.***

In certain circumstances, lawyers may reveal confidential information to prevent ***future crimes*** or harms by clients. The circumstances defined by the Model Code and Model Rules are quite different from one another. MR 1.6(b)(1) and DR 4-101(C)(3). The Model Rules' exception for future crimes retains the permissive language of the Model Code, but restricts the type of future crime that may permit revelation of confidential information. A lawyer ***may*** reveal information [relating to representation of a client] to the extent the lawyer reasonably believes necessary to prevent future harm that the lawyer believes is ***likely to result in imminent death or substantial bodily harm.*** MR 1.6(b)(1). This distinction between the Code and Rules is a significant one. If your course emphasizes distinctions between the Code and the Rules, this one is certain to be prominent.

☞ The crime-fraud exception to the attorney-client privilege is much broader than the future-crime exception to the duty of confidentiality. When a communication is within the crime-fraud exception to the attorney-client privilege but is not within the future-crime exception to the duty of confidentiality, the attorney-client privilege does not protect the communication, but the lawyer continues to have an ethical duty to maintain the confidence. If eventually a court rejects the assertion of the attorney-client privilege and orders the lawyer to testify, the "orders of court" exception to the duty of confidentiality will permit the lawyer to reveal the confidence.

☞ As long as all other requirements are satisfied, when a client reveals a ***past*** crime or fraud, that information is protected by the duty of confidentiality and the attorney-client privilege.

☞ When a client has committed a past crime or fraud, the lawyer's representation of the client is what the legal system expects the client to be afforded. When the lawyer knows the client intends to commit a future crime or fraud, and ***the lawyer's services are used to commit the crime or fraud,*** the lawyer will share both the moral and legal responsibility for the wrong.

Other Exceptions

☞ Lawyers may reveal confidences when required to do so by other law or by order of court.

☞ Even when some others in addition to the lawyer and client know the protected client information, the duty of confidentiality continues to protect the information. When the information ***is generally known,*** however, its continued protection by the lawyer will in some cases serve little purpose and most would say that the duty of confidentiality is lost as well.

☞ A wide range of lawyer duties impose requirements on lawyers only when the duty does not offend the duty of confidentiality. A number of ethics rules require or permit lawyers to disclose information that would otherwise be protected by the duty of confidentiality. Notice the frequent interconnectedness of the confidentiality duty with other rules and topics. Failure to account for the application of MR 1.6 when analyzing any of these other rules will produce errors.

Organizational Clients

Communications from agents of an ***organizational client*** are within the evidentiary privilege, and therefore within the duty of confidentiality, if two conditions are met: the information communicated is treated as confidential within the organization, and it is communicated to the lawyer so that the lawyer can give advice or counsel to the organization.

Because of the special public responsibilities of government agencies, government lawyers may strike a confidentiality balance somewhat more toward the public interest in disclosure of government wrongdoing.

Agents

Both lawyers and clients routinely use agents for communicating with each other. For purposes of the duty of confidentiality, client communication to a lawyer through a lawyer's agent is treated as if it were made directly to the lawyer. In addition, protected client information may be shared with other lawyers within the law firm or organization that represents the client. Communications from clients through agents to lawyers are treated as if they were made directly by the client to the lawyer.

Watch for the distinctions between the duty of confidentiality and the evidentiary privilege. It is critical that you watch the terminology in this area. Focus in on the distinctions between the duty of confidentiality and the evidentiary attorney-client privilege. Carelessly mixing those two in reading a question or writing an answer will produce error after error.

☛ To be protected by the evidentiary privilege, the information must come from the client or a client's agent. Information that the lawyer learns from third parties is protected by the duty of confidentiality but not the privilege. To be protected by the duty of confidentiality, the information need merely "relat[e] to representation of a client." MR 1.6(a).

☛ The duty of confidentiality applies to all information relating to the representation, not merely communications from client to lawyer.

☛ Lawyer observations are protected by the duty of confidentiality.

☛ Communications from third parties about the representation are protected by the duty of confidentiality.

☛ Lawyer thoughts and strategies about the representation are protected by the duty of confidentiality. They are also protected by the related discovery doctrine called the ***work product*** doctrine.

As a client's agent, a lawyer is generally restricted from using confidential information of the client either for the lawyer's benefit or to the client's detriment. Notice that the Model Rules' drafters placed this rule with the conflict of interests rules rather than with the confidentiality rule. Because of the overlap between these two areas, you need to discuss both when faced with a fact pattern that involves lawyer abuse of client information.

Exam Tips *on* CONFLICT OF INTERESTS

Conflict of interests is the most central, pervasive, complex, and important issue in the law governing lawyers. Consequently, it is also the most tested topic in the professional responsibility field. It is not unusual for a multiple-choice professional responsibility exam to include 30 to 50% of its questions in the form of conflicts questions of one variety or another.

The Question to Ask

When you analyze conflicts problems, ask yourself these questions:

1. What is the source of the conflict (third party interference, multiple client conflict, lawyer interests)?
2. Does the conflict meet its particular rule's threshold requirements, i.e., is there a conflict within the meaning of the appropriate rule?
3. Is the conflict one that imputes to the entire law organization?
4. If so, can the affected lawyer be effectively screened or isolated from the organization?
5. Is the conflict of a type that allows client waiver?
6. If so, what must occur for the waiver to be effective?

As you study, notice that some of the conflicts rules are like "nested dolls" that live inside one another. Take a fact pattern in which the lawyer has loaned the client money. You might first look at the financial assistance rule and conclude that it does not restrict the lawyer because there is no pending or contemplated litigation. MR 1.8(e). You might then notice that a loan of money is a business transaction and examine the business transaction rule. MR 1.8(a). If for some reason it does not restrict the lawyer either, you should then examine the general lawyer versus client interest rule (MR 1.7) and apply it. Treating each possible rule will add points to your score.

Always focus on the setting in which a question places you. The policies in the motion to disqualify setting will differ from those in the disciplinary setting, which will differ from those in the malpractice setting, and so on.

Loyalty

Basic to the lawyer-client relationship is the premise that lawyers owe clients a duty of *loyalty.* Lawyers owe clients a duty of ***independent professional judgment.*** When loyalty or independent judgment is threatened by some interest other than the client's, a conflicts question is present and requires analysis.

Many conflicts questions are primarily about breaches of confidentiality. When a question involves the potential for a confidentiality breach, you must analyze both the confidentiality issues and the conflicts issues. See Chapter 5.

Relatively easy cases of conflict of interest analysis occur when the lawyer attempts to represent directly adverse interests.

The application of many of the conflicts rules is triggered by a determination of whether there is a "significant risk" that the conflict "will materially limit[] the [lawyer's representation of the client]." See, e.g., MR 1.7(b). This standard is objective.

Waiver

Because true conflicts put client interests at risk and because client autonomy and decision-making are values worthy of some respect, clients are empowered to *waive* most but not all conflicts of interest.

☞ The general rationale of honoring client autonomy does not apply when the conflict is sufficiently gross to make any client waiver suspect.

☞ The general rationale of honoring client autonomy does not apply when the conflicts rule is less about the risk to client interests than it is about risks to justice system interests.

☞ At a minimum, conflict of interest waiver requires informed consent of the affected client. Some of the conflicts rules that allow waiver require more, such as confirmation of the waiver in writing, sometimes signed by the client.

☞ Whether a conflict is waivable is often the critical, deciding point. Be careful to distinguish between the conflicts that may be waived and those that may not. Recognize that when a conflict exists and is waivable, a lawyer will be subject to discipline if she goes forward with anything less than informed client consent. Many questions will have the lawyer giving notice to the client, or merely disclosing but not discussing the conflict with the client, neither of which satisfies the waiver requirements. Recognize that when the rule does not permit waiver, even when a question describes what would be an effective waiver, the conflict persists.

There are three primary sources of conflicts of interest: third party interference, lawyer interests, and multiple client interests. Identify the source of the conflict to locate the applicable Model Rule provision.

Third Party Conflicts

☞ *Third party interference* conflicts occur when someone who is not a party to the lawyer-client relationship seeks to affect or becomes positioned to affect the independence of the lawyer's judgment on behalf of the client. See MR 1.7(a)(2) for the general rule. Such conflicts may be waived if the client gives informed consent. A frequent third party interference fact pattern on exams involves a third party payer of a lawyer's fee. See MR 1.8(f) for the specific rule.

Lawyer versus Client

☛ The second major source of conflicts are *lawyer interests that conflict* with client interests.

　☞ Waiver of such a general conflict is possible if "the lawyer reasonably believes that the lawyer will be able to provide competent and diligent representation [despite the conflict] and the affected client gives informed consent." MR 1.7(b).

　☞ A variety of particular transactions between lawyers and clients are governed by specific conflicts rules.

　　☞ *Business transactions with clients,* Model Rule 1.8(a). This rule has enhanced waiver requirements.

　　☞ *Literary rights,* MR 1.8(d). No waiver of this conflict is permitted.

　　☞ *Drafting instruments that benefit the lawyer,* MR 1.8(c).

　　☞ *Sexual or amorous relations with clients,* MR 1.8(j).

　　☞ *Agreements limiting the lawyer's liability,* MR 1.8(h).

　　☞ *Settling claims with unrepresented clients,* MR 1.8(h).

　☞ Various restrictions on lawyer conduct, often interrelated with lawyer-client conflicts issues, are based on the doctrines of *champerty, barratry*, and *maintenance.*

　　☞ Lawyers are prohibited from advancing financial assistance to clients when there is pending or contemplated litigation, except that the lawyer may advance court costs. Client waiver of this "conflict" is not permitted. MR 1.8(e).

　　☞ A lawyer is prohibited from acquiring an interest in litigation or its subject matter, whether that interest is consistent or inconsistent with the client's interests. This prohibition is not a restriction on the lawyer's contract with a client for a reasonable contingent fee. Client waiver of a violation of this rule is not permitted. MR 1.8(i).

　　☞ A lawyer is prohibited from using information learned in the lawyer-client relationship to the detriment of the client. MR 1.8(b).

Multiple Clients

　☞ The third major source of conflicts is the interaction of *multiple clients'* interests. Multiple client conflicts can implicate not only concurrent representation of multiple clients but also conflicts between former and current clients, or prospective and current clients, or prospective and former clients.

　　☞ The easiest cases involve multiple representation of clients whose interests are in direct conflict. Such a direct conflict cannot be effectively waived by the clients on the theory that it is too gross a conflict.

　　☞ A lawyer may also find herself representing one client against a second client in a matter unrelated to the representation of the second client. In general, such a conflict may not be waived, but when the adversity is merely general, waiver has been permitted.

☞ Even multiple representation of clients who are at least initially on the same side of litigation or a transaction implicates conflicts analysis.

☞ Lawyers owe prospective clients a limited loyalty duty and the duty of confidentiality. Because confidentiality breaches are a primary consideration in multiple client conflicts analysis, conflicts analysis must be done on potential conflicts between prospective and current or former clients. Watch for fact patterns involving a prospective client who reveals information to a lawyer, but then does not retain the lawyer's services.

☞ Because lawyers owe clients a continued measure of loyalty after representation ends and because lawyers owe clients a full measure of the duty of confidentiality after representation ends, conflicts between former and current clients arise when their interests are directly adverse or when there is a *substantial relationship* between the two representations. Such a conflict may be waived by both clients by consent after consultation. MR 1.9.

☞ A lawyer who represents an organization, such as a corporation, a labor union, or a public interest organization, represents the organization, not its officers. At times, the interests of the organization and its officers may converge. Under such circumstances, a lawyer may represent both the organization and its officers, but the lawyer must withdraw if the interests of the organization and the officers diverge. MR 1.13.

Imputed Disqualification

As a general rule, when a lawyer has a conflict of interest, that conflict imputes to (transfers to, extends to) all of the lawyers in the law organization (usually a law firm) in which the lawyer works. MR 1.10. This *imputed disqualification* rule is mainly based on the notion that confidential information possessed by one lawyer is effectively possessed by all lawyers in the same firm.

☛ *Motions to disqualify* counsel, and entire law firms for which the disqualified lawyer works, have become a favored tactical device in litigation, effectively denying an opposing party her counsel of choice and preserving the integrity of the justice system from the threat of conflicts of interest. Such fact patterns allow an instructor to examine students in a way that goes beyond the Model Rules. When a court is considering a motion to disqualify, several factors may be considered in addition to the conflicts principles that are relevant in the disciplinary context. Expand your answer accordingly in a motion to disqualify situation.

☛ The increasing movement of lawyers from one practice setting to another, from one law firm to another, has dramatically increased the frequency and impact of imputed disqualification rules. Lawyers changing firms or moving from government to private practice are especially popular exam fact patterns.

Screening

☛ An increasing number of courts, supported by Model Rules 1.10, 1.11, and 1.12, have ruled that effective *screening procedures* will prevent the application of the imputed disqualification rules. Under such procedures, the conflicted lawyer is isolated from other lawyers in the organization by various devices.

☞ Special rules regarding imputed disqualification apply to former government lawyers and former judges.

Special Rules

Former judges' conflicts differ from those of lawyers who move from one practice setting to another, and they require special conflicts rules. MR 1.12. A former judge shall not engage in private representation in a matter in which the judge participated personally and substantially as a judge, unless all parties to the matter consent after consultation. MR 1.12.

☞ Judges are prohibited from negotiating for employment with lawyers who are currently representing parties before the judge's court if the judge is personally and substantially participating in the matter before the court. Similar, but waivable, restrictions apply to judicial law clerks. MR 1.12(b).

☞ Special, more relaxed imputed disqualification rules apply to the law firms for which former judges work. Effective screening procedures and notice to the judge's former court permit a former judge's law firm to continue with representation in which the former judge is disqualified from participating. MR 1.12(c).

Special conflicts rules apply to lawyers who move from government practice to private practice. MR 1.11.

☞ A former government "lawyer shall not represent a private client in connection with a matter in which the lawyer participated personally and substantially" as a government lawyer. MR 1.11. Notice that this conflict rule applies without regard to whether the lawyer has effectively changed sides in the matter.

☞ Three exceptions allow the former government lawyer to engage in the later private representation even when his participation in the government employment was personal and substantial.

  ☞ The conflicts rule excepts from its reach cases in which the law otherwise expressly permits the private representation to occur.

  ☞ The rule defines what it means by a "matter." It is only later private representation in connection with a government service "matter" that triggers a conflict of interest analysis. A matter includes a wide variety of instances and actions that engage the agency with a particular party or parties. The definition excludes rule drafting and other agency actions that have more general application.

  ☞ The agency may waive the conflict by giving its consent after consultation.

☞ Except when law otherwise expressly permits such representation, a former government lawyer is also prohibited from representing private parties who are adverse to parties about whom the lawyer has confidential information gained in the government practice that could be used against the adverse party. MR 1.11(c). The private party's interests are the ones at risk in such a case. As such, it is the private party and not the agency that must waive the conflict if the lawyer is to be permitted to proceed.

☞ Special, more relaxed, imputed disqualification rules apply when former government lawyers are the law firm lawyers who have a conflict.

Special conflict problems are associated with the occasion on which a lawyer is to be called as a witness. MR 3.7.

Exam Tips on
DUTIES TO THIRD PARTIES

☞ The duties owed to third parties operate as limits on the primary duty the lawyer owes to a client. In other words, they operate to form boundaries around acceptable, client-favoring actions by lawyers.

Truth-telling

☞ Rules governing lawyers' truth-telling duties outside the court context contrast with those that apply inside the court context. The outside-the-court truth-telling rules apply in a lawyer's dealings with opposing lawyers, opposing parties, witnesses, and anyone else with whom the lawyer communicates as a lawyer.

☞ For a statement to a third party to subject a lawyer to discipline, it must both be false and material. Lawyers are prohibited from making statements that are fraudulent or remaining silent when the statement or silence would amount to fraud under applicable tort principles.

Negotiation

☞ The negotiation setting presents a special circumstance within which the nature and effect of misleading statements must be analyzed. By its nature, an element of misleading is present in the negotiation process. The rules prohibit only certain forms of misleading.

☞ Statements made to other lawyers in negotiations (and arguably to very sophisticated non-lawyers) are regarded much differently from statements made to non-lawyers.

☞ Some statements made in the negotiation setting are not regarded as statements of fact because they are simply too nebulous to be called "statements of fact" or they are accepted parts of the negotiation game that ought to be evaluated for what they are worth by the other side.

☞ The process of reducing an oral agreement to writing poses special truthfulness problems.

Harassment

☛ Model Rule 4.4 prohibits a lawyer from using "means that have no substantial purpose other than to embarrass, delay, or burden a third person . . . ." The rule only prohibits actions that serve no substantial, legitimate purpose, but are merely done to embarrass, delay, or burden the third person.

　☞ Opposing parties are a special category of third party. Their interests are most directly contrary to those of the lawyer's client. Opposing parties are, therefore, routinely the object of a lawyer's client-favoring activities.

　☞ A great deal of lawyer conduct toward witnesses may be perceived by the witness as harassing.

　☞ Lawyers may not use unlawful means to gather evidence from witnesses. MR 4.4.

☛ Lawyers may investigate jurors' backgrounds by means of public records such as deeds, judgments, available voting records, and so on. Lawyers may not contact jurors either in person or through agents. MR 4.4.

☛ Remember that the language here is "merely to harass." Many client claims might be deemed to be harassing actions, but if the action has a substantial, legitimate purpose and both factual and legal merit, the claim will not be harassment.

☛ The Model Code includes a specific provision prohibiting threats of criminal prosecution "solely to obtain advantage in a civil matter." DR 7-105. Threatening criminal prosecution for reasons other than gaining an advantage in a civil matter is not prohibited by this rule. The Model Rule drafters did not include a specific provision on this subject in the Model Rules. Rather, they relied on the general, "Rights of Third Parties" rule to cover the use of inappropriate threats. MR 4.4. In effect, when a threat would amount to extortion, it is a prohibited threat under MR 4.4.

Represented Persons

☛ Watch for fact patterns in which lawyers contact third persons. The key distinctions will be whether the contacted person is or is not represented.

　☞ Lawyers are prohibited from communicating about the subject matter of a dispute with ***represented persons*** without first obtaining permission from the represented person's lawyer. MR 4.2. Opposing parties, however, may communicate with one another without offending MR 4.2, provided that the lawyer has not instructed the client to do so as a means of circumventing the rule.

　　☞ The rule includes represented persons, even if they are not formally parties to active litigation.

　　☞ No matter how much a particular witness's testimony is expected to favor one side in a dispute, a mere witness is not a represented party. Model Rule 4.2 does not apply to communication with mere witnesses.

　　☞ Organizations speak and function through individuals who are not in and of themselves the organization. When dealing with a represented organization, Model Rule 4.2 prohibits unauthorized communication between an opposing lawyer and employees with managerial responsibilities for the subject of the matter, employees whose acts or omissions may be imputed to the organization with respect to the matter, and employees whose statements may constitute an admission attributable to the organization. MR 4.2 Comment.

☞ Whether former employees may be considered as parties for purposes of MR 4.2 has been a controversial question. Both the ABA and the majority of decisions say that former employees are not parties under MR 4.2. Other courts have ruled to the contrary. The better approach is probably to distinguish cases based on the category of employee at issue and that employee's relationship to the matter.

☞ Members of a class, once certified, are treated as parties for purposes of MR 4.2.

☞ A lawyer may communicate with an opposing party about the subject matter of the representation if the lawyer is "authorized by law or by court order" to so communicate.

☞ In criminal practice, of course, the opposing party of the prosecutor is a criminal defendant. Two different aspects of this special configuration are worthy of note.

　☞ Fifth and Fourteenth Amendment due process rights and Sixth Amendment right to counsel protection restrain prosecutors' contact with criminal defendants in ways that go beyond the professional responsibility law constraints of Model Rule 4.2.

　☞ Prosecutors, especially federal prosecutors invoking not only Model Rule 4.2's "authorized by law" language but also the Supremacy Clause of the United States Constitution, have argued that their crime investigation activities are not restricted by Model Rule 4.2's requirements of consent by an opposing party's lawyer prior to communication.

Unrepresented Persons

☞ While not prohibited from communicating with **_unrepresented persons_** who are involved in a client's matter, lawyers are restricted in what they may say to such a person. MR 4.3.

　☞ A lawyer is under an affirmative obligation to refrain from stating or implying that the lawyer is disinterested in the matter about which the lawyer is communicating. Any effort to mislead an unrepresented person about the lawyer's interest subjects the lawyer to discipline.

　☞ When a lawyer "reasonably should know" that an unrepresented person misunderstands the lawyer's interest in the matter, the lawyer is obliged to make reasonable efforts to clarify his role.

　☞ Lawyers are prohibited from giving legal advice to the unrepresented persons with whom they inevitably come into contact, except to advise unrepresented persons to obtain counsel.

☞ Model Rule 4.3 does not prohibit fact gathering provided the lawyer does so without giving advice (other than advice to obtain counsel) to the unrepresented person.

Civil Liability

☛ In limited circumstances, a lawyer may have civil liability for wrongful or negligent lawyering activity to those outside the lawyer-client relationship.

☞ As a general rule, lawyers do not owe a duty to third persons that supports a negligence action.

☞ When a lawyer's work for a client is intended to benefit a third person, the lawyer owes a duty of care to that third person.

☞ When a lawyer's work for a client specifically invites the reliance of a third person, the lawyer owes a duty of care to that third person.

☞ When a lawyer does work for a client who is a fiduciary (such as a trustee of a trust for the benefit of a beneficiary), the lawyer owes a duty to the beneficiary requiring the lawyer to refrain from engaging in acts that assist the client in breaching the client's fiduciary duties.

☞ Lawyers who know that a client will harm a third person and fail to engage in reasonable steps to prevent the harm may have liability to the third person who is harmed by the client. This duty is highly controversial and not widely accepted.

Exam Tips *on*
DUTIES TO THE LEGAL SYSTEM AND SOCIETY

☛ The courtroom presents a dynamic, exciting setting for exam questions. If your course has emphasized courtroom and advocacy situations, you will have a significant percentage of questions from this chapter.

☛ Many of the lawyer's duties to the legal system or the public generally conflict with duties to client, and the discussion in this chapter is about rules that set the lines across which client favoring actions become unacceptably harmful to the legal system or the public.

Truth-telling

☛ Truth-telling inside the court context carries implications not present in out-of-court contexts, such as negotiation. When a lawyer misleads in court, the court itself is misled in addition to the opposing party.

☞ A lawyer is prohibited from knowingly making false statements of material fact to the court and from otherwise engaging in acts or omissions that amount to fraud. MR 3.3(a).

☞ Despite the duty of candor to the court, a lawyer is under no general obligation to reveal unfavorable facts to the court. Although a lawyer is under no general obligation to reveal unfavorable facts to the court, a lawyer must disclose material facts when disclosure is necessary to avoid assisting a criminal or fraudulent act by the client. MR 3.3; MR 1.2(d). The distinction between volunteering adverse facts and making affirmative, false statements is often tested. Notice that a lawyer who *does* volunteer adverse facts when not required to do so will be subject to discipline for breaching the duty of loyalty to the lawyer's client.

☞ On those occasions when a lawyer is permitted by law to engage in ex parte communications with the court, the lawyer must disclose to the court both favorable and unfavorable material facts. MR 3.3(d).

Perjury

☞ The perjury problem presents extraordinary difficulties for the lawyer, especially when the person committing the perjury is the lawyer's client. Perjury presents a common essay question topic, but is more difficult to frame as a multiple-choice question.

☞ A lawyer is prohibited from offering evidence the lawyer knows to be false. MR 3.3(a)(3). A lawyer "may refuse to offer evidence, except the testimony of a criminal defendant, that the lawyer reasonably believes is false." MR 3.3(a)(3). The distinction between evidence the lawyer knows is false from evidence the lawyer reasonably believes is false is subtle and much tested.

☞ When a lawyer knows that a witness other than the client has offered perjured testimony, the lawyer must promptly reveal the perjury to the court. MR 3.3(a)(3).

☞ Watch for the timing of the lawyer's knowledge of perjury.

  ☞ When the lawyer knows of the client's intention to commit perjury the lawyer must attempt to dissuade, attempt to withdraw, and finally, if the perjury occurs, take reasonable remedial measures. Reasonable remedial measures include disclosure of the perjury to the court.

  ☞ When the lawyer learns that the client's testimony was perjurious after the perjury occurs but before proceedings end, the lawyer must first attempt to persuade the client to rectify the matter by revealing the fraud and then testifying truthfully. If that effort fails, the lawyer has only the reasonable remedial measures option and according to the Model Rules Comment, must reveal the perjury if the lawyer learns of the perjury before the proceedings conclude.

  ☞ If the lawyer does not learn of the perjury until after the conclusion of the proceedings, then the lawyer has no obligation to reveal it.

☞ The Model Rule duty to rectify the perjury applies even if doing so would otherwise violate the duty of confidentiality under Model Rule 1.6. MR 3.3(c).

☞ Perjury issues in criminal representation present special problems because of the criminal defendant's right to testify in his own behalf, the obligation on the state to prove the defendant guilty beyond a reasonable doubt, the privilege against self-incrimination, and the right to counsel. A perfect mixture for an essay question.

☞ A lawyer is prohibited from making false statements of law to the court. MR 3.3(a). As an advocate, the lawyer need not reveal his objective analysis of the law to the court, but rather may make any nonfrivolous, client-favoring arguments regarding the law to the court.

Adverse Legal Authority

Lawyers are obligated to disclose to the court controlling, directly *adverse legal authority.* MR 3.3(a)(2).

☞ Only controlling authority, that is, mandatory authority that is controlling on the court currently making the decision, must be disclosed.

☞ Only directly adverse authority must be disclosed under this rule. Authority is directly adverse when it is applicable to the present case without extended analogy.

☞ Lawyers have no obligation to disclose adverse authority to opposing parties. Such disclosure occurs incidentally when it is made to the court.

Witness Compensation

☞ A lawyer is limited in the ways in which witnesses may be compensated and in instructing witnesses about whether to make themselves available for testimony or interview by the opposing side.

☞ Lawyers are prohibited generally from requesting or advising a witness to refrain from voluntarily cooperating with another litigant. MR 3.4(f). Under no circumstances may a lawyer dissuade a witness from appearing at a hearing or persuade a witness to secrete himself so that the witness will be unavailable. MR 3.4(a).

☞ A lawyer is permitted to request that a witness not cooperate voluntarily only if the witness is a relative, employee, or agent of the client and the lawyer reasonably believes that the request will not harm the witness. MR 3.4(f)(2).

☞ Lawyers may only pay nonexpert witnesses a statutory fee and reasonable expenses incurred by the witness in attending the trial or hearing.

☞ Expert witnesses may be paid the professional fee that someone in the expert's field charges for his or her time and reasonable expenses incurred by the witness in attending the trial or hearing. However, an expert may not be paid a fee that is contingent on the outcome of the matter.

Frivolous Claim

☞ Lawyers are prohibited from bringing actions or taking positions in litigation that are frivolous.

☞ Model Rule 3.1, in most respects tracking Federal Rule of Civil Procedure 11, prohibits lawyers from bringing or defending claims on a frivolous basis. In a frivolous claim situation, always discuss both Rule 11 and MR 3.1.

☞ In a criminal case, unlike a civil case, a defendant has a Due Process right to plead "not guilty" and require the government to be put to its proof. Model Rule 3.1 is not intended to prevent a lawyer from assisting a criminal defendant in the process of putting the government to its proof. Prosecuting lawyers have special obligations regarding the prosecution of charges that lack merit. (See Chapter 9 for this connection.)

☞ Frivolous discovery requests and those intended merely to delay are prohibited. MR 3.4(d).

☞ In general, lawyers are obliged to expedite litigation to the extent that such activity is consistent with the client's interests. MR 3.2. A violation of MR 3.2 rarely stands alone as the grounds for discipline.

Miscellaneous In-Court Restrictions

☞ Lawyers are prohibited from expressing their personal opinion to jurors about the justness of the client's cause, the credibility of a witness, or the culpability, guilt, or innocence of a party. MR 3.4(e).

☞ Lawyers are prohibited from undermining the evidence law policies by alluding to matters that are either irrelevant or will not be supported by admissible evidence. MR 3.4(e).

☞ The lawyer need not be certain that the evidence will be admitted. If the lawyer reasonably believes that the evidence will be admitted, then the lawyer may freely allude to the evidence.

☞ If evidence will only be admissible on a condition over which the lawyer in question has no control, the lawyer must not allude to that matter until the evidence is admitted.

☞ Once the court has ruled a piece of evidence inadmissible, a lawyer is prohibited from referring to it to the jury.

☞ Lawyers must obey court orders. Even when a lawyer knows that a judge is mistaken in making an order or ruling, the lawyer must obey the order, but may make reasonable efforts to preserve the record for later challenge on appeal.

☞ Although the First Amendment protects most lawyer expression, lawyers are subject to discipline for intemperate remarks that serve no useful purpose. Consider the court's contempt power in these situations.

☞ Lawyers generally and especially prosecutors are limited in what they may say to the media regarding pending litigation and criminal investigations. MR 3.6, 3.8(e) and (g).

☞ Because of such statements' possible effects on the judicial process, lawyers are prohibited from making out-of-court statements that a reasonable lawyer would expect to be disseminated by public communication and that the lawyer knows or should know will have a substantial likelihood of materially prejudicing the matter. MR 3.6(a).

☞ Only statements made out of court are restricted by this rule.

☞ Notwithstanding the general prohibition, statements in several distinct categories may safely be made without the risk of discipline. MR 3.6(b).

☞ When a lawyer reasonably believes that making a statement is necessary to counter the effects of a public statement made by the other side in the matter, the lawyer may make such a statement without being subject to discipline. MR 3.6(c).

Ex Parte Communications

☛ *Ex parte* (without the other party) *communications* seriously undermine the prospect of fair process in the justice system. As such, ex parte communication with decision-makers, both judges and jurors, is strictly regulated. Questions often place a lawyer in an innocently intended ex parte communication position. Such an ex parte communication is subject to discipline even though no harm is intended and none results.

☞ Except in very limited circumstances lawyers are prohibited from communicating ex parte with a judge. MR 3.5(b). Some ex parte communications are permitted because of their subject matter. Communications between lawyers and judges about matters unrelated to pending or impending litigation are not restricted by the rule. Such communications are not truly "ex parte" since they do not involve other parties at all. Ex parte communications regarding so-called housekeeping matters that relate to a pending case are permitted.

☞ Even innocently intended ex parte communications are prohibited.

☞ When authorized by law, lawyers are permitted to engage in ex parte communications. Such authorizations are typically found in rules governing requests for emergency restraining orders, for example. When such communication is authorized, a lawyer is under heightened candor-to-the-court requirements.

☞ All forms of communication are covered by this rule. A lawyer who sends a letter to the judge or files a paper with the court without serving a copy on opposing counsel is engaging in prohibited ex parte communications with the judge.

☛ Lawyers are strictly prohibited from communicating with jurors outside the courtroom before and during jurors' duties. Even communication about matters other than the current proceedings is prohibited. Lawyers must refrain from even innocent communication with sitting jurors.

☛ Lawyers are prohibited from communicating with jurors after the jurors' duty ends, with some exceptions. Lawyers are prohibited from harassing jurors at any time. MR 3.5. Once proceedings have ended, lawyers may have very limited contact with jurors for benign purposes such as to determine whether the lawyer's presentation manner is effective.

☛ A lawyer is under an affirmative obligation to report to the court in which the proceedings are being had juror misconduct or others' misconduct with respect to jurors. Failure to do so subjects the lawyer to discipline.

Pro Bono

☞ Amendments in 1993 and 2002 to Model Rule 6.1 have come as close as the organized bar has to imposing a requirement on individual lawyers to render pro bono service. Nonetheless, even the 2002 version of MR 6.1 remains aspirational and not mandatory. A lawyer is not subject to discipline for failing to render pro bono service.

Exam Tips on
SPECIAL ROLE-RELATED DUTIES

☞ When a lawyer in a fact pattern is filling a particular role, *special duties and rules will apply.*

Prosecutors

☞ Criminal prosecutors have ethical responsibilities in addition to those of other lawyers. Prosecutors do not represent the crime victim or a complaining witness. Charged with representing the public's interests rather than those of an individual litigant, prosecutors are required to seek justice rather than mere victory in their work.

☞ Prosecutors are prohibited from prosecuting charges that the prosecutor knows are not supported by probable cause, the usual standard below which judges will not issue warrants and will dismiss charges at preliminary hearings. MR 3.8(a).

☞ Prosecutors are charged with the responsibility to make reasonable efforts to assure that defendants are advised of their right to counsel. MR 3.8(b).

☞ Prosecutors must not unfairly extract waivers of important pretrial rights, such as jury trial, right to counsel, and self-incrimination, from the unrepresented accused. MR 3.8(c).

☞ Prosecutors must timely disclose ***exculpatory evidence*** and mitigating circumstances regarding sentencing. MR 3.8(d).

☞ Prosecutors are required to respect the lawyer-client relationship by refraining from unnecessarily issuing subpoenas that call on lawyers to give evidence about past or present clients. MR 3.8(f).

☞ A prosecutor is obliged to pursue investigative leads even-handedly, without regard to whether they might favor or damage her case.

Supervisors and Subordinates

☞ Under certain circumstances, ***supervising lawyers*** will be ethically responsible for the acts of their ***subordinates,*** both lawyer and non-lawyer. Under certain circumstances, subordinate lawyers will be relieved of ethical responsibility for their actions.

☞ Subordinate lawyers are not relieved of the duty to follow the rules of professional conduct merely because they are supervised, nor for that matter merely because the misconduct in which they might engage is ordered by the supervising lawyer. MR 5.2.

☞ A subordinate lawyer is not subject to discipline when she "acts in accordance with a supervisory lawyer's reasonable resolution of an arguable question of professional duty." MR 5.2(b).

☞ The distinction between supervisory lawyers (who may or may not be partners) and law firm partners (who may or may not be supervising the specific subordinate involved) triggers different levels of duty. Watch for this subtle distinction.

☞ Separate from the acts of lawyer subordinates, supervising lawyers are subject to discipline if they fail to provide adequate supervision.

☞ Supervisory lawyers are subject to discipline for the conduct of lawyer subordinates that violates the rules of lawyer conduct when the supervisory lawyer orders the subordinate lawyer to engage in the misconduct, when the supervisory lawyer ratifies the subordinate lawyer's misconduct, or when a lawyer who is either a partner or the subordinate's direct supervisor learns of the misconduct at a time when its effect could be avoided or mitigated and yet fails to take reasonable remedial action.

☞ Lawyers are responsible for providing reasonable supervision of nonlawyer subordinates on the same terms as they are responsible for supervising lawyer subordinates.

Ancillary Business

☛ Lawyers are subject to the rules of professional conduct for lawyers while providing ancillary services when either of the following two conditions is present: When the services provided are not distinct from the lawyer's legal services, MR 5.7(a)(1), or when the services are provided by a separate entity either controlled by the lawyer or by the lawyer with others, and the lawyer fails to communicate clearly to the client that the services are not legal services and are not subject to the normal protections of the lawyer-client relationship. MR 5.7(a)(2).

Exam Tips on ADVERTISING AND SOLICITATION

☛ More than in any other area of Professional Responsibility law, case law is at the center of advertising and solicitation law. Change your exam strategy to take this into account without completely disregarding the Model Rules provisions, which have been fairly effectively amended to keep pace with successful court challenges.

☞ **Warning:** The Model Code advertising and solicitation provisions are misleading. DR 2-101, 2-102, 2-103, 2-104, 2-105. The Code was amended during the 1970s to reflect some of the earliest constitutional limitations on the regulation of client-getting. But because the Model Code has not been updated and amended by the ABA since the Model Rules' adoption in 1983, many of its provisions do not reflect recent court decisions that render enforcement of some of its provisions unconstitutional.

☞ The ethics rules distinguish between *advertising* and *solicitation.* Categorizing a particular client-getting activity as one or the other is the first step to analyzing whether or not the activity is permitted.

☞ The term *advertising* has traditionally referred to widely distributed, public statements about the services available from a particular lawyer or law organization.

Solicitation

☞ The term *solicitation* has traditionally referred to narrower communications directed at one or a small group of identified recipients who are known to need a particular service.

☞ Direct, personal, but form, mail to people known to have particular legal needs partakes of some of the attributes of both advertising and solicitation. Since the *Shapero* case, such communications are treated as advertising by the Model Rules. Written or recorded communications to those known to be in need of specific services must include the words "Advertising Material" on the outside of any envelope used and at the beginning and end of any recorded communication. MR 7.3(c).

☞ The Model Rules treat advertising and solicitation in separate rules (MR 7.2 for advertising and MR 7.3 for solicitation). They also create general restrictions that apply to both advertising and solicitation in MR 7.1, 7.4, and 7.5.

Commercial Speech

☞ Advertising and solicitation are speech. As such, some First Amendment protection is provided to these activities, effectively limiting the states' authority to prohibit and regulate them. Commercial speech, such as advertising, is given some protection under the First Amendment.

☞ Restrictions on commercial speech must further a substantial government interest and must be no broader than necessary.

☞ The government has a substantial interest in protecting the public from being misled or coerced by lawyer communications.

☞ Regulating commercial speech based on its "dignity" or "taste" is constitutionally *impermissible.*

☞ Despite the constitutional limitations on its power to restrict lawyer commercial speech, a state may prohibit lawyer client-getting that is false or misleading, that is coercive, or that promotes transactions that are themselves illegal.

☞ Some restrictions apply equally to all forms of client-getting, whether denominated as advertising or solicitation.

False or Misleading Statements

☞ False or misleading statements in lawyer client-getting communication are subject to discipline. MR 7.1.

☞ *Self-laudation* that is either unverifiable or misleading-but-true is subject to discipline as false or misleading. Statements that are unverifiable are deemed misleading. Self-laudation is subject to discipline as being misleading-but-true when, although verifiable and true, the statement misleads the reader or viewer, usually because it appears to be more important than it would be if it could be put into a full context.

☞ Firm names may be misleading when they untruthfully imply a relationship to a government or other institution. MR 7.5.

☞ Since *Bates,* lawyers' statements about fees have been constitutionally protected. Like other advertising statements, they may be restricted only when they are false or misleading.

Specialization

☛ Until the 1970s, state bars were quite restrictive in their regulation of lawyers' indications of practice concentration, *specialization*, or certification in areas of practice. As long as the words used by the lawyer to designate areas in which the lawyer practices fairly communicate those areas, they will be protected commercial speech and will not subject the lawyer to discipline. An unqualified statement of certification may mislead the reader into thinking that the state has certified the lawyer in a particular area. However, a state may not impose a blanket prohibition on statements of certification.

☛ In an effort to guard against the potential for lawyer overreaching of accident victims and their families, some states have imposed waiting periods before any otherwise protected targeted communications may be made. Narrowly drawn waiting-period restrictions are constitutional.

Some restrictions have particular applicability to advertising.

☞ Lawyers, of course, may pay reasonable costs associated with advertising. MR 7.2(b). This rule states what may seem to be the obvious because outside of the advertising context, lawyers may not pay others for recommending the lawyer.

☞ All advertisements must include the name and address of at least one lawyer or law firm responsible for the advertisement's content. MR 7.2(c).

More on Solicitation

☛ In-person and live telephone solicitation are subject to prophylactic rules that are much more restrictive than the advertising rules.

☞ Although all client-getting communication is subject to discipline if it involves duress or coercion, restrictions on in-person and live telephone client solicitation are meant to protect prospective clients from special dangers of lawyer coercion and duress that attend such communications.

☞ Computer, auto dial, and recorded telephone solicitations are restricted only by the advertising rules and by the general, false, and misleading and actual duress or coercion limitations.

☞ Subject only to the general limitations on client-getting speech, lawyers may solicit people with whom the lawyer has a family or prior professional or close personal relationship. MR 7.3(a).

☞ The specific restrictions on in-person and live telephone solicitation apply only when a significant motive for the solicitation is pecuniary gain for the lawyer. MR 7.3(a).

☞ Once a prospective client makes known her desire not to be contacted by the lawyer, the lawyer may not contact that prospective client. MR 7.3(b)(1).

Barratry and Champerty

☛ Lawyers have long been restrained by both ethics rules and criminal statutes from engaging in barratry, maintenance, and champerty.

☞ **Barratry** is a term that refers to stirring up controversy and thereby litigation. Its relationship to client-getting activities is the connection between soliciting clients and generating the prospective clients' interest in pursuing litigation.

☞ Lawyers are limited in the ways in which they may maintain, that is, support financially, their clients. In terms of client-getting, a lawyer is prohibited from using offers of financial support of a client to induce the client to retain the lawyer.

☞ **Champerty** law restricts lawyers from acquiring an interest in the subject matter of litigation. In terms of client-getting, champerty law restricts lawyers from buying into client claims for the purpose of attracting the client to retain the lawyer.

Runners and cappers monitor accidents and other events likely to produce legal work, and then direct potential clients to the lawyer for whom the runner or capper works. Lawyers who employ runners or cappers are subject to discipline. MR 5.3(c). In many states, employment of runners or cappers is also a criminal violation.

Exam Tips *on*
JUDICIAL CONDUCT

☛ The Multistate Professional Responsibility Exam typically devotes 10 to 15% of its questions to judicial conduct. Some Professional Responsibility teachers attempt to mirror this ratio.

☛ Disqualification and waiver are the prime topics for judicial conduct questions.

Different Focus

☞ Judicial conduct law is fundamentally different from lawyer conduct law because the judge and lawyer roles are fundamentally different. For example, judges are neutrals not partisans, so the lawyer's duty of loyalty to a client is simply not a part of a judicial conduct discussion. Likewise, judges are not confided in by either of the parties, so the lawyer confidentiality discussion drops out of judicial conduct discussions.

☞ The law governing judges comes from a wide range of sources.

☞ The American Bar Association has adopted a ***Model Code of Judicial Conduct*** (CJC). Like its lawyer conduct models, the CJC is not directly applicable to anyone. Rather, it becomes so when adopted by a state's legislature or court system as the applicable rules of judicial conduct for the particular jurisdiction.

☞ Most judges are also lawyers and to the extent they remain relevant to the judge's role, the professional ethics rules governing lawyers apply to judges as well.

☞ Although a lack of integrity is rarely the sole ground for imposing judicial discipline, a fundamental expectation of judges is that they have integrity. CJC Canon 1.

☞ Most of the assumptions underlying our judicial system hinge on the impartiality of judges.

Appearance of Impropriety

☞ Public perception of judges has a significant effect on the public confidence in the justice system. As such, the notion of avoiding even the ***appearance of impropriety*** has greater force in judicial conduct law than it does in lawyer conduct law. CJC §2A Comment.

☞ Judges' misconduct that violates law violates the "comply with law" standard of the CJC. CJC §2A.

☞ A judge's contrary to law conduct need not result in a conviction before judicial discipline is imposed.

☞ A judge can be subject to discipline for repeatedly failing to follow the law in his own decisions.

☞ Judges are prohibited from lending the prestige of their offices to private interests.

☞ Because of the judge's potentially excessive influence on a fact finder, there are some limitations on the use of judges as witnesses. The limitations, in fact, however, are minimal. As long as the judge is not presiding over the proceeding, a judge may be called as a fact witness. A judge is prohibited from voluntarily testifying as a character witness. CJC §2. A judge must be subpoenaed in order to obtain her presence and testimony as a character witness.

☞ A judge is not permitted to be a member of an organization that "practices invidious discrimination on the basis of race, sex, religion or national origin." CJC §2C.

☞ Within certain constraints, judges are permitted to teach, speak, and write about the law, the legal profession, and the justice system. CJC §3B.

☞ Judges are required to be cautious in their discussion of pending cases. They must refrain from making either public or nonpublic comments that risk the fairness of the proceedings.

☞ Judges may serve as directors, board members, or trustees of not-for-profit organizations unless the organization would be likely to come before the judge's court or will regularly be involved in litigation in any court. CJC §4C. Judges may not engage in direct fundraising for such organizations. CJC §4C(3)(b).

☞ Except for such services performed for family members, a judge is prohibited from serving as executor, administrator, trustee, guardian, or other fiduciary. CJC §4E.

☞ Except for serving interests of herself or her family members, full-time judges are not permitted to practice law. CJC §4G.

☞ When judges are permitted to earn outside income (teaching, writing, speaking, etc.), such income must be limited to reasonable amounts for the services rendered and must not appear to compromise the judge's integrity and impartiality.

☞ Judges may not accept gifts or favors from a person whose interests are or are likely to be before the judge. Gifts that are appropriate to special occasions (wedding or anniversary, for example) are permitted.

☞ Perhaps the most central attribute of the judge's role in our justice system is impartiality. All of the other rules and assumptions flow from this central notion.

☞ Judges are required to be diligent in the discharge of their duties. CJC §3A(5).

☞ Judges must also have and maintain competence in the law and decision-making. CJC §3B(2).

☞ Judges are authorized and required to maintain courtroom decorum. CJC §3B(3). Watch for fact patterns with out-of-control lawyers. In maintaining courtroom decorum and conduct, judges are required to restrain lawyer bias, though not to the extent of prohibiting legitimate argument. CJC §3B(6).

Bias and Prejudice

☞ In order to remain impartial, a judge must avoid bias and prejudice. CJC §3B(5).

☞ Except in limited circumstances, judges may not engage in ex parte communications. When ex parte communications occur, discuss both the lawyer's and judge's misconduct.

☞ In the absence of evidence to the contrary, a private communication between a judge and a lawyer with a matter pending before the judge will be presumed to have been about the pending matter.

☞ A case continues to be a pending matter until its final disposition. As such, even after a trial judge has ruled, the judge is not permitted to have ex parte communications with counsel while appeals are pending.

Ex Parte Communications

☞ The CJC permits ex parte communications in a few distinct situations.

☞ Communications for scheduling or administrative purposes do not violate the ex parte communication rules provided the judge "reasonably believes that no party will gain [an] advantage [from the communication] and the judge promptly notifies all parties and affords them an opportunity to respond." CJC §3B(7)(a).

☞ Judges may consult with other judges and with disinterested experts on the law if the judge identifies the person consulted to the parties and affords the parties an opportunity to respond. CJC §3B(7)(b).

☞ Judges may consult with clerks about the law in the absence of the parties without restriction. Even judicial clerks, however, may not do independent fact investigation and then communicate the results to the judge. CJC §3B(7)(c).

☞ Other law authorizes ex parte communications in various, limited circumstances, such as requests for emergency temporary restraining orders.

☛ Judges are prohibited from making public or private comments regarding pending matters that risk the fair outcome of the matter. CJC §3B(9).

☛ Aside from expressing appreciation of jurors' service, judges may neither compliment nor criticize jurors' decisions. CJC §3B(10).

Reporting Misconduct

☛ Judges have an obligation to report other judges' misconduct under certain circumstances. CJC §3D(1).

☞ Judges "should take appropriate action" (which may in the judge's discretion mean reporting misconduct) when a judge receives information that raises a "substantial likelihood that another judge" has violated the CJC. CJC §3D(1).

☞ A judge "shall inform the appropriate authority" when the judge "has knowledge" that another judge has committed misconduct "that raises a substantial question" about that judge's fitness for office. CJC §3D(1).

☛ Judges are required to report certain lawyer misconduct as well. CJC §3D(2).

☞ Judges "should take appropriate action" (which may in the judge's discretion mean reporting misconduct) when a judge receives information that raises a "substantial likelihood that a lawyer" has violated her state's professional ethics rules.

☞ A judge "shall inform the appropriate authority" when the judge "has knowledge" that a lawyer has committed misconduct "that raises a substantial question" about the lawyer's honesty, trustworthiness, or fitness as a lawyer in other respects.

☞ A judge's report of misconduct is absolutely privileged from civil actions for damages.

Disqualification

☛ Disqualification is among the most important and most litigated areas of judicial conduct. Both CJC Canon 3E and federal statutes govern this topic. A judge who voluntarily removes herself from hearing a matter is said to have ***recused*** herself. 28 U.S.C. §§47, 144, 455.

☞ The basic standard for judicial disqualification is an objective one. "A judge shall disqualify himself or herself [when] the judge's impartiality might reasonably be questioned . . . ." CJC §3E(1). The central federal statute is similar. 28 U.S.C. §455. However, a judge also must be subjectively free from bias.

☞ Occasionally, an issue arises that would disqualify every judge that is sitting on a court with jurisdiction to resolve the issue. When this phenomenon occurs, the "***rule of necessity***" says that judges are not disqualified.

☞ Naturally, a judge's bias may be reason to question her impartiality. Bias, however, only will be grounds for disqualification when the bias is against a party as opposed to the legal rules governing the case and when the bias against a party arises from a source outside the present litigation.

☞ A wide variety of personal and professional relationships may cause a question to be raised regarding the judge's impartiality.

  ☞ When the judge was formerly a lawyer on the same or a substantially related matter, the judge is disqualified.

  ☞ When the judge was associated with one of the lawyers while the lawyer was representing the party in the same or a substantially related matter, the judge is disqualified. CJC §3E(1)(b).

  ☞ When a judge has been a material witness in a matter, the judge is disqualified. CJC §3E(1)(b).

  ☞ When a judge has prior personal knowledge of disputed evidentiary facts regarding the matter, the judge is disqualified. CJC §3E(1)(a).

  ☞ A judge is disqualified from hearing the matter when she has more than a de minimis (very small) economic interest in the outcome of the matter.

  ☞ The disqualifying interest under this rule must be economic; it may be in either the subject matter of the controversy or in a party to the proceeding. CJC §3E(1)(c).

  ☞ The disqualifying interest may be held by the judge personally or as a fiduciary or by a member of the judge's family residing in the judge's household or by the judge's spouse or a person within the third degree of relationship to the judge.

  ☞ The interest must be one that "could be substantially affected by the proceeding." However large the interest might be, minor or highly speculative effects on it are not disqualifying. CJC §§3E(1)(c), 3E(1)(d).

  ☞ A de minimis (very small) interest in the subject matter or a party to the proceeding is not disqualifying. CJC §§3E(1)(c), 3E(1)(d).

  ☞ Only those interests that are known to the judge are disqualifying, but a judge has a duty to keep informed about the judge's and the judge's spouse and minor children's economic interests. CJC §§3E(1)(c), 3E(1)(d), 3E(2). The judge also has a duty to make reasonable efforts to be informed of the economic interests of family members.

Waiver

☞ Most sources of disqualification can be waived by the parties and the judge permitted to continue in the matter, provided the appropriate procedures are followed. CJC §3F; 28 U.S.C. §455.

☞ Under the CJC, parties may not waive the judge's personal bias regarding a party. They may waive any other form of disqualification.

☞ Under 28 U.S.C. §455, the parties may waive disqualification when it follows only from the general standard, that is, when the judge's "impartiality might reasonably be questioned." They may not waive any of the more specific reasons for disqualification. For the waiver to be effective, the judge must disclose the nature of the disqualifying interest on the record, and the parties must all agree on the record, without the participation of the judge, that the judge should continue in the matter. CJC §3F.

Judicial Immunity

☛ When judges engage in the core judicial function of deciding cases, they are absolutely immune from civil damage suits. Even when a judge errs in judicial decision-making, the judge is immune from damage actions. The immunity does not extend beyond the judicial function. Administrative actions by judges also fall outside the protection of absolute judicial immunity.

SHORT-ANSWER QUESTIONS
AND ANSWERS

SHORT-ANSWER QUESTIONS

CHAPTER 1

INTRODUCTION AND THE ROLE OF LAWYER

1. Lawyer knows that his client, Sally, has committed the crime with which she is charged. He advises her of all her options, but because the evidence against her is weak, he tells her that he thinks she should plead not guilty. Has Lawyer acted immorally? _____

2. Lawyer's client, Dr. Bob, admits to Lawyer that he made a mistake during surgery on one of his patients. His patient is unaware of the mistake and has not yet suffered any harmful side effects from the mistake. In fact, the odds are good that whatever problems the patient does develop will not be traceable to Dr. Bob's mistake. Dr. Bob wants Lawyer's advice on how to handle this situation. If Lawyer is a morally activist lawyer, what would she counsel Dr. Bob to do? _____

3. Assume that the same facts apply as in the previous question. If Lawyer were a businessperson lawyer, how would she respond? _____

CHAPTER 2

REGULATION OF THE LEGAL PROFESSION

4. John is applying for admission to the bar in the state of Wythe. As part of the application, he is required to complete a questionnaire designed to determine whether the applicant has the good character necessary for the practice of law. The questionnaire asks the applicant to list and explain any arrests or convictions. While a 19-year-old college student, John was arrested and convicted for trespassing and theft as a result of his participation in a fraternity prank. Three years after his arrest, the incident was expunged from his record. Must John list this incident on his bar application? _____

5. Jim has come to Sally, an attorney, asking for her help in resolving his dispute with a car dealership. Sally has determined that the best course of action would be to file suit in the state of Orange. Unfortunately, Sally is licensed to practice law only in the state of Blue. Must Jim find a new lawyer in the state of Orange or can Sally represent him? _____

6. Assume in the question above that the Judge denied Sally's pro hac vice petition to represent Jim in the state of Orange after giving the petition only a cursory reading. Have either Sally's or Jim's due process rights been violated? _____

7. Richard has been a real estate agent for 15 years. He is well acquainted with the steps involved in preparing the documents necessary for closing a real estate sale. He can prepare these documents for his clients for one half the amount it costs to have an attorney do so. May Richard prepare the documents for his clients? _____

8. Bill is a licensed attorney sharing an office with Amy. He is aware that there is a dispute over a missing document in one of Amy's cases. As a result of overhearing a conversation in the lobby between Amy and one of her clients, Frank, Bill has become aware that Amy is in possession of the document requested during discovery but is claiming that it cannot be located. Bill has become close friends with Amy over the years and does not want to cause her any trouble. Must Bill report Amy to the appropriate professional authority? _____

9. In the state of Wythe, membership in the state bar association is mandatory. State bar members must pay yearly dues. The state bar association wants to pay the traveling expenses for a group of attorneys to travel to the state capital to lobby against a bill requiring more stringent application procedures for gun owners. May the state bar use the money collected from the payment of yearly dues to pay for the traveling expenses of the lobbyists? _____

10. Mary resides near the border of her state and wishes to open a solo practice upon receiving her license to practice law. She would like to have the broadest client base possible and is considering applying to the bar in her home state as well as the neighboring state. Is it possible for Mary to be licensed in two states at once? _____

11. Alice retained an attorney, Bob, to file a medical malpractice suit against her Doctor and Hospital. Bob assured her that everything was under control, but in actuality, Bob forgot to file the suit and missed the deadline, effectively prohibiting Alice from ever filing suit. Bob has already been disciplined by the state bar. Does Alice have any further recourse? _____

12. Mary is a licensed lawyer in the state of Marshall. Marshall requires applicants to the state bar to furnish the admission authorities with recommendations from currently licensed lawyers. Mary has recently been contacted by her former college roommate, Joan, and asked if she will provide a recommendation for Joan's son, Bob, who is applying to the state bar. Mary has never met Bob and knows nothing about him other than what his mother has told her. Can Mary write the recommendation for Bob as a favor to Joan? _____

13. Sam has recently been admitted to practice law in the state of Wythe. The state of Wythe's ethics code is based on the ABA Model Rules. Sam is faced with a difficult ethical question. He is unable to find any state ethics opinions that help answer the question, but there is an ABA ethics opinion that provides guidance. As Sam is not an ABA member, must or should he give any weight to the ABA's ethics opinion? _____

CHAPTER 3

CONTROLS ON LAWYER CONDUCT

14. Sarah retains a lawyer to represent her in a product liability case. Sarah gives her lawyer the blender that malfunctioned and caused her injury. The lawyer takes the blender home and puts it in her garage. Later, the lawyer accidently discards the blender while preparing

for a yard sale. As a result of the loss of this evidence, Sarah loses her case. What course of action against the lawyer is available and what are the likely results? _____

15. Joe is one of the most successful criminal defense attorneys in the state and has always been careful to ensure that his actions as an attorney always fall well within the bounds of the ethics rules. However, Joe has had two arrests for driving under the influence in the past year and has also been arrested for spousal abuse. May the bar discipline Joe for these arrests? _____

16. In exchange for a reduced hourly rate, Jane has signed a written agreement not to sue her attorney for malpractice that may occur during the representation. Is the attorney subject to discipline? _____

17. Joan is a tax attorney with an advanced degree in tax law. One of her clients has brought a malpractice suit against her as a result of tax advice Joan gave the client. To what standard will Joan be held? _____

18. Overruling her client Joe's preference, Amy decided not to put Material Witness on the stand during Joe's civil trial. She felt that Material Witness' testimony would do more harm than good because of certain credibility problems of Material Witness. The jury decided against Joe. Several of the jurors said one of the influences on their decision was the fact that Material Witness did not testify. Will Joe prevail in his malpractice suit against Amy? _____

19. Tom brought a malpractice case based on a tort theory against his attorney, Bob. Tom was able to prove that but for Bob's actions he would have won the matter that Bob had undertaken for Tom. However, he would have only won nominal damages. What damages can Tom get from Bob? _____

20. During the trial of his client, Joe felt that the judge clearly misapplied the rules of evidence in refusing to let him use the written statement of the police officer to refresh the officer's memory of the license plate he saw at the scene of the crime. Joe was vigorously representing the interests of his client when Joe gave the witness the document anyway and loudly instructed the witness to use the document to refresh his memory despite the judge's contrary ruling. The judge ordered Joe to pay a $500 fine for contempt of court. Does Joe have any immediate recourse? _____

21. Lisa's opposing counsel has made a motion to have her disqualified from the case because of a conflict of interest. In addition to the general interests meant to be furthered by the ethics rules on conflict of interest, what interests may the judge take into consideration in deciding whether to grant the motion? _____

CHAPTER 4

FORMAL ASPECTS OF THE LAWYER-CLIENT RELATIONSHIP

22. Rachel is on retainer to Bob. Bob comes to Rachel and asks her to represent him in a personal injury claim. After investigating, Rachel comes to believe that the potential

claim is frivolous. Bob demands that the claim be filed. Is Rachel required to represent Bob because of the retainer agreement she signed agreeing to represent Bob in all of his legal affairs? _____

23. Jack's client, Sally, does not have enough money to pay Jack for representing her in her divorce. Sally suggests a fee arrangement whereby she will pay Jack an agreed-on percentage of any alimony she is awarded. Jack feels that this is a fair arrangement. Will Jack be subject to discipline if he enters into this agreement with Sally? _____

24. Jill comes to Jack, an attorney, with a legal problem in an area he has never worked on. It is not a complex problem and Jack is aware of several sources where he can find the information he needs to represent Jill. Provided he charges Jill a reasonable rate for the time it takes him to become familiar with the law governing Jill's problem, will Jack's acceptance of this case subject him to discipline? _____

25. Larry is representing Janet in a personal injury case on a contingent fee basis. Larry has had a number of cases against the opposing counsel in Janet's case, and he knows that they often offer settlements that turn out to be thousands of dollars lower than Janet could get if the case goes to trial. The opposing counsel makes a settlement offer. Larry knows that it would be in Janet's best interest to reject the offer. However, he knows that if Janet heard the offer, she would be so impressed by the amount she would probably want to accept it. Larry decides to reject the offer without telling Janet, and eventually he wins a much larger verdict after a trial. Will any of Larry's actions subject him to discipline? _____

26. Sam has received a court appointment to represent Joe who has been charged with assault. Sam does not want to take the case because the amount he will be paid by the court is substantially less than the rate he normally bills and he is trying to save money to take a vacation at the end of the year. During Sam's initial meeting with Joe, Sam realizes that Joe is the former husband of a woman that Sam represented in a divorce case 10 years ago. One of the allegations during the divorce was that Joe had assaulted his wife. Can Sam decline the court appointment? _____

27. At a party, Kelly, a lawyer, is talking to an acquaintance, Sam, who tells her that he is considering consulting a lawyer because of a problem he has been having with his landlord. He tells Kelly all the details of the problem and asks whether she thinks he has grounds for a suit. Kelly tells him that the situation poses an interesting legal question that she could not answer without doing some research and talking to her friend, a housing attorney. Has a lawyer-client relationship begun between Kelly and Sam? _____

28. What factors may be taken into consideration when determining whether an attorney's fee is reasonable? _____

29. Sarah is a solo practitioner who employs a paralegal, Joe, to help her with a variety of tasks. Joe is paid a set salary for the work he does as the office manager, but when he works on specific cases with Sarah he receives a set percentage of any fee Sarah collects. Sarah and Joe both feel that this is a fair arrangement. Will this fee arrangement subject Sarah to discipline? _____

30. Jane has represented Harry and his family in all their legal matters for a number of years. Jane has recently become aware that Harry is using her services to commit fraud. She wants to withdraw as his counsel, but she signed a retainer agreement in which she agreed to represent him in all his legal matters. The agreement covers the next six months. Jane also knows her withdrawal will result in a material adverse effect on Harry and his family. May Jane withdraw? _____

CHAPTER 5

CONFIDENTIALITY

31. Henry met his lawyer for lunch at a popular local restaurant. At the salad bar, Henry discussed his role in the crime for which he has recently been indicted. Does the attorney-client privilege protect the information that Henry told his lawyer during lunch? _____

32. Bob and Sue are charged with committing a crime together. Bob confesses everything to his lawyer and waives the attorney-client privilege. Sue doesn't want Bob's lawyer to be able to reveal the communication because it would implicate her in the crime and she plans to argue that she didn't take part. Can Sue prevent the revelation of the communication by invoking the attorney-client privilege? _____

33. Joe told his attorney that he was outside of the building acting as a lookout when the crime was committed. Joe has chosen to testify during his trial. While on the witness stand, the Prosecutor asks Joe if he was outside of the building at the time the crime was committed. Can Joe invoke the attorney-client privilege to avoid answering the question? _____

34. Jim told his attorney that he committed the crime and threw the gun in the woods. Lawyer goes to the woods and sees the gun, but he does not touch it or disturb it in any way. The prosecutor asks the lawyer if he knows where the gun is. Does the lawyer have to reveal the location of the gun without revealing how he knows where it is located? _____

35. Assume that the same situation existed as in the above Question, except that the lawyer picked up the gun and took it back to his office. What would be protected by the attorney-client privilege in this situation? _____

36. Joe and Sam go to Lawyer to ask him to help them reach an agreement on a business deal they are considering entering. What effect does this arrangement have on the creation of the attorney-client privilege? _____

37. Attorney is investigating the circumstance surrounding the crime with which his client, Bill, has been charged. During the investigation, Bill's friend tells the attorney where Bill was on the night the crime occurred. Is the communication between the client's friend and the attorney protected by the attorney-client privilege? _____

38. Four years ago, Nick came to Lawyer and confessed that he had committed a murder and asked Lawyer to represent him if he was ever charged with the crime. Nick was never arrested for the murder and Lawyer's unrelated representation of Nick ended three years ago. John has recently asked Lawyer to represent him. John has been charged with committing the murder that Nick confessed to Lawyer four years ago. What should Lawyer do? _____

39. Lawyer represented Jack and, in the course of the representation, he learned that Jack had saved a substantial amount of money. Lawyer has been unable to collect his fee from Jack and has filed suit against Jack to collect the fee. During the trial, Jack claims that he has no money with which to pay the rest of the fee. Revealing the information would certainly help Lawyer's case, but would be detrimental to Jack. Must Lawyer keep quiet? _____

40. Lawyer represents a corporation that is considering building a large park in an area that is currently rural. If the park is built, the property near the park will rapidly increase in value. Lawyer is considering buying property near the proposed park site. Is the Lawyer violating any ethics rules by buying this property? _____

41. Sarah storms into Lawyer's office and says, "When I leave your office I'm going to find Joe and shoot him." Lawyer believes Sarah is telling the truth. Is this communication protected by the attorney-client privilege or the duty of confidentiality, and does Lawyer have any responsibility to warn Joe? _____

42. An attorney working for a government agency becomes aware that agency personnel have illegally accepted thousands of dollars in trips and gifts from assorted lobbying groups. Is Lawyer bound by the attorney-client privilege not to reveal the violations? _____

CHAPTER 6

CONFLICT OF INTERESTS

43. Alan and Bill were car-pooling to work one morning when they were involved in a car accident. Alan was driving. Alan and Bill both believe the other driver to be primarily at fault, but Alan was fumbling with his seat-belt at the time—an issue that the fact-finder may find relevant, especially in their comparative negligence state.

Alan and Bill approach you, seeking joint legal representation. Are there any circumstances under which you may represent both Alan and Bill, rather than advising one of them to seek other counsel? _____

44. Assume that the facts are the same as those given in the above question. Alan and Bill seek joint representation for their suit against the other driver in a car accident. However, in this case, interviews with the prospective clients and two different witnesses reveal that Alan had been drinking prior to the incident and may have been largely at fault for the collision. After a full consultation, Alan and Bill still insist that they wish to be jointly represented and they waive any possible conflicts. Can you represent them? _____

45. Judge Bennett recently moved from the bench to private practice with XYZ law firm. XYZ is approached by Chemical Corp. for legal representation. While still acting as a judge, a motion came before Judge Bennett involving the same case against Chemical Corp. The Judge ruled that Chemical Corp. had not complied with discovery request deadlines and ordered the Corporation to either turn over the requested materials or face contempt charges. Is Judge Bennett disqualified from this representation?

_____

46. Ann approaches Lawyer Fred concerning a possible lawsuit against a local real estate agency. In fact, the agency is owned and managed by Fred's wife, and some of the couple's personal funds were invested to start the business. Fred is confident, however, that he can remain neutral and, after a complete consultation with Ann, Ann voluntarily agrees to waive the conflict of interest. Is Fred's representation of Ann against the agency a violation of the ethics rules? _____

47. Brian, an attorney in private practice, takes a pro bono tort case for an indigent client. Because his client is poor, Brian offers to cover the expenses involved in taking several depositions, including a very expensive expert-witness doctor. One of Brian's friends questions whether Brian can do this under the rules, but Brian assures his friend that he had the client sign a waiver of the conflict of interest. Does Brian's paying for the depositions violate the ethics rules? _____

48. Sandra, a one-time attorney with the Environmental Protection Agency, has recently moved to a private environmental law practice. While with the EPA, Sandra participated in a case against CleanCo. for its violations of several major environmental laws. Her participation in the case allowed her access to confidential business information about the company, as well as a lot of information about its system of environmental compliance and the difficulties it has had in implementing and maintaining the system. Now, Sandra is approached by a citizens group that wishes to bring suit against CleanCo. for violations of a completely different environmental statute. Can Sandra act as their attorney?

_____

49. An attorney with the Labor Department learns of a case in which the Circus Workers Union has figured out a loophole to one of the Department's regulations. In response to the Union's activity, the attorney launches an initiative that results in an amended regulation preventing further Union activity. Now that she is in private practice, may the attorney represent the Union in defending an agency-brought action based on the regulation? _____

50. As you attempted to cross the street in the safe haven of a crosswalk one afternoon, a driver ran a stop sign and hit you. You suffered severe injuries and incur sizable medical bills. Seeking redress, you go to Lawyer Jill. You give her all of the basic details about the accident, your insurance coverage, and your medical history and problems. Lawyer Jill believes you have a claim but regretfully declines to represent you when she discovers a potential conflict of interest. If you discover that Jill later agreed to represent the driver in the accident, is Jill subject to discipline? _____

51. You are injured in a car wreck in which your friend was driving. You and your friend both believe the other driver was at fault. You decide to join together to sue the other driver and go see attorney Paul. Paul listens to the details of the accident and tells you that you two could have conflicting interests in the case. However, Paul says he can still represent you both if you sign waivers. Is Paul subject to discipline?

_____

52. You have a casual attorney friend named Alex. You like Alex, but recently you have learned of some disturbing activity in which Alex was involved. You know that lawyers are prohibited from drafting instruments in which they are personal beneficiaries. However, you have discovered that Alex recently drafted his aunt's will in which he is named as one of the beneficiaries. Do you have a duty to report Alex? _____

53. You are planning to defend Denise against criminal charges. Denise is suffering financial difficulties in addition to her criminal problems, and you agree to do the work pro bono. Later in the week, however, her brother calls and offers to pay your fee. What must occur in order for you to accept her brother's proposal? _____

54. The state of Robbins is governed by a statute allowing uncontested divorce parties to "share" the same attorney when it is reasonable to do so. Attorney Julie has in the course of her divorce practice represented several such couples, acting as a successful intermediary. Today, Paul and Alison enter her office, and they seem perfect for the same situation. They have no children, no hard feelings, and have already divided the assets. In light of their situation, Julie has them sign a contract for services without any further discussion. They begin to discuss the specific details of the divorce. Has Julie violated any rules? _____

CHAPTER 7

DUTIES TO THIRD PARTIES

55. Lawyer Anne represents a man accused of murder. Several days before trial, the prosecutor and Anne sit down and negotiate in an attempt to reach a plea bargain. The prosecutor tells Anne that he believes the evidence against Anne's client is so strong that the jury will not only convict him but also impose the death penalty. The prosecutor convinces Anne that his case is unbeatable, so she tentatively agrees to a deal that will leave her client in prison for a large portion of his life. Later, before meeting with her client to discuss his reaction to the tentative deal, she goes over the prosecutor's case again and finds large holes in the prosecutor's theory. Is the prosecutor subject to discipline for misleading Anne regarding the strength of his case? _____

56. During negotiations, Attorney Carl is sometimes prone to slight exaggeration. He believes it makes things more interesting and that other lawyers not only expect such puffery but are doing the same thing. During a recent negotiation conference concerning a car wreck, Carl stretched the truth in several respects. He said that his client had sought the advice of seven doctors who all concurred on the severity of his client's injuries, and he said he didn't think his client would accept less than $75,000. In reality, Carl's client has consulted only two doctors, and he knows perfectly well that his client would be extremely happy to receive $50,000. Are Carl's negotiating tactics subject to discipline? _____

57. Lawyer's Client wishes to buy an expensive piece of beach-front property but would like to get a lower price than the seller is willing give. Lawyer has a friend pose as an Environmental Protection Agency inspector and tell the seller that the adjacent property is contaminated and that his own property may decline in value as a result. The seller acts quickly but, rather than sell to lawyer's client, seller finds a third party to pay full price. The seller, therefore, was apparently not harmed by the false EPA report. Should the lawyer be subject to discipline? _____

58. Lawyer is sorting through jury forms, trying to decide which potential jurors seem likely to be sympathetic to his arguments. She notices that one of the jurors lives next door to an old college friend. She calls her friend, asking about the potential juror's views on many topics. Her friend even asks the potential juror some of the lawyer's questions and reports back. Is lawyer subject to discipline? _____

59. Husband and wife are involved in protracted divorce proceedings with no end in sight. Wife's attorney discusses the proceedings with her client. The wife's attorney is concerned that husband would be more willing to reach settlement without constant pressure from his lawyer not to "give in on anything." Wife's attorney remarks that she thinks sometimes people would reach agreements more easily without such acrimonious influences. After considering her attorney's statements, wife contacts husband to attempt to reach a settlement without their attorneys present. Is wife's lawyer subject to discipline? _____

60. Following an even more bitter divorce, a custody battle rages between ex-husband and ex-wife. Husband plans to have his girlfriend as his main witness, who will testify about all the bad behavior she has witnessed ex-wife display in the past. Following girlfriend's deposition, ex-wife's attorney notices a couple of confusing things and calls the girlfriend to clear them up. Is ex-wife's attorney subject to discipline? _____

61. You represent an injured employee of Corporation. The employee worked in the chemistry laboratory, under the Products Development Division. Not knowing much about the Corporation generally, you wish to get a little background information. To that end, you interview a neighbor of yours who is a midlevel manager in a department of Corporation that is unrelated to the subject matter of your representation. Before conducting the interview, you notify Corporation's lawyer of your intentions. You tell the neighbor whom you represent and the nature of your interest in talking with him about Corporation. Assuming that the employee you chose may not make a statement that could be admissible as an admission of Corporation, have you violated any disciplinary rules? _____

62. Lawyer is hired to sue a drunk driver in a car accident in which a single mother was injured. Lawyer does a poor job and gets the mother a very limited damage recovery. Several years later, the mother dies of an unrelated cause. Her children come to you seeking to sue the lawyer for malpractice because his poor lawyering served to decrease their possible inheritance. What is your advice for them? _____

63. During negotiations, a rental car company agrees to buy 2,000 new cars from a car manufacturer. The two parties orally agree to some of the terms. At the end of the meeting, the car manufacturer's attorney (Attorney A) offers to draw up the agreement. The rental car company attorney (Attorney B) agrees, and asks that while drawing up the agreement, Attorney A refer to the notes that Attorney B had taken during the meeting; essentially, Attorney B had already drawn up a draft agreement. Attorney A takes the notes, and notices that in B's draft, the car rental company agreed to buy 200, rather than 2,000 cars. A changes this figure to 2,000. In making this alteration, can A be subject to discipline? _____

64. Lawyer is representing a man in a slip and fall incident that occurred at a local bar. One evening, Lawyer goes to the bar and sits with a few of the regulars, the waitresses, and the bartender. They talk for a while, and Lawyer asks them questions like whether the waitresses often spill beer and make the floor slippery, etc. He does not identify himself as an attorney, nor does he affirmatively lie and give another reason for his curiosity. Is the lawyer subject to discipline? _____

65. Lawyer represented Client in a medical malpractice action against Doctor. After a flurry of pretrial discovery, Lawyer and Client concluded that there was little or no chance of proving Doctor's liability. They therefore agreed to let the case lie dormant for a time, to see if Doctor's insurance carrier might offer a modest sum in settlement. Ultimately, Doctor moved for summary judgment, won the motion, and had the case dismissed. Then he sued Lawyer for malpractice, claiming that Lawyer had brought a baseless lawsuit against him, thereby injuring his reputation in the community and among members of the medical profession. Is Lawyer liable to Doctor for malpractice? _____

CHAPTER 8

DUTIES TO THE LEGAL SYSTEM AND SOCIETY

66. Lawyer is defending a man accused of criminal charges stemming from a hit and run accident. While trying to put his case together, he learns several facts that may be material to the outcome of the case. For example, he learns that there is a very big dent in the defendant's front fender. He also discovers that his client consumed a great deal of alcohol on the night of the incident. Finally, Lawyer interviews a witness who says that shortly before the accident, the client rushed out of a bar upon learning how late it was. Which, if any, of these facts is the lawyer under an obligation to reveal to the court? _____

67. Attorney Richard is working on a large antitrust claim. He is furious because one of his law clerks assigned to do legal research missed a critical, recent case in that area decided by their state's supreme court. The case is highly favorable to his client and signifies a new direction in the law. Richard discovered the omission the day before a motion that he is to argue in court. Richard is scrambling to revise the draft of his motion memorandum to the court that he will submit tomorrow at the motion hearing. Richard is also angry at opposing counsel, Robin, because the case the law clerk missed had been argued by a partner in Robin's firm. Therefore, there is no way that Robin was not aware of this new turn in the law favoring Richard's client. Richard has not yet seen Robin's memorandum to the court; it will also be submitted to the court tomorrow at the motion hearing. But Richard and Robin met a week ago to try to settle the matter. Despite having obviously known about the case, Robin said nothing about it to Richard when they met. Richard asks for your advice on whether he can file for sanctions against her for failure to disclose to him this controlling, directly adverse (to Robin's side) legal authority.

68. Attorney Anne is representing an accused drug dealer. Anne has been over her client's story many times and doesn't think that it rings true. There are no glaring inconsistencies and her investigation has not revealed any directly contrary evidence; she simply thinks that her past experience with clients makes her able to read clients well enough to suspect when a client is lying. Anne still has no evidence to the contrary, however, and decides that her client's best strategy is to testify. Anne puts her client on the stand to testify. Is Anne subject to discipline? _____

69. Attorney David feels some anxiety about the conflict between his ethical duties to the court and his obligation to his client. He defended the client in a criminal assault charge arising out of an altercation between his client and another man. The jury eventually acquitted David's client despite the other man's grave injuries because they apparently believed (on the strength of David's client's testimony) that David's client was a relatively innocent bystander who was unwillingly pulled into the fight. Several days after the verdict, however, David overheard his client laughingly describe how he lured the victim into the fight. David is concerned and asks you whether he must come forward and tell the court that his client committed perjury. _____

70. Attorney represents plaintiff in a personal injury case resulting from a car accident. Plaintiff's friend is one of the witnesses to the accident, who happened to be walking down the street at the time of the collision. There are other witnesses available to testify about what they saw as well. Plaintiff's friend is painfully shy and would prefer not to testify. If she did testify, her testimony would be against her friend, the plaintiff. The discomfort of testifying unfavorably to her friend adds to her misgivings about testifying. Because her testimony would not be the only evidence available of what happened in the accident, plaintiff's attorney tells the friend that she needn't testify and that she might want to "make herself scarce" during the weeks leading up to the trial. Is the attorney subject to discipline? _____

71. Attorney is preparing a case for trial and determining which witnesses will need to testify. Discussing the matter with Client, they agree that Client's doctor should testify regarding doctor's examination of Client's physical condition, that Client's psychologist should testify regarding Client's mental state during the time in question in the litigation, and that the Client's next door neighbor should testify regarding Client's character and reputation for truthfulness. Client instructs attorney to pay each witness $1000 to compensate them for their time in testifying. May attorney follow Client's instruction? _____

72. During closing arguments, an attorney makes the following statements:

> It is obvious that my client is innocent. You heard from a witness who testified that she saw my client several miles away from the crime scene at the time in question. Moreover, that witness believes my client is innocent based on a conversation the witness had with a mutual friend. The prosecution's witness gave a very different story, but which one do you think is more believable? It seems to me that the prosecution witness is the one with a reason to lie, and I can tell that the witness did lie.

Evidence of the conversation between the witness and the mutual friend was excluded because it was based on inadmissible hearsay. What ethical problems are there with the lawyer's closing argument? _____

73. Attorney Claire comes to you for advice. While trying a case before Judge Rock, Claire believed that she discovered wrongful conduct on the part of the judge. She made her charges public, but they turned out to be based upon misinformation and were false. Judge Rock found her in contempt for making the false charges, and she believes she will also be disciplined by the bar. What arguments can she make in her defense?

_____

74. In prosecutor's opening statements, the prosecutor says the following:

> The accused lives in a house on Maple Street with his wife and children. After this crime was committed, investigators spent several weeks collecting evidence, all of which led to the defendant's arrest. He was questioned on May 7 and arrested shortly thereafter. The accused has been charged with first-degree murder. Testimony will show that the accused knew the victim and that his romantic relationship with her had recently ended.

A reporter in the courtroom reports all of these statements, and they are widely disseminated in the media. For which of these statements will the prosecutor be subject to discipline for the publicity generated? _____

75. Attorney has an emergency. A family problem has come up, and she is required to leave town quickly. However, she has a motion argument in two days, and she is not even halfway through preparation for it. Without thinking, she grabs the phone and calls the judge at home. She explains her emergency situation and tells the judge that this motion is critically important to the case. He agrees to push the hearing date back by a week. Can the attorney be subject to discipline for this communication? _____

76. Lawyer is at a restaurant, eating lunch during a break from her trial. She is absorbed in her notes, until she looks up to see two jurors standing beside her table. They seem eager to be friendly, and they ask her a couple of questions about where she is from and how she likes the town. Lawyer worries that by not replying, the jurors will be offended and her client will be jeopardized. May she answer these questions, which have nothing to do with trial matters? _____

CHAPTER 9

SPECIAL ROLE-RELATED DUTIES

77. You are a prosecutor with the State Attorney's office. In an extremely well-publicized case, a famous actor's girlfriend is murdered. The actor often plays unsavory characters, and this may help explain the public outcry that the actor be arrested. There is a racial element as well, in that the actor is white and his girlfriend was black. People are insisting that justice demands that the actor be arrested. However, you have little or no evidence to tie him to the crime beyond the public opinion polls. To prevent bad publicity and possible racial disturbances, may you bring charges and then drop them if nothing substantial is uncovered in the investigation? _____

78. Bill, a state prosecutor, goes to see Defendant Jay, who will soon be tried for assault. Jay refused his court-appointed attorney in favor of self-representation. Bill knows that

Jay makes a very sympathetic witness and is worried about going to trial. Bill would like to advise Jay to forego the jury in favor of a bench trial. What advice can Bill give Jay? _____

79. Prosecutor Steve has a very strong case against Defendant, with excellent evidence and accurate, reliable witnesses. Steve believes his case would be bolstered just a little bit more ("the last nail in the coffin," in Steve's words) with testimony from the Defendant's former attorney concerning things that fell outside the attorney-client privilege. May Steve subpoena the defendant's former lawyer? _____

80. Prosecutor Scott is involved in the investigation of a drug smuggler. The investigator reports on several possible leads. Two are promising: a report of the phone calls the Defendant made in the last month and a source that can relate Defendant's recent travels. Other leads look less helpful: several witnesses intimated that others were involved in the crime and minimized Defendant's role. If Scott directs the investigator to look at the phone records and travel logs but not follow up on the witness information, has he violated any ethical duty? _____

81. Anne, fresh out of law school, is a new attorney in Barbara's firm. Assigned to work on a case with Barbara, Anne gathers documents to release in response to the opposing party's request for the materials. Barbara praises Anne's diligence but nevertheless pulls several documents from the stack because "the other side wouldn't be interested." Anne disagrees. Because it's a huge firm, Anne is able to covertly ask several attorneys in the firm hypothetical questions about the exclusion of this type of document in response to a request for documents. All of these attorneys confirm Anne's view that the documents should be included. What are the consequences if Anne says nothing? _____

82. XYZ law firm has a long-standing practice. Although the firm's young attorneys in their first three years of practice are allowed to handle some of their own cases and clients, they must go to their supervisors and discuss each case from the beginning. The supervisors are expected to remain on top of the case and guide the younger attorneys through the unfamiliar terrain. Yvette, a new attorney at XYZ law firm, decides to represent a friend in an action against her friend's landlord. She does not take the case to her supervisor, deciding that she can handle it herself. However, the court rules that the claim is frivolous. Will Yvette's supervisor be subject to discipline? _____

83. Assume the facts are as detailed in the question above. This time, however, a partner from a different division learned of the frivolous claim the day before it was to be filed. He waited, however, until the following week to discuss it with Yvette. Is the partner correct in assuming that because he does not directly supervise Yvette, he has not violated any conduct rules? _____

84. Brenda is buying a house, and Attorney Ann is representing both her and Watson Realty Co., the brokers in the transaction. Ann's role as intermediary is compromised when the deal falls through, and Brenda decides to sue Watson for breach of contract. Ann withdraws and is dismayed when Brenda subpoenas her to testify to statements Watson made during the deal. Ann asserts attorney-client privilege. Will she be successful?

85. Lynn, a young attorney relatively new to her firm, has just been assigned a secretary. Lynn becomes involved in a contentious case with an older, experienced attorney who succeeds at intimidating her every chance he gets. One day the older attorney phones and begins yelling that his request for production of documents did not yield what he had been looking for. Terrified, Lynn quickly hands the phone to the secretary, instructing her to tell the older attorney that no such documents exist. Actually, Lynn had found the documents past the deadline, and was too afraid to turn them over late. Lynn feels badly for putting her secretary on the spot. Will Lynn be subject to discipline? _____

Chapter 10

ADVERTISING AND SOLICITATION

86. A legal aid lawyer represents a client who is alleging that the housing complex has been discriminating on the basis of race in making repairs. The lawyer decides to go door to door in the housing complex to find out if other tenants have had similar experiences and whether they are willing to bring suit. Will the lawyer be subject to discipline for her actions? _____

87. Joe represents the state of Marshall and is defending the state's ethics code sections dealing with lawyer advertising and solicitation against a claim that they violate the constitutional right to free speech of lawyers. What must Joe demonstrate to have the provisions declared constitutional? _____

88. Bob and Sally want to enter private practice in the state of Wythe, specializing in labor law. They want to have a unique name for their firm, so rather than use their last names, they have decided to call themselves Wythe Labor Relations Legal Services. Will they be subject to discipline for the name of their firm? _____

89. Bob is a personal injury attorney, and he knows how hard his clients sometimes struggle to pay all of their expenses until they reach an agreement with the insurance company. Bob wants to offer potential clients a weekly stipend to live on until the case is settled. If the clients win their cases, they will be required to reimburse him. If they lose, he is willing to absorb the cost of the weekly stipends. Bob wants to run an ad clearly and truthfully explaining his policy for his clients. Will Bob be subject to discipline for his ad? _____

90. Allen, a former state trooper, is now an attorney. He plans to run an advertisement stating his background as a former state trooper with the statement, "I can fix your drunk driving problems." Will Allen be subject to discipline for this advertisement? _____

91. Jane decides to place an ad in the local newspaper. In addition to listing her specialties and educational background, she decides to include the phrases, "one of the state's toughest litigators" and "well respected by state and federal judges." She believes the statements to be true and thinks that lawyers are entitled to do a little self promotion. Will Jane be subject to discipline for the advertisement? _____

92. Peter is planning to send form letters to a select group of individuals that has recently been denied Social Security benefits, proposing that they hire him to represent them at their hearing. Is Peter's letter permissible? _____

93. Joan is an attorney at a law firm that has decided to place an advertisement in the Yellow Pages. Joan is in charge of designing the ad. Because of the large number of distinguished partners in her firm, Joan has decided to only use the firm's name and address in the ad. None of the named partners are currently practicing. Will the firm be subject to discipline for the ad? _____

CHAPTER 11

JUDICIAL CONDUCT

94. Judge is accused of trying to bribe someone in a matter wholly unrelated to his judicial functions. An abundance of evidence substantiates the charge. Nonetheless, no criminal charges are brought against Judge. Is judge correct in his belief that because no criminal charges were brought, he will not lose his position on the bench? _____

95. Alice's neighbor, Bob, is a judge. One evening, someone breaks into Alice's house. Bob remembers seeing someone suspicious on the street earlier in the evening. Bob volunteers to testify to the approximate time he spotted the shady character, as well as to the prowler's appearance. Does Bob's conduct violate the Judicial Code of Conduct? _____

96. Judge Smith's docket is getting a little bit backed up. In fact, he has cases that are three months behind where they should be. Judge Smith realizes that part of the reason he's behind is that he has had to end his court sessions early three days a week in order to be on time for a course he teaches at the nearby university. He prefers teaching to being a judge but realizes it's important to maintain his status as a judge because the university gives special consideration to this status and pays him two and a half times the average teaching salary. What, if any, rules have been violated? _____

97. Attorney Carl is trying a case in Judge Douglas's court. Carl and Judge Douglas run into each other one evening while each is dining alone. Carl does not join the judge's table, but he does stop by and talk for approximately 20 minutes. A party on the opposite side of the case is present at the restaurant and witnesses the discussion. If neither Carl nor Judge Douglas is willing to testify that he was not discussing the case, will the judge be considered to have violated a rule of conduct? _____

98. Judge Amy and Judge Brenda are friends who both belong to the local country club. Amy has lately heard some disturbing rumors around the club about Brenda, specifically, that Brenda took a bribe to acquit a wealthy white collar criminal defendant. The rumors come from very reliable sources. Amy has no direct evidence, but she does notice that Brenda has been avoiding her and suddenly began living in a fairly ostentatious manner several months ago. Amy knows their judges' salaries would not support such a lifestyle. What are her duties in terms of reporting Brenda? _____

99. While a judge's chambers are being redecorated, he is forced to use the public restrooms down the hall. One day, he accidentally overhears a last-minute emergency meeting between the attorney and criminal defendant presently before his court. The judge hears the attorney discussing his participation with the client in an attempt to bribe and/or coerce members of his client's jury. What are the judge's reporting requirements?

_____

100. Judge has an old friend from childhood who is charged with criminal conduct in a case pending in Judge's court. Judge and his friend see each other often, keep in frequent contact, and consider themselves close. Judge honestly believes, however, that despite this friendship, he can remain neutral. His higher duty, he understands, is to uphold the law. Is the Judge correct in deciding that he need not disqualify himself?

_____

101. Local Democratic party leaders approach Judge about running for the state senate. It is a fairly small state, and Judge's popularity assures that she will have to invest only a small amount of time and effort on the campaign. For almost the entire timetable of the campaign, she foresees no effect on her judicial duties. For how long may she remain on the bench? _____

102. Judge presides over a complex civil suit that takes several weeks to try. The issues are very difficult, and although her law clerks work overtime to keep her current and knowledgeable, she is struggling with this unfamiliar area of the law. In the end, she applies an incorrect legal standard, wrongly causing B to prevail over A. The appeals court overturns the judge's decision, noting the judge's error. What action can A bring against the judge in order to recover the costs of the appeal? _____

103. Judge owns stock in BIG Manufacturing Corp. (BMC). The value of his shares is approximately $500, and BMC is a large, Fortune 500 company. BMC is sued in tort by a plaintiff who claims to have been injured while visiting one of BMC's job sites. The plaintiff is asking for $34,000 in damages. Should the judge be disqualified for hearing the case? _____

104. Judge has in the past made statements condemning the current laws that offer too little protection for abortion clinics from their vigorous protestors. Now, several abortion protest defendants are to appear in Judge's court. Should Judge be disqualified?

_____

105. Judge is presiding over a case against BCD Corporation. The case involves a sexual harassment claim against BCD and several of its former high-level managers. While the judge was still in private practice, one of his fellow attorneys at a law firm litigated a matter against BCD in a completely unrelated labor dispute over wages. BCD argues that the judge should be disqualified because of his former associations. Are they correct? _____

ANSWERS TO SHORT-ANSWER QUESTIONS

1. No. Certain roles that are important to the continued existence of an ordered society implicate moral choices for those in particular roles. If these choices are consistent with the effective execution of the role, they are by definition moral. It is important to the functioning of the criminal justice system that the accused have a lawyer to zealously represent and protect the accused's interests.

2. The morally activist lawyer would counsel Dr. Bob to do what is morally right—to tell the patient of the mistake and the potential consequences. If Dr. Bob refuses to take this course of action, Lawyer, as a morally activist lawyer, would probably refuse to continue representing him.

3. The businessperson lawyer would do a cost-benefit analysis and would advise Dr. Bob to tell the patient only if it is the most efficient course of action.

4. Yes. Any past conduct may be considered by the admission authorities, including arrests and convictions that have been expunged from records. An applicant to the bar may not make any material false statement and must not "fail to disclose a fact necessary to correct misapprehension known by the [applicant] to have arisen in the matter. . . ." M.R. 8.1(b). By failing to include his arrest and conviction on his application, John is leading the admissions authorities to believe that he has never been arrested or convicted, a fact he clearly knows is not true.

5. It is possible for Sally to represent Jim in the state of Orange. Before she can represent Jim in a state in which she is not licensed to practice, she must apply to the state's courts to request admission pro hac vice. If Sally's request is granted, she may represent Jim in the state of Orange's courts until the dispute with the car dealership is resolved.

6. No. The right to appear pro hac vice is within the discretion of the state. Neither Sally's or Jim's have a due process right to a certain quality of consideration of their application. A number of states grant pro hac vice applications only to lawyers whose home state has a policy of reciprocating when its lawyers apply to practice in the applying lawyer's state. Some states require the out-of-state lawyer to associate, for purposes of the case, with a lawyer who is licensed in the state.

7. No, Richard is not an attorney and therefore cannot practice law within the state. Preparing the necessary documents in this situation is legal work that can be performed only by a licensed attorney.

8. Yes, Bill is under a duty to report Amy's misconduct, and a failure to do so is an ethical violation on Bill's part. Model Rule 8.3(a) states that "[a] lawyer who knows that another lawyer has committed a violation of the Model Rules of Professional Conduct that raises a substantial question as to that lawyer's honesty, trustworthiness, or fitness as a lawyer in other respects, shall inform the appropriate professional authority." Even though Amy has not directly informed Bill that she is withholding the document, he has personal knowledge of her actions based on the conversation between Amy and Frank and the circumstances surrounding the case.

9. No. Although state courts and legislatures are permitted to require membership in and dues payment to the state bar association for all licensed attorneys, a mandatory bar

may not expend members' dues to advance political or ideological positions. Keller v. State Bar of California, 496 U.S. 1 (1990).

10. Yes, Mary may hold licenses to practice in as many states as she wishes, provided she complies with the licensing requirements in each state. States' efforts to require in-state residency by attorneys wishing to gain a license to practice have been held unconstitutional.

11. Yes. The law of a wide variety of other areas forms an essential part of the law of lawyering. Depending on the circumstances of the case, Alice may bring suit for breach of contract or a tort suit for malpractice.

12. No. Licensed lawyers may not "knowingly make a false statement of material fact" in connection with a bar admission application. MR 8.1(a). It would be a misrepresentation of a material fact for Mary to state to the admission authorities that Bob was a qualified applicant if she did not have personal knowledge of the applicant. If Mary investigates and determines Bob to be a qualified applicant, she may write the recommendation, provided the recommendation truly represents her knowledge of Bob.

13. Yes, Sam should consider the ABA opinion even though he is not a member. The ABA's views on issues affecting the law of lawyering and its Model Rules are very influential, even though it is a voluntary organization with no direct regulatory authority over lawyers. However, even though Wythe's code is based on the ABA model, it is the state adopted code and not the ABA model that actually controls. The best way for Sam to determine how the Wythe's State Bar would resolve the question is to ask the state bar to issue an ethics opinion. Both the ABA and the state bar associations will issue nonbinding ethics opinions. These opinions are often generated by submitting a hypothetical question to a state bar committee whose responsibility it is to answer the question and publish the opinions.

14. Sarah could begin a malpractice action against the lawyer and file a bar disciplinary complaint. She will prevail on her malpractice claim if she can prove that she would have won her initial case had her lawyer not lost the blender, but the lawyer probably will not be disciplined by the bar if this is an isolated event.

15. Yes, discipline may be imposed for conduct outside of the lawyer's role if the conduct is criminal and reflects adversely on the lawyer's fitness to be a lawyer, as these acts do.

16. Yes, unless such agreements are permitted by law in the relevant jurisdiction and Jane was represented by impartial counsel in making the agreement.

17. Because Joan is a specialist in her field, she will be judged by the knowledge and skill of tax specialists rather than the standard of the ordinary, reasonably knowledgeable lawyer.

18. A lawyer is not liable in malpractice for reasonable strategy choices. As such, Joe will not win because Amy will not be held liable for reasonable strategy choices. Strategy choices such as these are the lawyer's to make and not the client's. Thus, Joe's preference to have Material Witness testify is irrelevant.

19. Bob's actions did not cause any actual damages so Tom will be unable to recover anything from Bob.

20. No. A judge may act immediately and without a hearing to punish contempt of which he or she has personal knowledge.

21. Judges may consider a wide range of interests in ruling on conflicts-based disqualification motions including the following: court delay and inefficiency resulting from the time that new counsel would need to become sufficiently familiar with the case; timing of the motion and whether the party filed the motion merely to gain an advantage in the litigation; the attorney preference of the party against whom the motion was filed.

22. Rachel is not required to represent Bob on this matter. Indeed, she has a duty to decline representation if she believes Bob's claim is frivolous.

23. Yes, because contingent fees are prohibited in most domestic relation cases, including this type.

24. No, the duty of competence does not require Jack to possess expertise at the beginning of representation if he will be able to acquire the necessary knowledge with reasonable diligence.

25. Yes, Larry was obliged to communicate the offer to Janet and did not have the authority to reject the settlement offer without Janet's agreement.

26. No, the financial burden is not unreasonable and the representation is unrelated to Sam's former representation of Joe's wife. As a result, Sam may not decline the appointment.

27. Yes, if Sam reasonably believes that Kelly was going to look into his legal problem. No formal agreement need be entered for a duty to arise and it is irrelevant that there was no discussion of fee arrangements. It does not matter that Kelly never intended to take Sam as a client and was just making conversation at a party. If her actions gave rise to Sam's reasonable belief that she would research his issue and answer his question, then Kelly owes a lawyer duty to Sam.

28. Model Rule 1.5 lists a number of factors to be considered, including, for example, the following: the number of years the lawyer has been a member of the bar and the lawyer's experience in similar matters; the type of case and the legal issues raised; the time and labor involved in the representation; the nature of the professional relationship between the lawyer and client; and customary charges for such services in the locality.

29. Yes, except in very limited circumstances outlined in Model Rule 5.4(a), fee sharing with nonlawyers is prohibited.

30. Even though Jane's withdrawal will cause a material adverse effect on the client, Jane is required to withdraw if she knows that Harry is using her services to commit fraud. If, after knowing that her services are being used to commit fraud, she does not withdraw, she will have civil liability to those whom Harry defrauds with her services.

31. No. The evidentiary privilege is not created when the communication is made in circumstances that do not indicate a desire for confidentiality by the client. Keep in mind that the duty of confidentiality still protects the information. The lawyer should have warned Client that the communication would not be protected by the attorney-client privilege.

32. No. The attorney-client privilege between Bob and his lawyer belongs to Bob, and he has chosen to waive it.

33. No. Joe must answer the question truthfully. The attorney-client privilege would allow Joe to refuse to answer a question about whether he told his attorney that he was outside of the building, but the privilege does not work to shield all information that a client reveals to his attorney.

34. No. The lawyer's observation of the gun's location was a direct result of the communication with the client and, therefore, it is protected by the attorney-client privilege. Requiring a lawyer to reveal the location of the gun in this situation without revealing the source of the information would undermine the purpose of the privilege. Clients would not be able to speak freely with their lawyers. Keep in mind that if Jim chose to testify, waiving his Fifth Amendment privilege against self-incrimination, and he was asked where the gun was, he would have to answer truthfully under penalty of perjury.

35. The lawyer would have to turn the gun over to the authorities. It is not privileged. The gun's location would also not be privileged because the lawyer has disrupted the opposing party's (here the government's) opportunity to discover the location. Effectively, the lawyer has destroyed the evidence of location. The client's communication to the lawyer would remain subject to the privilege. The lawyer could not be required to reveal how he found the gun because that would reveal the privileged communication.

36. When acting as an intermediary between clients, the lawyer must disclose to both that the attorney-client privilege is not available to either client for purposes of restricting the other's testimony regarding client communications to the lawyer.

37. No, unless the friend is an agent of the client. However, the friend's communication and the information he conveyed is covered by the duty of confidentiality.

38. The Lawyer is bound by the attorney-client privilege and the duty of confidentiality not to reveal Nick's confession to either John or the police. Lawyer may not accept representation of John. To do so would require Lawyer to either breach Nick's confidences or fail to serve John's interests fully.

39. No. A lawyer is permitted to reveal and use for her own benefit information that would be protected by the duty of confidentiality "to establish a claim or defense on behalf of the lawyer in a controversy between the lawyer and the client." Model Rule 1.6(b)(3). The lawyer is permitted to reveal only those facts necessary to present her claim.

40. Yes. The Model Code expressly prohibits a lawyer from using confidential information of the client, either to the client's detriment or to the lawyer's gain. DR 4-101(B)(2), 4-101(B)(3). The Model Rules prohibit a lawyer from using confidential information to a client's detriment. MR 1.8(b). Lawyer's act creates too great a risk of detriment to the client. If the client consents to lawyer's acts, lawyer may go forward with his purchase.

41. The attorney-client privilege in evidence law does not protect communications that further future crimes or frauds. Sarah's communication is not protected by the privilege. Further, both the Model Code and the Model Rules provide an exception to the duty of confidentiality for future crimes. Under the Code, a lawyer may reveal the intention of his client to commit a crime and the information necessary to prevent it. However, an ABA opinion indicates that "may" in this case means "must" if a lawyer is certain about the client's intention to commit a serious crime. The Model Rules use the word "may," but restrict the type of future crime that permits the revelation of confidential information to prevent future harms that the lawyer reasonably believes are likely to

result in imminent death or substantial bodily harm. MR 1.6(b)(1). Therefore, if Lawyer believes that Sarah is telling the truth, this communication is not protected by the duty of confidentiality and Lawyer should take steps to prevent Sarah from carrying out her threat.

42. Although the attorney technically represents the interests of agency, the attorney, as a public employee, also represents the interests of the public. The special public responsibilities of government agencies require lawyers to strike a confidentiality balance more toward the public interest in disclosure of government wrongdoing. In this case, the attorney would not be disciplined for revealing the violations.

43. Yes, provided that you receive each client's informed consent. In this case, the clients should be informed of how comparative negligence works and the fact that Bill will have to give up any of his possible claims against Alan, which could preclude Bill's full recovery. However, as long as no "gross conflict" exists, you may represent them with consent. Nonetheless, if conflicts develop during representation, you will likely have to withdraw from representing both Alan and Bill.

44. No. Joint representation requires both consent AND a reasonable belief that representation will not be adversely affected (MR 1.7(a), MR 1.7(b)). You must not only personally believe that the representation will not be adversely affected but the belief must be one that would be shared by an objective, reasonable attorney.

45. Yes. A judge who has participated personally and substantially in a matter is disqualified from later representation of either party. Ruling on a pretrial motion of significance should be considered such a personal and substantial involvement. MR 1.12.

46. Yes. When competing interests are at stake, a lawyer must not only get client consent but must also hold a reasonable belief that the representation will not be adversely affected. Here, such a belief is not reasonable.

47. No. An attorney is permitted to advance the costs of litigation to his client, even without an assurance that they will be paid regardless of the outcome. Moreover, no waiver was necessary in this situation because advancing litigation costs created no conflict. However, Brian could not advance any other financial assistance to his client (e.g., living expenses while the case is pending), and no waiver of this rule is allowed.

48. No, unless Cleanco consents, an unlikely prospect. Sandra is not permitted to represent a private party with interests adverse to a party about whom she gained confidential information while still in government practice. Here, although the environmental statutes are different, the confidential information Sandra gained about CleanCo. while with the EPA could be used unfairly and to CleanCo.'s disadvantage.

49. Yes. Even though the government attorney's participation in this was personal and substantial, an exception is made when her participation did not involve a "matter." A matter generally involves instances and actions that engage that agency with a particular party or parties. Drafting regulations does not fit under this category.

50. Yes. Lawyers owe a duty of confidentiality even to prospective clients. Although Jill did not represent you, she also owes you a limited loyalty duty and must avoid a conflict of interest in your case. No formal lawyer-client relationship need be formed to implicate these duties.

51. Yes. An informed client waiving a conflict of interest should know not only of the existence of the conflict but also the possible consequences that may result from the waiver. Here, Paul should have explained issues such as a possible inability to get a full recovery if your friend is found partially at fault and any possible claims against your friend you would be waiving.

52. No, because Alex has not violated any professional conduct rules. Lawyers cannot draft documents that make a substantial gift to the lawyer or close relative. However, an exception is made when, as here, the donee is related to the donor. MR 1.8(c).

53. You must cover several bases in order to accept payment from a third party for Denise's legal expenses. First, Denise must consent to the arrangement after consultation. Then, you must make clear to Denise's brother that Denise is still your client, regardless of who is paying the fees. Denise will still get to call the shots, and you will owe your lawyer duties such as confidentiality to Denise alone.

54. Yes. In order to represent both parties in a divorce, both a consultation on the common risks and effect on confidentiality and the consent of the clients are needed. Even with these safeguards, the potential for an escalated conflict still exists, and if this happens Julie will have to withdraw as counsel.

55. No. The prosecutor may have put his case in its most favorable light in order to convince her to negotiate, but unless the prosecutor has made material, false statements of fact, he will not be subject to discipline. Anne is presumed to be a competent attorney. This should have enabled her to make her own professional judgment, and she was not entitled to rely on the prosecutor's mere puffery.

56. Yes. Statements about the estimated value of a case are not considered facts but rather parts of negotiation strategy that each side is expected to take into account. However, specific factual statements, when false and material such as Carl's lie about the number of doctors consulted, subject a lawyer to discipline under Model Rule 4.1.

57. Yes. Lawyers are prohibited from engaging in unlawful acts on behalf of their clients, and his actions through his friend were intended to fraudulently induce the seller to lower his price. The prohibitions on using unlawful means and on making material false statements exist regardless of whether any actual harm results from the actions, so the lawyer should still be subject to discipline.

58. Yes. It does not matter that lawyer had a legitimate contact in the juror's next door neighbor; by initiating the contact between her friend and the juror, her friend became an agent. MR 3.5 and 4.4 prohibit the lawyer to contact any jurors or potential jurors in this manner.

59. No. Wife's attorney only expressed her view that opposing counsel was making negotiations difficult and that divorces in general might sometimes go easier without outside influences of this type. Had wife's attorney directed wife to contact husband to work out an agreement, then a violation would have occurred. Here, wife's attorney did not direct the meeting, so no improper communication with the represented husband occurred.

60. No. Even though girlfriend is husband's prime witness, she is still an unrepresented party. As such, MR 4.2 does not prohibit communication between the girlfriend and the opposing counsel. A violation would occur, however, if the ex-wife's attorney attempted to use the girlfriend as an intermediary in an attempt to communicate with the ex-husband.

61. No. Attorneys are prohibited from having contact only with employees who are managers relative to the subject of the matter, who may make statements that would be attributable to the organizational party, or whose acts or omissions may be attributable to the organizational party. Here, the neighbor's department is not involved in the subject of the matter. Had the neighbor fallen into any of the above categories, however, mere notice to the Corporation's lawyer would have been insufficient. To avoid discipline, the attorney would need to receive actual approval from Corporation's lawyer, rather than merely give notice. (The need to get consent to communicate with an opposing party is always present and not limited only to the organizational party context.)

62. The children will not be permitted to sue because they are third parties, and the lawyer did not owe them a duty to exercise care. The mother was the direct beneficiary of the lawsuit. Even though the outcome affected them adversely, they were not intended beneficiaries of the lawyer's work, such as would be the case if the lawyer drafted a shoddy will, poorly carrying out the mother's intention to leave them her estate. (In the will-drafting case, the lawyer would owe a duty of care to the children, as the ones intended to benefit.)

63. No. The question states that 2,000 cars was the actual figure that the parties had already agreed upon. As long as Attorney A is confident of this fact, he has not intentionally altered agreed-to terms. Therefore, A should not be disciplined.

64. While the lawyer did not affirmatively lie to the people in the bar, he failed in his duty to unrepresented persons to notify them of his interest in the matter. MR 4.3. By sitting and drinking with the others in the bar, he implied that his purpose was not an investigative one. While easier questions are those in which lawyers actually lie about their motives, this lawyer would be subject to discipline under MR 4.3.

65. No, Lawyer is not *liable for malpractice* to Doctor because Doctor was not Lawyer's client and was not a third party intended to benefit from Lawyer's legal services to Client. For a lawyer to be liable for malpractice, there must first be some duty that the lawyer owes to the malpractice plaintiff. Here Lawyer owed no such duty to Doctor. As an opposing party to Lawyer's client, Lawyer owed no duty to prevent harm such as this to Doctor. Under certain circumstances, however, a lawyer may be liable for malicious prosecution.

66. The lawyer is under no obligation to reveal any of these facts. Generally, there is no obligation to reveal unfavorable facts. The lawyer is, however, prohibited from making false statements about any of these facts. In addition, the lawyer would have to reveal all material information, regardless of how unfavorable, if in an ex parte setting with the judge.

67. No. A lawyer is under a duty to disclose controlling, directly adverse legal authority only to the court. Although this case appears to be controlling and directly adverse, Robin was under no duty to disclose it to Richard. While Richard would find out about the new case when Robin disclosed it to the court, the rule's object is for the benefit of the court, not the individual opposing attorney.

68. No. While a lawyer must not knowingly offer false evidence, Anne's instincts standing alone are insufficient to support the conclusion that she knows her client will commit perjury. Further, a lawyer "may refuse to offer evidence that the lawyer reasonably believes is false." MR 3.3(a)(3). Ordinarily, Anne has discretion to offer evidence that she reasonably believes, but does not know, is false; however, a lawyer may not refuse to let her criminal defendant client testify if she reasonably believes, but does not know, that the client will testify falsely. MR 3.3(a)(3). Allowing her client to testify despite her suspicions, therefore, would not violate the Model Rules.

69. No. After legal proceedings have concluded, a lawyer has no obligation to reveal perjury. MR 3.3(c). This rule applies only when the lawyer does not learn of the perjury until after the proceedings. If David had learned of the perjury before the conclusion of the trial, he would have been obligated to take reasonable remedial measures, including, if necessary, coming forward to reveal the perjury.

70. Yes. Lawyers are prohibited from advising witnesses to avoid the service of a subpoena. MR 3.4(a), MR 3.4(f). Witnesses do not belong to only one side or the other, and defendant is entitled to have access to the witness without disruption by plaintiff. The fact that the friend's testimony would not be the only such testimony available is irrelevant. Attorney is subject to discipline.

71. Client's desire to pay each witness for his or her testimony violates witness payment rules. Regarding the next door neighbor, payment to lay witnesses will be provided for in a state statute. Such a fee will be considerably less than $1000. Attorney must not follow Client's instruction to pay a lay witness in excess of the statutory fee. For both the doctor and psychologist, if they are testifying as experts rather than mere occurrence witnesses, MR 3.4(b) allows payment of whatever professionals in the field charge for that time period and services, respectively. If they are to be experts, they may be paid as such.

72. First, it violates Model Rule 3.4(e) in alluding to matters not supported by admissible evidence. It was proper for the lawyer to summarize the witness's actual testimony but improper to allude to a conversation that was not allowed to be heard by the jury. The lawyer could have had no reasonable belief that such evidence was admissible, because the ruling was already made (this is a closing argument). In addition, the lawyer violated MR 3.4(e) by impermissible expression of personal opinion as to the credibility of the prosecution witness. It was proper to point out any possible bias by the witness but not to argue that the lawyer, personally, did not believe the testimony.

73. Two opposing considerations compete here. There is a need to criticize judges to check the judiciary and attempt to improve the overall legal system. However, lawyers are expected to use discretion when deciding whether to publicly criticize judges. Lawyers do receive some limited First Amendment protection when criticizing judges, so the fact that Claire did not make the charges maliciously but instead believed them to be true will be relevant to her defense.

74. None of them. The rules limiting publicity apply only to out-of-court statements. Because these were all made in opening trial statements, they do not violate the trial publicity rules, regardless of the reporter's story. Had the prosecutor made the statements in a press conference, rather than the courtroom, some would be problematic. It is permissible to state the nature of the crime and the identity of the defendant, information in the public record, the defendant's address and family status, and when he was arrested. The prosecutor could not discuss the defendant's past relationship and history with the victim because this has a substantial likelihood of materially prejudicing the matter.

75. Yes. The attorney's conversation with the judge involved more than a mere housekeeping-type matter. Although scheduling matters such as this are normally considered housekeeping matters that are permitted to be communicated about ex parte, here the lawyer made reference to the critical nature of the motion under the judge's consideration.

76. No, she will be subject to discipline if she responds to such questions. Communications with jurors outside the court are prohibited completely both before and during a trial, regardless of the subject matter. She should not respond, report the incident to the judge, and get an instruction that the lawyer's silence should be interpreted only as compliance with the rules of ethics.

77. No. Prosecutors are prohibited from prosecuting charges that the prosecutor knows are not supported by probable cause. Although a public interest is identified here (the avoidance of racial tensions, etc.), bringing charges would subject the lawyer to discipline.

78. Bill cannot advise Jay to give up a jury trial. As an unrepresented accused, Bill has a special duty to protect Jay and to not have Jay waive substantial trial rights. MR 3.8(c).

79. Steve should not subpoena the lawyer in this case. Generally, when such testimony is not a necessity to the case (as here), a prosecutor should if at all possible avoid calling a former attorney to testify. MR 3.8(e).

80. Yes. If Scott pursues all of his favorable leads without looking into possible exculpatory evidence, he will violate an ethical obligation. Prosecutors must investigate leads even-handedly, without regard to the possible help or hindrance they might become in the case.

81. It is likely that Anne has violated an ethical duty. Anne's position as a subordinate does not relieve her of a duty to follow professional conduct rules. One exception is created: Anne could escape disciplinary liability if Barbara's decision is the reasonable resolution of an arguable question of professional duty. MR 5.2(b).

82. Yvette's supervisor should not be subject to discipline for Yvette's actions in this case. Partners and supervisory lawyers are required to take reasonable efforts to establish systems in an attempt to prevent violations of the rules. Here, a system was in place to prevent the filing of frivolous claims, and Yvette's violative conduct went around the system. If her supervisor made reasonable efforts to maintain the supervision, her supervisor will not be subject to discipline.

83. No, the partner may be subject to discipline. Although reasonable systems were in place, both direct supervisors *and* partners have a responsibility to take steps to avoid or mitigate the effects of any subordinate's misconduct when they learn of it. The partner is not Yvette's supervisor, but his status as a partner means that once he learned that Yvette planned to file a frivolous claim, he had a duty to stop it.

84. No. When representing two parties concurrently, no evidentiary privilege exists as between the commonly represented parties. The two parties should have consented to this after a consultation, thus effectively waiving these privileges.

85. Yes, Lynn is subject to discipline. Model Rule 5.3(c)(1) dictates that an attorney will be subject to discipline for the misconduct of non-lawyer subordinates when, among other things, she orders the subordinate to engage in the misconduct. Lynn's status as an associate rather than a partner is irrelevant; as a supervisor, she is subject to discipline.

86. No. The Supreme Court has ruled that lawyers may solicit clients in person if the lawyer is doing so not for pecuniary gain but rather to further political and ideological goals. In re Primus, 436 U.S. 412 (1978). The lawyer would be subject to discipline, however, for any actual coercion or duress.

87. Joe must demonstrate that the provisions further a substantial government interest and are no broader than are necessary to achieve that interest.

88. Yes. The name of Bob and Sally's firm misleads the public into assuming they are associated with the government or a nonprofit law firm. Firm names that are false or misleading violate Model Rule 7.5. Firm names may be misleading when they untruthfully imply a relationship to a government or other institution.

89. Yes. A lawyer is prohibited from offering a client financial support to induce the client to retain the lawyer. MR 1.8(e).

90. Yes. Advertisements cannot give rise to unreasonable expectations or refer to illegal activity. Allen's ad implies that Allen will use his connections as a former state trooper to fix his clients' tickets. Model Rule 7.1 Comment 4.

91. Yes. The ad violates the ethics rules because Jane made claims that are not susceptible to verification. Statements that are unverifiable are deemed to be misleading. Model Rule 7.1.

92. Advertising has traditionally referred to widely distributed public statements about services available from a particular lawyer or law organization. Solicitation has traditionally referred to narrower communications directed at one or a small group of identified recipients who are known to need a particular service. As a result of the Court's decision in Shapero v. Kentucky Bar Association, 486 U.S. 466 (1988), Peter's letter would be considered to be advertising and is permissible if it is not false or misleading and if it bears the words ADVERTISING MATERIAL on the envelope.

93. No. Model Rule 7.2(c) requires all advertisements to include the name and address of at least one lawyer or law firm who is responsible for the advertisement's content. Joan's firm's ad complies with this rule.

94. No. No conviction or criminal charge is necessary to support judicial discipline. There is sufficient evidence that the judge's conduct was contrary to law. There would be special concern about the judge's fitness for office because the charges are directly related to the judge's integrity and honesty.

95. No. A judge is permitted to be a fact witness, as long as the judge is not presiding in the matter. Had the testimony concerned Alice's character, Bob could not have testified voluntarily but instead would have to be induced by a subpoena.

96. Several rules are implicated here. CJC §3A(5) requires diligence in judicial proceedings. Judges are also limited to only a "reasonable amount" of outside income, and the judge's large outside salary may be problematic with this standard. Finally, judicial duties must take precedence over other commitments that a judge undertakes. CJC §3B.

97. Yes. Canon 3A(4), 1972 CJC prohibits judges from engaging in ex parte communications. Moreover, absent evidence to the contrary, their conversation will be presumed to be about the pending matter.

98. Amy should be held to a permissive reporting standard. That is, she "should" take appropriate action, which allows her discretion in whether to report or not. Because this involves permissive and not mandatory reporting, Amy could take other forms of action, such as confronting Brenda in an effort to resolve the matter.

99. The judge has a mandatory requirement to report the attorney's conduct. CJC §3D(2). The judge "shall" inform the disciplinary authorities when he has knowledge that a lawyer committed misconduct that raises a "substantial question" about the lawyer's honesty, trustworthiness, or fitness as a lawyer.

100. No. Under CJC §3E(1)(a), the standard in this case has both an objective and a subjective element. Therefore, regardless of the judge's individual belief in his neutrality, he must disqualify himself when his impartiality might reasonably be questioned by an objective observer.

101. The judge may not remain on the bench for any length of time. The judge is required to resign when she becomes a candidate for any nonjudicial office.

102. A cannot bring any action against the judge. Judges are absolutely immune from civil damage suits when engaging in their core judicial functions. The immunity covers the judge even when there is an error in decision-making.

103. The judge should probably not need to be disqualified. His interest in the company is small, and any possible harm to the value of his shares is both speculative and negligible in amount.

104. No. The judge's statements in the past concerned the general legal rule, and not the parties themselves. Bias is only grounds for disqualification when directed at a specific party, as opposed to the legal rules governing the case.

105. No. Normally, a judge is disqualified for personal representation of or against a party in his courtroom. CJC §3E(1)(b). However, the prior representation must have taken place in the same or a substantially related matter. Here, the two matters are wholly unrelated, causing no conflict.

MULTIPLE-CHOICE
QUESTIONS AND ANSWERS

MULTIPLE-CHOICE QUESTIONS

These multiple-choice questions are designed to prepare students for the Multistate Bar Exam.

1. Attorney Smith represents a commercial fisherman who was being prosecuted for violating a statute prohibiting salmon fishing at a particular time of year. In preparing for trial, Smith hoped that the government agent who had cited the Defendant could not identify him. He decided to test the witness' identification.

    Next to him at counsel table, Smith placed Mr. Jones, who resembled the Defendant, and had Jones dressed in outdoor clothing consisting of denims, heavy shoes, a plaid shirt, and a jacket-vest. Defendant wore a business suit and large round glasses and sat behind the rail in a row normally reserved for the press.

    Smith neither asked the court's permission for, nor notified the court or government counsel of, the substitution.

    On Smith's motion at the start of the trial, the court ordered all witnesses excluded from the courtroom. Jones remained at counsel table.

    Throughout the trial, Smith acted as if Jones was the Defendant. He gestured to Jones as though he were his client, gave Jones a yellow legal pad on which to take notes, and referred to Jones as "my client." The two conferred. Smith did not correct the court when it expressly referred to Jones as the Defendant and caused the record to show identification of Jones as Defendant.

    During trial, two government witnesses misidentified Jones as Defendant. Following the government's case, Smith called Jones as a witness, Jones testified that he was not Defendant, and Smith disclosed the substitution.

    Is Attorney Smith subject to discipline?

    (A) Yes, because a client is entitled to zealous advocacy.
    (B) Yes, because the attorney disclosed the misrepresentations before the trial ended.
    (C) Yes, because a lawyer may not make a false statement of material fact to a tribunal.
    (D) Yes, but only if the court first finds the attorney to be in contempt.

2. During the trial of a civil case, Attorney Jones was examining a witness for his client when opposing counsel objected to a question on the ground of hearsay. The trial judge sustained the objection, and Attorney Jones asked if he might approach the bench. A conference was held, during which Attorney Jones cogently explained why the judge's ruling was erroneous. Attorney Jones was correct; the trial judge's ruling was erroneous. Not persuaded, the trial judge reiterated his ruling sustaining the objection. Attorney Jones, still out of the jury's hearing, said, "Judge, I mean no disrespect but you are wrong. This information is vital to my client's case and the jury must have it." At this point, Attorney Jones approached the witness and quietly told the witness to answer the question. The witness answered the question, and opposing counsel again objected and moved that the answer be stricken. The trial judge granted the motion to strike and instructed the jury to disregard the answer. The trial judge later in private berated Attorney Jones. The trial continued without further incident.

Is Attorney Jones subject to discipline?

(A) Yes, because a lawyer may not advise a client to disregard a ruling of the court.
(B) No, because a lawyer may not fail to seek the client's lawful objectives.
(C) No, because a lawyer may advance a position that is supported by existing law.
(D) No, because a lawyer may take reasonable steps in good faith to test the validity of a court's ruling.

3. An indigent client came to see Attorney Jones for advice and counsel regarding a dispute with his landlord. After examining the circumstances, Attorney Jones advised the client to give notice to the landlord and move out. Attorney Jones reasonably anticipated that no litigation would ensue. Because the client did not have the funds, Attorney Jones loaned him $250 to make a deposit on a new apartment. Is Attorney Jones subject to discipline?

(A) Yes, because an attorney may not loan money to a client.
(B) No, because the attorney was not seeking to take unfair advantage of the client.
(C) No, because no attorney-client relationship was formed.
(D) Yes, if the attorney failed to obtain the client's informed consent in writing to this business transaction.

4. Attorney Smith is an accomplished trial lawyer and writer. She has been approached by a murder defendant who wants her representation. Smith says that she will represent the defendant if the defendant grants Smith publication rights to the defendant's story. The defendant agrees and is effectively represented by Smith. Is Smith subject to discipline?

(A) No, because the representation was effective.
(B) Yes, because the attorney failed to make full disclosure to the defendant before obtaining defendant's consent.
(C) Yes, because a lawyer is prohibited from acquiring an interest in publication rights with respect to the subject matter of a client's representation.
(D) Yes, because a lawyer is prohibited from acquiring an interest in publication rights with respect to the subject matter of a client's representation until the representation is completed.

5. Attorney Jones is one of only three lawyers in town who are experienced criminal defense lawyers. He was approached by Daryl Thompson, who has been charged with breaking into the home of Irving Trumbull, the president of the "Only Bank in Town." The Bank is one of Jones' only repeat customers, and Jones has dealt with Mr. Trumbull regarding much of the Bank's collection business for the last four years. Thompson is a man of modest means but is not indigent. Attorney Jones told Mr. Thompson that he would not represent him because of Jones' representation of the Bank.

Is Attorney Jones subject to discipline?

(A) Yes, because the financial hardship to Jones is insufficient to excuse his duty to represent Mr. Thompson.
(B) No, because representing Mr. Thompson would have created a conflict of interests.
(C) Yes, because Jones failed to seek Mr. Thompson's informed consent.
(D) No, because, with few exceptions, none of which is present here, a lawyer is under no duty to represent every prospective client.

6. In which of the following situations would the information received by the attorney be covered by *both* the attorney-client privilege and the ethical duty to preserve the client's confidential information?

I. Lawyer L is representing Client C in a personal injury claim. L and C attend the same church. At a church social, while walking through the buffet lunch line, C tells L that his injuries are much less serious than he had previously thought.

II. L is representing C in a boundary line dispute with C's neighbor. When combing through the county land records, L discovers that C's grantor apparently had no legal title to the land he purported to grant to C.

III. L is defending C in a first degree murder case. In the course of her investigation, L talks to a taxi driver who tells L that he remembers that on the night in question, C rode in his taxi to an address near the scene of the murder.

IV. L represents C in an action for breach of an oral contract. When preparing the case for trial, L stumbles across an old newspaper clipping reporting C's conviction of a felony in a distant state 15 years ago.

(A) All of the above
(B) II, III, and IV only
(C) I only
(D) None of the above

7. Edgar was charged with a felony after the police found marijuana plants growing in his vegetable garden. The police search was of doubtful legality. Edgar implored his friend and neighbor, Attorney Joyce, to defend him in the case. Joyce warned Edgar that her regular practice was limited to worker's compensation law, that she had never handled a criminal case before, and that she had little time to prepare herself to handle his defense. Edgar said he understood all that, and Joyce reluctantly agreed to represent him. At the time, she intended to do the necessary research on criminal procedure, but the pressure of her regular work prevented her from doing it. A reasonably prudent criminal defense lawyer would have moved to suppress the evidence resulting from the police search. Because of her ignorance of criminal procedure, Joyce did not make a motion to suppress. The evidence was admitted at Edgar's trial, and he was convicted. Which of the following is most nearly correct?

(A) Joyce is not subject to discipline since it is uncertain whether a motion to suppress would have granted.
(B) Joyce is not subject to discipline since she duly warned Edgar of her lack of time and her lack of experience in criminal defense work.
(C) Joyce is subject to discipline since a motion to suppress might have been granted.
(D) Joyce is liable to Edgar for malpractice since she failed to do the research needed to handle the case competently.

8. Lawyer represented Client in a lawsuit completed over a decade ago. Lawyer has not represented Client since. Plaintiff, who was not involved in the prior litigation with Client, seeks to retain Lawyer to sue Client in another matter that, although distinct from the prior litigation, is ancillary to it and involves in part the same facts and circumstances, some of which are confidential.

It is proper for Lawyer to:

(A) Decline to represent Plaintiff.

(B) Refer the matter to his law partner, who was not involved in the prior litigation and who became associated with Lawyer only a year ago.

(C) Accept the representation after notifying Plaintiff and notifying Client.

(D) Refer the matter to Smith, a lawyer in another firm, in exchange for 10% of the fee that Smith will charge Plaintiff.

9. John Doe requested that Attorney defend him in a murder charge. Attorney told Doe that he restricted his practice to civil matters, so he gave Doe the names of three good criminal defense lawyers. As Doe was leaving, Doe told Attorney the facts leading to his arrest, including an admission that he shot the victim. Doe then asked Attorney what his reactions were. Attorney briefly discussed temporary insanity as a defense. Doe subsequently hired another lawyer. Attorney did not charge Doe any fee. The prosecutor learned of Doe's conversation with Attorney and has subpoenaed Attorney to appear as a witness in Doe's trial.

Is it proper for Attorney to testify that Doe admitted shooting the deceased?

(A) Yes, because an attorney-client relationship was never formed between Doe and Attorney.

(B) Yes, because Attorney did not charge Doe any fee.

(C) No, because the lawyer-client evidentiary privilege extends to prospective clients, and a lawyer may not disclose the confidences or secrets of a prospective client.

(D) No, because Attorney told Doe that Attorney did not handle criminal matters.

10. Attorney Jones is the majority shareholder of Collection Agency, Inc. If Collection Agency's collection efforts are not successful, Jones has authorized Collection Agency's Manager, who has graduated from law school but not been admitted to the bar, to write a letter which, in Manager's best judgment, is appropriate. The letter is on Jones' legal letterhead. The letter may, if Manager so decides, contain a statement that the matter has been referred to Attorney Jones and that suit will be filed in five days if payment is not received. Manager is authorized to sign Attorney Jones' name to the letter. Jones does not personally review each letter before it is sent.

Is Attorney Jones subject to discipline?

(A) Yes, because Attorney may not threaten suit to gain advantage in a civil case.

(B) Yes, because the letter is a threat.

(C) Yes, because Collection Agency, through Manager, is engaging in the unauthorized practice of law.

(D) No, because Manager is authorized to act as Jones' agent.

11. Lawyer Smith represents Client Jones in a personal injury case. During negotiations with the defendant's counsel, Smith said, "Mr. Jones just can't accept anything less than $50,000 to settle this claim." In fact, Smith had been authorized by Jones to accept as little as $35,000.

Is Smith subject to discipline?

(A) Yes, because a lawyer is prohibited from making a false statement of fact.

(B) Yes, because he has failed to carry out his client's directive.

(C) No, because such statements in negotiations are not generally regarded as statements of fact.

(D) No, because the statement was made in good faith.

12. Lawyer Green was contacted by criminal defendant Junior. Junior asked Green to represent him and told Green that Junior's father would be paying Green's fee. Green contacted father who confirmed that he would pay the fee. Green proceeded to represent Junior.

    Is Green subject to discipline?

    (A) No, because the father agreed to pay Green's fee.

    (B) No, because Junior knew that his father was paying the fee.

    (C) Yes, because a lawyer is prohibited from accepting payment for legal services from a third party.

    (D) Yes, because Green failed to obtain Junior's informed consent to the arrangement.

13. Lawyer Black believes that he can earn a good living by serving in an efficient manner scores of black lung victims. Black sends a tasteful, direct mail advertisement of his services to all 25-year veterans of coal mining in Black's home state.

    Is Black subject to discipline?

    (A) No, because the First Amendment protects lawyer advertising to the same extent as it protects any other speech.

    (B) No, because the advertisement is tasteful.

    (C) Yes, because this activity amounts to direct solicitation in writing.

    (D) No, because the First Amendment protection of lawyer advertising as commercial speech is sufficient to prohibit the state's blanket prohibition on direct mail advertising.

14. Attorney Youngblood is a public defender representing an armed robbery defendant. The case was called for trial after several previous postponements. The district attorney advised the judge that a key prosecution witness was missing and asked for another postponement. The judge was greatly upset about the effect of this further postponement on the administration of justice and on his calendar and gave the prosecution a one-day postponement to find the witness. The judge said that if the witness was not produced and the prosecutor was not ready to go forward the next day, the indictment would be dismissed. No one said anything to Youngblood, and she said nothing, other than announcing that she was ready for trial.

    The next day the D.A. announced to the judge that the police had found the witness by checking his forwarding address at the post office. In talking to the witness, the D.A. had learned that since moving, he had been in touch with the public defender's office and that, in fact, Youngblood knew where he was.

    Is Youngblood subject to discipline?

    (A) Yes, because a lawyer may not fail to disclose that which the lawyer is required by law to reveal.

    (B) No, because a criminal defendant is entitled to zealous advocacy.

    (C) Yes, because a lawyer may not interfere with the discovery of evidence by an opponent.

    (D) No, because a lawyer is under no duty to assist an opponent's effort to locate evidence.

15. Lawyer Lawrence was contacted by Client Clarence. Clarence told Lawrence about an emergency situation in which Clarence was involved that would warrant Lawrence's filing an application for a temporary restraining order to be issued against Clarence's adversary. Clarence tells Lawrence of material facts that are adverse to Clarence's position. When Lawrence approached the local judge with his ex parte application for the temporary restraining order, he did not disclose these adverse facts to the court.

Is Lawrence subject to discipline?

(A) No, because a lawyer is under no duty to disclose facts that are adverse to the lawyer's client.

(B) No, because a lawyer cannot be compelled to testify against the lawyer's client.

(C) Yes, because a lawyer is prohibited from making false statements of fact to a tribunal.

(D) Yes, because a lawyer must disclose material adverse facts to a court when making an ex parte presentation.

16. Attorney Jones worked for two years for the Veteran's Administration. While there, his main function was to investigate claims filed by veterans. During the course of his employment, he once investigated a claim filed by Charles, a Korean War veteran. After Jones left the Veteran's Administration, the agency denied Charles' claim. Charles comes to Jones, who is now engaged in private practice, and asks him to represent him in a suit against the Veteran's Administration for the benefits to which Charles believes he is entitled. Is Jones subject to discipline if he accepts Charles' case?

(A) No, because Jones has left the Veteran's Administration.

(B) No, if Jones was not privy to confidential information regarding Charles arising from his employment at the VA.

(C) Yes, because Charles' case was pending while Jones was employed at the VA.

(D) Yes, if Jones had substantial and personal responsibility for Charles' VA claim while in his VA employment.

17. Attorney Jones represents Porter in a civil law suit. Attorney Smith represents the opposing party. Smith notices that Jones has been unduly contentious during the discovery phase of the case and has offended the judge to whom the case is assigned for trial. Also, she believes that Jones has made several questionable tactical decisions. She honestly believes that Porter stands a good chance of being hurt by Jones' conduct. May Smith discuss this matter with Porter?

(A) No, because Porter is represented by Jones.

(B) No, unless she believes Jones' conduct amounts to a disciplinary violation.

(C) Yes, if it will not hurt Smith's client.

(D) Yes, if Smith gets the informed consent of her own client first.

18. Bob is a financial planner. He is not licensed to practice law. He has recently been helping his clients prepare their wills as part of his estate planning service. Has Bob committed unauthorized practice of law?

(A) No, because will preparation is an integral part of financial planning and Bob is an expert in his field.

(B) Yes, because preparing legal documents is considered to be practicing law.

(C) Yes, because financial planning is best done by a tax lawyer.

(D) No, because Bob is careful to ensure that all his clients know he is not an attorney.

19. The state of Wythe has decided to limit those it admits to the practice of law in its state to only those that either reside in the state or maintain an office in the state. Will the state's requirement withstand a constitutional challenge by a nonresident who does not wish to maintain an office in the state?

    (A) Yes, because it is within the authority of the state to determine who it will permit to practice law in its courts.

    (B) No, because this requirement violates the Constitution's Privileges and Immunities Clause.

    (C) No, because this requirement violates the equal protection guarantee of the Fourteenth Amendment.

    (D) Yes, because the state has a substantial interests in ensuring that its lawyers know the local rules, are available for court appearances, and do their share of volunteer and pro bono work in the state.

20. Sally is an attorney who wishes to defend her client against charges that have been brought against him in a state in which she is not licensed to practice. Which of the following are true?

I. The only way for Sally to represent her client is for her to receive a license to practice in the state.

II. Sally may represent her client if her pro hac vice application is granted.

III. Sally may be required to associate with a local attorney for the purposes of the case.

    (A) I, II, and III

    (B) II and III

    (C) I and III

    (D) None of the above

21. The state of Wythe has recently decided to make membership and annual dues to the state bar mandatory. Joan doesn't feel that she should be forced to belong to the bar and required to send them annual dues if she wants to practice law in the state. She brings suit arguing that the requirements are unconstitutional. Will Joan prevail?

    (A) No, it is within the authority of the state to require membership in and dues payment to the state bar.

    (B) Yes, requiring Joan to join the bar to gain her license is a violation of her First Amendment rights.

    (C) Yes, this type of requirement is prohibited by the Supreme Court's 1990 decision in Keller v. State Bar of California.

    (D) No, the Model Rules permits the states to require bar membership.

22. Lawyer represents Client in a civil matter. Representation is completed, and three years later, Client dies. Following Client's death, in conjunction with a criminal investigation of Grand Jury Target, Prosecutor requests Lawyer's files on Client's matter. If Lawyer resists Prosucutor's request, will Lawyer be successful?

    (A) Yes, because Client is not the subject of Prosecutor's investigation.

    (B) Yes, because the lawyer-client evidentiary privilege extends even beyond the client's death.

(C) No, because former clients receive a diminished lawyer-client evidentiary privilege.

(D) No, if Prosecutor's need for the material is great.

23. Beth and Dave are opposing counsel in a civil trial. During depositions, Beth's client gets caught in an inconsistency. When questioned further on the matter, Beth's client alleges that Beth told him to change his story if he wanted to reduce his liability. A friend of Dave's works for the same firm as Beth. Dave's friend told him that he knows that Beth has allowed her clients to perjure themselves on the stand. If Dave believes Beth has committed attorney misconduct, must he do anything about it?

(A) He does not have to report Beth because he does not have direct knowledge of her misconduct.

(B) He does not have to report Beth because her actions, even if true, do not raise a substantial question as to the lawyer's honesty, trustworthiness, or fitness as an attorney.

(C) He must report her misconduct or he will be in violation of the ethics rules.

(D) He should report her misconduct because it will give him an advantage in the litigation.

24. Bob, a CEO of a large corporation, meets with the Corporation's legal counsel. Bob's executive assistant is present during the entire meeting. During the meeting, the CEO discusses the corporation's strategy in a recently filed lawsuit as well as the status of his divorce, in which he is represented by other counsel. Is the information Bob told the attorney regarding his divorce protected?

(A) The information is protected by the attorney-client evidentiary privilege and the duty of confidentiality.

(B) The information is protected by the duty of confidentiality but not the attorney-client privilege because the presence of the executive assistant during the discussion of Bob's divorce precluded the creation of the attorney-client privilege.

(C) The information is protected by the evidentiary privilege only.

(D) The information is not protected.

25. Sally talked to the neighbor of her client and learned where her client was on the night the crime for which he was arrested was committed. Her client refused to tell Sally where he was that night. Is the lawyer's knowledge of the location subject to the attorney-client privilege?

(A) No, because the evidentiary privilege was never established.

(B) No, but Sally may still be subject to discipline for violating the duty of confidentiality if the court orders her to testify and she does so.

(C) Yes, the information is covered by the attorney-client privilege and the court may not override this evidentiary privilege.

(D) Yes, but the Judge can order the client to reveal the information.

26. Stan's client confesses to him that he stole a large amount of cash from his employer and hid it on his property. Stan goes to his client's property and locates the money. If Stan does not want to reveal the location of the money and does not want to violate any ethics rules, what should he do?

(A) Put the money in a safety deposit box.

(B) Take the money to his office, count it, write down the serial numbers, and return it to where he found it.

(C) Leave the money where it is.

(D) Turn the money over to the police and refuse to tell the police how or where he found it.

27. Bart feels he is being treated unfairly at work. He goes to his lawyer's office and tells him that he owns a gun and he's going to shoot his boss. Bart leaves the office and his lawyer calls the boss to warn him. On the way to his boss' office, Bart calms down and changes his mind. The boss is understandably distressed and fires Bart. Bart reports his lawyer to the bar for violating the duty of confidentiality. Will the lawyer be subject to discipline?

(A) Yes, because Bart is the only person with the right to waive the duty of confidentiality.

(B) No, because the lawyer was required by law to warn the boss.

(C) No, because the future crimes exception to the duty of confidentiality permits the lawyer to reveal information the lawyer reasonably believes necessary to prevent reasonably certain death or substantial bodily harm.

(D) Yes, because the lawyer was not reasonable in his belief that Bart was going to shoot his boss.

28. Jill has represented Jack's construction company for a number of years. In the course of that representation, she has prepared a number of contracts for him. Jill has learned that Jack is using the contracts that she has prepared for him to defraud his customers. She has learned that Jack is adding clauses to the contracts that permit him to carry out his fraudulent scheme. Jack has recently requested that Jill prepare several more agreements between him and his clients. Jack's company accounts for over half of Jill's business. Can she continue to represent him?

(A) Jill can continue representing Jack because the Constitution guarantees the right to legal representation.

(B) Jill must withdraw because Jack is using her services to further his fraud.

(C) Jill can continue to represent Jack as long as she does not directly commit a crime or fraud.

(D) Jill must withdraw only if she will directly profit from Jack's fraud.

29. Which of the following conflicts are NOT waivable?

(A) Third party fee payment.

(B) Conflict between two current clients.

(C) Lending clients money when litigation is pending or contemplated, other than advancing litigation costs.

(D) Conflict between a current and a former client.

30. Lawyer Adam and Client Bill wish to enter a joint business venture. To achieve this and satisfy the conflict rules, Adam puts everything in writing—both Bill's consent and the transaction itself, which Adam also takes care to put into terms that Bill can understand. On these facts alone, which statement is true about the transaction?

(A) It satisfies the conflict rules because everything is in writing.

(B) It satisfies the conflict rules because the language is that which Bill can understand.

(C) It fails to satisfy the conflict rules, because it must also be objectively reasonable and because Bill must be advised that it would be desirable and have the opportunity to seek independent legal counsel.

(D) Both A and B.

31. Corporation C hired Firm in 1995 to assist with a corporate restructuring. Firm also helped to draft several employment contracts for high-ranking executives. Firm's representation of Corporation C ceased. In 2002, a Client approaches Firm, wishing to be represented in a personal injury matter against Corporation C. Which statement is true?

    (A) The Firm cannot represent the Client against Corporation C because it owes the Corporation a duty of loyalty.

    (B) The Firm can represent the Client if both Client and Corporation give informed consent.

    (C) The Firm can represent the Client because his interests are not directly adverse to the former Corporation client.

    (D) The Firm can represent the Client because there is not a substantial relationship between the two representations.

32. Assume the same facts as those found in Question 31, but assume that Client's proposed representation arises from the employment contract drafted by Lawyer D at Firm. May Lawyer F, also with Firm, represent Client?

    (A) Yes, because the matters are not substantially related.

    (B) Yes, because the interests are not directly adverse.

    (C) No, because Lawyer F and all the lawyers at Firm are disqualified based on Lawyer D's prior representation in a substantially related matter.

    (D) Yes, if Lawyer F is in a different practice section of the law firm.

33. When may a former judge engage in private representation in a matter in which he was involved while formerly on the bench?

    (A) When the judge was not involved personally and substantially.

    (B) When the parties consent after consultation.

    (C) When the parties settled the matter during proceedings so that the judge was prevented from ruling on the merits.

    (D) Both A and B.

34. An investigator working on a prosecutor's rape case uncovers information about another possible suspect. As the investigation continues, the probability increases that the new suspect, rather than the man arrested for the crime, is the guilty party. What is the prosecutor's ethical obligation?

    (A) Immediately request a hearing with the judge assigned to the case.

    (B) Immediately request an ex parte meeting with the judge assigned to the case.

    (C) Turn the information over to the defense attorney in a timely manner.

    (D) Continue to investigate the new suspect until he is sure that the new suspect is the guilty party before revealing the information to the defense.

35. Partner in a law firm discovers that a secretary in a different section of the firm is continuously leaking confidential client information. The firm has each new employee

watch a video on client confidentiality and sign an agreement to abide by the confidentiality rules. Does the Partner violate any rules by not stopping the Secretary's conduct?

(A) Yes, because as a partner he has a duty to take reasonable remedial action to stop further breaches once he learns of them.
(B) Yes, because the firm's systems to prevent such conduct were not reasonable.
(C) No, because the partner is not the secretary's direct supervisor.
(D) No, because the firm has reasonable systems in place to prevent such confidentiality breaches.

36. You are a divorce attorney, and Nathan and Lynn come to your office seeking a divorce. They believe they've worked out an amicable preliminary settlement and need you only for the technicalities. Your state allows such representation, and you agree. The next day, Lynn calls and discusses a family heirloom that she and Nathan both want, and she muses about her chances of prevailing in a lawsuit. What action should you take?

(A) Explain to Lynn that if things progress to litigation, you will be forced to withdraw from representing either side.
(B) Withdraw as counsel for both.
(C) Withdraw as counsel for Nathan only.
(D) Withdraw as counsel for Lynn only.

37. Lawyer places an advertisement containing the statement "Most experienced criminal lawyer in the state—I produce results." This statement:

(A) is permitted because it is mere puffery.
(B) will subject the lawyer to discipline because it is unverifiable and therefore misleading.
(C) false and will subject the attorney to discipline.
(D) refers to an illegal activity and will subject the attorney to discipline.

38. A private law firm chooses the name Immigration Legal Services of California. This name:

(A) will subject the attorneys to discipline because it does not contain the name of at least one of the attorneys in the firm.
(B) is permitted because it is protected commercial speech under the First Amendment.
(C) will subject the attorneys to discipline as misleading because it untruthfully implies a relationship to the government or other institutions.
(D) is permitted because neither the Model Code nor the Model Rules addresses permissible firm names.

39. As a result of the Supreme Court's decision in In re Primus, 436 U.S. 412 (1988), which of the following is true?

(A) Lawyers have no First Amendment right to solicit clients in person.
(B) States may not ban advertisements containing true claims of certification of specialization by a bona fide organization.
(C) A lawyer may solicit clients in person if it is to further political or ideological goals and not for pecuniary gain.
(D) States may prohibit lawyers from contacting accident victims for 30 days after the accident.

40. A lawyer wants to include information about his fees in his advertisement. Such information:

- **(A)** is permitted as long as it is not false or misleading.
- **(B)** receives no constitutional protection after the Court's decision in Bates v. Arizona State Bar, 433 U.S. 350 (1977).
- **(C)** may be prohibited by the states because it is inappropriate for the profession.
- **(D)** is permissible only if the fees are described in general terms such as "reasonable and moderate" rather than in actual dollar figures.

41. Form letters written to a specific group of clients identified as being in need of certain legal services are:

- **(A)** treated essentially as advertisements as a result of the Supreme Court's decision in Shapero v. Kentucky Bar Ass'n in 1988.
- **(B)** not protected speech because of concerns for the potential for overreaching and undue influence.
- **(C)** prohibited by the Court's decision in Ohralik v. Ohio State Bar Ass'n in 1988, which reaffirmed that the First Amendment does not protect in-person solicitation.
- **(D)** considered to be the equivalent of in-person solicitation and permitted, provided the letters are not false or misleading.

42. Judge is the treasurer of a local charitable organization. He is shamefully removed from this position on suspicion of embezzlement, although he is never formally charged. Can judge be removed from his position on the bench?

- **(A)** No, because the problem was in the context of the Judge's personal involvement in the organization, rather than any official functions.
- **(B)** Yes, because it is inappropriate for a judge to hold office in the organization.
- **(C)** No, because the Judge was neither charged nor convicted.
- **(D)** Yes, because the episode bears on his integrity.

43. Judge is involved in a discussion with Attorney Camille. Judge recently ruled on a case in which Camille represented one of the parties, and now Camille is asking advice regarding the appeal. Judge believes that justice will be served by giving Camille the advice, and his personal role in the case is over. Is this ex parte communication proper?

- **(A)** Yes, the case is no longer pending before the judge's court.
- **(B)** Yes, the judge has a good faith motivation in discussing the case.
- **(C)** Yes, the discussion is only on housekeeping matters.
- **(D)** No, the ex parte communication is not proper.

44. Judge is the treasurer for a local charitable organization. During the charity's annual fund-raising drive, judge asks some of his friends and associates to buy tickets to a dinner dance. He is careful to avoid using the auspices of his office to pressure anyone into contributing; in fact, no one with whom he speaks is connected to his judicial role. Has any judicial conduct rule been violated?

- **(A)** Yes, Judge violated the rule prohibiting him from being an officer in an organization.
- **(B)** Yes, Judge is prohibited from directly fundraising for an organization.
- **(C)** Yes, Judge is not permitted to have a membership in a local organization.
- **(D)** No judicial conduct rule was violated.

45. Mike's house is broken into and some of his valuables are stolen. When Mike, a lawyer, files a claim with his insurance company, he overstates the value of the stolen property and includes property that was not stolen. Mike receives a payment from the insurance company for several thousand dollars more than the true value of his stolen property. Can Mike's actions subject him to discipline by his state's bar?

- **(A)** No, even though Mike was not honest with the insurance company, dishonest acts outside the lawyer's role will not subject a lawyer to discipline.
- **(B)** Yes, Mike has acted fraudulently, and his conduct will subject him to discipline.
- **(C)** No, only criminal conduct committed when acting as an attorney will subject Mike to discipline.
- **(D)** No, Mike's act says nothing about his fitness as a lawyer.

46. Julie has observed Beth, her opposing counsel, engage in behavior that clearly violates an ethics rule and raises a substantial question about Beth's fitness as a lawyer. Julie feels she is obligated to report Beth to the disciplinary authorities. What should Julie do first to start disciplinary proceedings against Beth?

- **(A)** File suit in state court.
- **(B)** Report Beth to the judge hearing their case.
- **(C)** File a complaint with the bar disciplinary committee.
- **(D)** File suit in federal court if their case is in federal court.

47. Sam filed a bar disciplinary complaint against his former attorney, James, because Sam felt that he lost his case as a result of James' lack of due care. The disciplinary proceedings were recently dismissed. Sam does not feel that the Bar adequately considered all the relevant evidence. How can Sam appeal the decision by the Bar?

- **(A)** Sam cannot appeal the bar decision, but he may bring a malpractice suit against James.
- **(B)** Sam may appeal the decision to the state trial court.
- **(C)** Sam may appeal the decision to the state court of last resort.
- **(D)** Sam may appeal the decision in federal court.

48. Disciplinary proceedings have been started against Alex. Alex feels that his actions did not amount to disciplinary violation and feels that his best course of action would be to have a jury trial. Will his timely request for a jury trial be granted?

- **(A)** Yes. He has a constitutional right to a jury.
- **(B)** No. There is no right to a jury trial in a disciplinary proceeding.
- **(C)** Yes. All state bars guarantee a right to a jury.
- **(D)** It depends. It is within the discretion of the bar committee whether to grant his request, but there is no constitutional right to jury trial in disciplinary cases.

49. Bill and Abby are solo practitioners on the same floor of a small office building. Although they specialize in different areas, they often consult one another about the legal issues on which they are working. A client comes to Bill with a legal problem that Bill knows is within the area that Abby specializes in. Bill obtains the client's permission to consult with Abby about the matter. After the client leaves, Bill talks to Abby about the client's problem, and Bill and Abby agree that Abby will do the substantive legal work for Bill for an agreed-upon hourly rate. Bill will continue to serve as the client's counsel. Will the arrangement between Bill and Abby subject them to discipline?

(A) No, fee splitting is permitted by lawyers that work together.

(B) No, provided the client agrees in writing and the fee is reasonable.

(C) Yes, the bar permits fee sharing only if the lawyers are members of the same firm.

(D) Yes, because Bill is not competent in the area of the law raised by the client's problem.

50. Joe is starting a biotech firm and goes to see Beth, a lawyer and an old friend, for legal advice regarding patents, corporate trademarks, and taxes. Beth has spent the 20 years since law school writing wills and working on domestic relations issues. Can Beth represent Joe?

(A) No. A lawyer has a duty to decline representation when she lacks competence.

(B) Yes. Joe approached Beth and asked for her services.

(C) Yes, as long as Beth can achieve the requisite level of expertise in the new field by reasonable preparation.

(D) No. Because Beth has been friends with Joe for over 20 years, she will have a conflict of interests in representing him.

MULTISTATE-STYLE EXAM ANSWERS

1. C	11. C	21. A	31. D	41. A
2. A	12. D	22. B	32. C	42. D
3. D	13. D	23. C	33. D	43. D
4. D	14. D	24. B	34. C	44. B
5. D	15. D	25. A	35. A	45. B
6. D	16. D	26. C	36. B	46. C
7. D	17. A	27. C	37. B	47. A
8. A	18. B	28. B	38. C	48. D
9. C	19. B	29. C	39. C	49. B
10. C	20. B	30. C	40. A	50. C

ESSAY EXAM QUESTIONS
AND ANSWERS

ESSAY EXAM QUESTIONS

QUESTION 1

Several employees of Microchips Incorporated filed a class-action suit against Microchips for sex discrimination. Darlene DeLesio, an attorney in Microchip's in-house legal department, began to work on the defense of the suit. In the course of her preparation, DeLesio obtained information from Microchips about its personnel practices. As DeLesio explained later, "I obtained specific information from the personnel department concerning salaries and hiring practices. . . . I participated in a conference with outside consultants hired by the corporation to prepare statistical information regarding employment. I obtained intraoffice memoranda . . . regarding the case."

DeLesio decided not only that the plaintiffs had a good case against Microchips but that she herself had been the victim of sex discrimination by Microchips. She elected to join the very class-action suit against Microchips that she had been preparing to defend. Accordingly, DeLesio asked the plaintiffs' counsel to represent her, and she resigned from her position at Microchips.

Plaintiffs' counsel agreed to represent DeLesio, and she joined the litigation as a plaintiff. Microchips' new counsel then moved the court to disqualify plaintiffs' counsel, alleging conflict of interests. Should the motion be granted? Explain. Is DeLesio subject to discipline for her conduct?

For a discussion of the issues raised, see Hull v. Celanese Corp., 375 F. Supp. 922 (S.D.N.Y. 1974), *aff'd,* 513 F.2d 568 (2d Cir. 1974).

QUESTION 2

During a recess from trial, Defense Counsel finds Potential Witness in the courthouse lobby. PW is a friend of Defendant who has said that he witnessed the crime and that Defendant was not present and therefore could not have committed the crime. Potential Witness says to DC, "When it's my turn, I know what to do. I'll stick with the story just the way I told it to you." Defense Counsel responds, "You must tell the truth." A discussion ensues during which Defense Counsel comes to believe that PW's favorable story for Defendant is false and that PW intends to commit perjury. DC says, "You're not doing your friend any favors. I won't call you as a witness."

Unnoticed by DC, Prosecutor has overheard her last comments to PW. Prosecutor, misinterpreting the comments, now believes that PW would testify to a version of the events that favors the government and that DC was berating PW in an effort to persuade PW to testify falsely for the Defendant.

Trial is resumed moments later and Prosecutor calls PW as his witness. Much to Prosecutor's chagrin, PW testifies to the Defendant-favoring version of the events that DC believes is false. DC does not cross-examine PW, and PW is excused. Trial continues to a conclusion with no more mention of PW.

Is Prosecutor subject to discipline? Is Defense Counsel subject to discipline? Both? Neither?

ESSAY EXAM ANSWERS

SAMPLE ANSWER TO QUESTION 1:

Because of her work as a lawyer for Microchips, Ms. DeLesio has both a continuing duty of loyalty to Microchips and confidential information of Microchips, her former client. These two realities drive the analysis of her possible discipline and the disqualification of her new lawyer.

When a court considers a motion to disqualify, it will consider a range of interests beyond the usual policies of the conflicts rules. For example, the equities of the motion's timing, the interest of the opposing party in having counsel of choice, and judicial economy will be factors. Here, the equities probably favor Microchips. It does not appear that Microchips has delayed the motion to gain a litigation advantage, the case is at a relatively early stage, so substituting new Plaintiff's counsel is unlikely to result in substantial delay, and there is no indication that Plaintiff's counsel somehow screened Ms. DeLesio. (As a plaintiff rather than a new lawyer, screening her may have been impossible in any event.)

In some sense, Ms. D is like a lawyer switching sides. It is as if she has represented one side in litigation and then switched to represent the other side. If she is viewed this way, she would clearly be disqualified from representing the Plaintiffs herself. Her association with the Plaintiff's counsel could result in her disqualification imputing to Plaintiff's counsel, thus disqualifying them as well. Such a gross conflict (a lawyer switching sides in the same litigation) would not be waivable. Even though some respect should be paid to client autonomy, allowing clients to waive most conflicts by giving informed consent, some gross conflicts such as this one are not waivable. Even if this conflict were waivable, waiver in this instance is beyond imagining. The affected client is Microchips. Far from being amenable to giving a waiver, Microchips is moving to have Plaintiff's counsel disqualified (i.e., have the effects of the conflict enforced).

It is true that she is not really switching sides as a lawyer but rather has gone from being a lawyer for one side to being a party on the other side. The lawyer-implicated result is much the same, however. The confidences of her former client will presumably be revealed to the other side in the litigation. The key question (discussed below) may be whether she is permitted to reveal Microchips' confidences. If so, then she will not be subject to discipline for revealing confidences and the conflicts implications will be much reduced.

She might argue that she is not revealing confidences of Microchips in her role as lawyer, but rather as a private person. That argument is unavailing. She gained the confidences as a lawyer. She only had access to the information because of her work for Microchips as its lawyer. A lawyer's duty of confidentiality does not stop when the lawyer is not acting as a lawyer. Rather, it stays with the lawyer when the lawyer goes out to dinner with friends or makes business decisions. A lawyer may not use confidences of a client to disadvantage the client. MR 1.8(b). That duty applies even after the lawyer-client relationship has ended. This prohibition would, for example, keep a lawyer from using confidences of a client to buy property adjacent to property the client plans to buy and develop. Again, the client can waive this prohibition, but surely Microchips is not inclined to waive in these circumstances. Here, Ms. D is using Microchips' confidences to disadvantage Microchips and advantage herself.

A better argument for Ms. D might be an analogy to the duty of confidentiality exception for self-defense and fee collection. A lawyer may reveal a client's confidences to the extent reasonably necessary to collect the lawyer's fee, or to self-defend against charges (criminal, disciplinary, or civil) against the lawyer. Here, Ms. D is using Microchips' confidences not to collect her fee but to enforce employment rights against Microchips. Ms. D was not only Microchips' lawyer, but also its employee. She is entitled to pursue lawful claims against her former employer as any other employee would. The only way for her to pursue those lawful claims is to use her former client's confidences. The policies favoring her are essentially the same as in the case of the lawyer using confidences to collect her fee or self-defend. A client's wrongdoing (failing to pay a fee or bringing wrongful claims against a lawyer) ought not to be advantaged by protection of confidences that might undo the wrongful conduct. Here, Ms. D believes she was the target of gender discrimination by Microchips. Microchips ought not to be advantaged in defending against such charges by being able to enforce the confidentiality rules against the victim (Ms. D) of its misconduct.

The self-defense exception ought to apply to allow Ms. D to pursue her claim. This exception, however, permits only so much revelation of confidences as reasonably necessary to self-defend. As such, Ms. D could not use Microchips' confidences to assist the other plaintiffs. If she has revealed to plaintiff's counsel broader information than necessary to pursue her own case, then she is subject to discipline. As well, because of the extreme difficulties of determining or monitoring the measure of information she has or would in the future reveal to plaintiff's counsel, she should not be permitted to join the plaintiff's case and plaintiff's counsel should be disqualified from continuing in the matter. Ms. D may retain her own counsel and pursue her claim using only such information as necessary to pursue her own claim. Cooperation with plaintiff's counsel, revealing Microchips' confidences to them, would subject her to discipline.

SAMPLE ANSWER TO QUESTION 2:

The central issues here involve the possibility that PW has committed perjury. Neither DC nor Prosecutor has knowingly offered false testimony. DC may have a duty to report PW's suspected perjury, but that responsibility is diminished since DC neither called nor examined PW. DC was careless in allowing her conversation with PW to be overheard, but that error in judgment is insufficient to subject her to discipline. DC acted properly in handling PW and was under no obligation to consult with her client before deciding not to call PW as a witness. Finally, Prosecutor's mistaken but perhaps reasonable belief that DC was suborning perjury may create a duty for Prosecutor to report DC's "misconduct."

Perjury, especially in a criminal matter by a defendant or a defense witness, presents a serious challenge for lawyers and the justice system. Perjury is an especially significant affront to the court and lawyers are expected to take some responsibility for the integrity of judicial proceedings. Revealing perjury, especially a client's perjury, is an especially grave breach of trust and confidentiality.

Lawyers are prohibited from knowingly offering false testimony. MR 3.3(a)(3). Here, DC did not offer this evidence and indeed, did not cross-examine PW when PW was called by Prosecutor. Had DC taken advantage of the situation by asking PW questions that further elaborated on what DC believed was a false story, the situation would be strikingly different. But under the circumstances in the fact pattern, DC has not offered false evidence. Neither has Prosecutor. Although Prosecutor called PW as his witness, Prosecutor did so expecting truthful, government-favoring testimony to result. Prosecutor was mistaken. While Prosecutor may have offered false evidence, he has not done so knowingly.

Lawyers have discretion to decline to offer evidence they reasonably believe, but do not know, to be false. This discretion does not extend to a decision to decline to call a criminal defendant client, but PW is not the defendant. Some might argue that this narrowing of discretion should apply to defense witnesses. The rationale for the narrowing of discretion is based on the defendant's right to testify on his own behalf, but a defendant also has a right to the use of compulsory process (i.e., calling witnesses on defendant's behalf). Based on the compulsory process right, a reasonable argument exists for taking from defense counsel the discretion to decline to offer defense witnesses. Nonetheless DC operated in compliance with MR 3.3(a)(3) and handled PW properly in this respect. DC is not subject to discipline for declining to call PW as a witness.

Once called by Prosecutor, DC arguably had a duty to inform the court of her expectation that PW was about to perjure himself. However, DC could not know what PW would do, having been called as a witness by Prosecutor. When a lawyer has not offered the false evidence, the duty to report exists only when the lawyer "knows" that the evidence will be or has been false. DC could not be said to have known PW's testimony would be false in advance, once PW was called by Prosecutor. What DC should have done after the testimony is a somewhat closer question. At this point, PW has testified to what DC came to believe was a false version of the events. Still, she may not know that PW's testimony is false. Unless DC has more powerful indications than her sense of her conversation with PW, it seems more accurate to say that she believes but does not know that PW has testified falsely. Remembering that she did not cross-examine PW, and since the question says that the trial ended without further mention of PW, I assume that DC did not argue PW's version of the facts to the jury, she had no duty to reveal PW's perjury to the court. (The duty to reveal perjury of which a lawyer knows continues to the conclusion of the proceeding, which means until the final judgment has either been affirmed on appeal or the time to appeal has passed. MR 3.3 Comment 13.)

Arguably, since DC did not know that PW's testimony was false and since DC represents a criminal defendant and since PW was called not by DC but by Prosecutor, DC had a duty to her client to argue a reasonable defense theory based on PW's testimony. Such choices, however, if they are reasonable tactical choices, are within the discretion of the lawyer. Lawyers must defer to their clients about the goals of representation, but have discretion to make reasonable tactical choices. Likewise, DC was not obliged to consult with her client regarding her decision to decline to call PW as a witness.

DC should not have engaged in the conversation with PW in a place where they could be overheard. That sort of error, if it had resulted in damage to a client, might support a malpractice action by a client against a lawyer. But such an error is not so grave as to subject DC to discipline for lack of competence. MR 1.1.

Prosecutor believed that DC was suborning perjury. Prosecutor was mistaken, but his belief was based on his personal knowledge (the conversation he overheard) and the belief, though mistaken, was his. Lawyers have a duty to report the misconduct of other lawyers when that conduct raises substantial questions about the honesty, trustworthiness, or fitness of the lawyer. Further, the reporting lawyer must know of the misconduct in order for the duty to report to arise. Suborning perjury is the sort of serious misconduct that must be reported. Prosecutor would have a duty to report DC's conduct if it can be said that Prosecutor knows of it. Here, once PW has testified, Prosecutor must surely be left unsure of what had happened in the lobby between PW and DC. As such, it seems that Prosecutor's knowledge of any misconduct probably falls short of the rule's requirements. If Prosecutor did report the conduct, thus mistakenly reporting DC to the bar discipline authorities, Prosecutor could successfully assert a claim of privilege to any defamation claim brought by DC.

Neither Prosecutor nor DC is subject to discipline.

Index

Table of Cases

Table of Statutes, Rules, and Opinions

**Model Code of Professional Responsibility
Disciplinary Rules**